International Political Economy Series

Series Editor
Timothy M. Shaw, University of Massachusetts Boston,
Boston, USA;
Emeritus Professor, University of London, London, UK

The global political economy is in flux as a series of cumulative crises impacts its organization and governance. The IPE series has tracked its development in both analysis and structure over the last three decades. It has always had a concentration on the global South. Now the South increasingly challenges the North as the centre of development, also reflected in a growing number of submissions and publications on indebted Eurozone economies in Southern Europe. An indispensable resource for scholars and researchers, the series examines a variety of capitalisms and connections by focusing on emerging economies, companies and sectors, debates and policies. It informs diverse policy communities as the established trans-Atlantic North declines and 'the rest', especially the BRICS, rise. NOW INDEXED ON SCOPUS!

More information about this series at
http://www.palgrave.com/gp/series/13996

Md Saidul Islam · Edson Kieu

Climate Change and Food Security in Asia Pacific

Response and Resilience

palgrave
macmillan

Md Saidul Islam
School of Social Science and Asian
School of the Environment
Nanyang Technological University
Singapore, Singapore

Edson Kieu
Singapore Management University
Singapore, Singapore

ISSN 2662-2483 ISSN 2662-2491 (electronic)
International Political Economy Series
ISBN 978-3-030-70752-1 ISBN 978-3-030-70753-8 (eBook)
https://doi.org/10.1007/978-3-030-70753-8

This Palgrave Macmillan imprint is published by the registered company Springer Nature Switzerland AG
The registered company address is: Gewerbestrasse 11, 6330 Cham, Switzerland

To my lovely and only daughter, Ulfat Tahseen, and wonderful sons, Rawsab Said and Musab Said, who feel pain for the hungry people and climate refugees in this planet.

—Md Saidul Islam

To my family, Yen Shing, Eileen, and Edgar, for their unconditional love and immeasurable support in all my pursuits.

—Edson Kieu

Acknowledgments

Climate Change and Food Security in Asia-Pacific: Response and Resilience was made possible by Tier-1 grants from the Ministry of Education, Singapore. We acknowledge our debt to Nanyang Technological University Singapore, Singapore Management University, and Massachusetts Institute of Technology. We are grateful to the Series Editor, Commissioning Editor, and Editorial Assistants of Palgrave Macmillan for their crucial and diligent support and timely response to every phase of this publication. Special thanks to Balaji Varadharaju and the production team.

We are thankful to our interviewees who voluntarily and enthusiastically participated in this study and shared their deep insights with us. A special "thank you" to all the research assistants who worked for the Tier-1 and URECA projects namely Nigel Selvanathen, Yeo Kai Qing Joanne, Yuvaranjini D/O Mathiazakan, Teng Kuan Yung, Teo Xin Yi Belicia, Furqan Akram Khan, Mangharam, Shrutika Ajit, Andrea Ting Wong, and few more.

Our family members and friends have been a constant source of encouragement and enthusiasm throughout our life, particularly during this study. We believe, this work could not be made possible without the continued emotional support from our family members. We are also grateful to Palgrave Macmillan for publishing this book.

Praise for *Climate Change and Food Security in Asia Pacific*

"In this ground-breaking work, Islam and Kieu examine the power of regional initiatives in meeting the threats of climate change and food insecurity. Indeed, these challenges are fundamentally regional: they are nearly identical for adjacent nations, but widely differing at the global scale. Regional alliances enhance the political and financial leverage of their members, while holding a tighter focus is possible for global alliance. Islam and Kieu apply the analytical methodology of multi-sited ethnography, through case studies of specific Asia-Pacific initiatives. This work will be valued by policy makers and practitioners tackling the two greatest challenges of our age."

—Professor John H. Lienhard, V, *Director, Abdul Latif Jameel Water and Food Systems Lab (J-WAFS), Massachusetts Institute of Technology*

"The authors provide a very detailed and insightful analysis of the complex relationships between climate change and food (in)security in the large Asia-Pacific region, going beyond common efforts to demonstrate how the former is impacting the latter by also focusing on the impact of food systems on climate change. They do this via in-depth analyses of three large Asian-Pacific Initiatives aimed at promoting food security across differing parts of the region, as well as paying special attention to China and India, urban food security and the role of green movements in achieving equitable as well as sustainable food security. With a keen eye toward policy implications, they help point the way to a more sustainable food system in this vital region."

—Riley E. Dunlap, *Past-President, Research Committee on Environment and Society, International Sociological Association*

"*Climate Change and Food Security in Asia-Pacific: Response and Resilience* is a very timely volume with a focus on one of the key regions in the new global economy. Providing insights on regional initiatives for mitigations and resilience to climate change and food security in Asia Pacific, this book is key not only for those who are interested in the responses to climate change to address food security concerns, but also for international relations and politics experts who are interested in this strategically very important geography. Authors warn us about the dangers of "resource wars" among the have and have not nations, threats of green-washing by some of the key actors who are not genuine in their efforts to address the threats and speak of the necessity of robust public policies and participation of the poor to make meaningful changes towards food security."

—Mustafa Koc, *Professor, Department of Sociology and the Centre for Studies in Food Security, Ryerson University, Toronto, Canada*

"A very timely book. Climate change, food security and resilience are central to the challenge of addressing food insecurity in some of the fragile economies of Asia Pacific. The two dominant countries of the region—China and India—present an interesting contrast."

—Chandra A. Madramootoo P.Eng., *James McGill Professor, Faculty of Agricultural and Environmental Sciences, McGill University, Canada*

"*Climate Change and Food Security in Asia Pacific: Response and Resilience* is a timely contribution for a better understanding of how regional organizations can shape climate change mitigation policies in view of ensuring food security. Md Saidul Islam and Edson Kieu provide key insights on the possible pathways for a sustainable food system in the Asia-Pacific region."

—Stefano Ponte, *Professor of International Political Economy and the Director of the Centre for Business & Development Studies, Copenhagen Business School, Denmark*

Contents

Acronyms

ACCI	ASEAN Climate Change Initiative
ACEF	All-China Environment Federation
ACP-EU	Technical Centre for Agricultural and Rural Cooperation
ADB	Asian Development Bank
ADLI	Agricultural Development-Led Industrialization
AEC	ASEAN Economic Community
AFCD	Agricultural, Fisheries and Conservation Department
AFED	Arab Forum for Environment and Development
AFSIS	ASEAN Food Security Information System
AFSRB	ASEAN Food Security Reserve Board
AIFS	ASEAN Integrated Food Security
AIPP	Asia Indigenous Peoples' Pact
AMAF	ASEAN Ministers on Agriculture and Forestry
AMIS	Agricultural Market Information System
AMME	ASEAN Ministerial Meeting
ANGOC	Asian NGO Coalition
APEC	Association of Protection of Environment and Culture
APN	Arab Group for the Protection of Nature
APTERR	ASEAN Plus Three Emergency Rice Reserve
ASCC	ASEAN Socio-Cultural Community
ASEAN	Association of Southeast Asian Nations
AusAID	Australian Aid
AVA	Agri-food and Veterinary Authority of Singapore
AWGCC	ASEAN Working Group on Climate Change
C	Carbon
CCA	Climate Change Adaptation

CCP	Chinese Communist Party
CDM	Clean Development Mechanisms
CEC	Center for Environmental Concerns-Philippines
CESDI	Center for Environment and Sustainable Development
CF	Contract Farming
CIDP	Community Initiatives for Development in Pakistan
CIF	Climate Investment Fund
CO_2	Carbon Dioxide
COP	Conference of the Parties
CROP	Council of Regional Organizations in the Pacific
CSISA	Cereal Systems Initiative for South Asia
CSO	Civil Society Organizations
CUTS	Consumer Unity and Trust Society
DAFO	District Agricultural and Forestry Office
DRR	Disaster Risk Reduction
DWA	Dalit Welfare Association
EASEP	East Amman Society for Environment Protection
ECOT	Ecumenical Coalition on Tourism
ECTET	Ecumenical Coalition on Third World Tourism
EDA	Emirates Diving Association
EEG	Emirates Environmental Group
EFS	Environment Friends Society
EGA USAID's	Economic Growth and Agriculture
ENSO	El Niño-Southern Oscillation
ESDF	Environmental and Societal Development Foundation
ESDO	Environmental and Social Development Organization
ESO	Environmental Society of Oman
EU	European Union
FAO	Food and Agriculture Organization of the United Nations
FFA	Forum Fisheries
FSPWG	Food Secure Pacific Working Group
FTA	Foreign Trade Agreements
GAIA	Global Alliance for Incinerator Alternatives
GBS	Gram Bharati Samiti
GDP	Gross Domestic Product
GEF	Global Environment Facility
GEIDCO	Global Energy Interconnection Development and Co-operation Organization
GHG	Greenhouse Gases
GMO	Genetically Modified Organisms
GV	Global Voices
HEAD	Human Environmental Association for Development
HRS	Household Responsibility System

HSA	Health Sciences Authority
IAPH	International Association of Ports and Harbours
IC	Inorganic Carbon
ICEJ	International Christian Embassy Jerusalem
IGEG.CC	Inter-governmental Expert Group on Climate Change
IHRC	International Human Rights Commission
IICI	Indo OIC Islamic chamber of commerce and industry
ILEC	International Lake Environment Committee Foundation
IMAECSED	International Movement for Advancement of Education Culture Social and Economic Development
IMF	International Monetary Fund
INTACH	Indian National Trust for Art and Cultural Heritage
IPCC	Intergovernmental Panel on Climate Change
IPFSP	Industry Partners for a Food Secure Pacific
IRRI	International Rice Research Institute
ITP	Industrial Tree Plantation
JES	Jordan Environment Society
MAC	Marine Aquaculture Centre
MEP	Minimum Export Prices
MEWR	Ministry of Environment and Water Resource
MOU	Memorandum of Understanding
MRV	Measurement, Reporting and Verification
MSP	Minimum Support Prices
MSW	Municipal Solid Waste
MWC	Mahindra World City
N	Nitrogen
NAFTA	North American Free Trade Agreement
NAMAs	Nationally Appropriate Mitigation Actions
NARS	National Agricultural Research System
NATO	North Atlantic Treaty Organization
NCCC	National Committee on Climate Change
NDRC	National Development and Reform Commission
NEA	National Environment Agency
NFN	NGO Federation of Nepal
NGO	Non-Governmental Organization
NO_2	Nitrogen Dioxide
NOAA	National Oceanic and Atmospheric Administration
NPO	Non-Profit Organization
NTU	Nanyang Technological University
NWHO	New World Hope Organisation
NYAA	National Youth Achievement Award
OWTF	Organic Waste Treatment Facilities
PCCR	Pacific Climate Change Roundtable

PDS	Public Distribution System
PICTs	Pacific Island Countries and Territories
PIF	Pacific Island Forum
PIFS	The Pacific Islands Forum Secretariat
PIFSC	Pacific Islands Fisheries Science Centre
RADP	Rural Area Development Programme
REDWO	Rural Educational Development and Welfare Organization
SAARC	South Asian Association for Regional Cooperation
SAFE	South Asian Forum for Environment
SCOPE	Society for Conservation and Protection of Environment
SEE	Society of Entrepreneurs and Ecology
SEZ	Special Economic Zone
SFA	Singapore Food Agency
SINAM	Sadayanodai Ilaignar Narpani Mandran
SIS	Pacific Islands Forum's Smaller Island States
SLR	Sea-level Rise
SPA-FS	Strategic Plan of Action on Food Security for the ASEAN Region
SPC	Secretariat of the Pacific Community
SPNL	Society for the Protection of Nature in Lebanon
SPREP	Secretariat of the Pacific Regional Environment Programme
SPTO	South Pacific Tourism Organization
SRI	System of Rice Intensification
SRS	Sembawang Research Station
SSJFZ	Sino-Singapore Jilin Food Zone
TAC	Treaty of Amity and Cooperation
TEBTEBBA	Tebtebba Foundation Indigenous Peoples International Policy Research and Education
TEI	Thailand Environment Institute
TLL	Temasek Life Sciences Laboratory
UAE	United Arab Emirates
UFSS	Urban Food Systems Strategies
UK	United Kingdom
UN	United Nations
UNCCD	United Nations Convention to Combat Desertification
UNDESA	United Nations Department of Economic and Social Affairs
UNDP	United Nations Development Programme
UNFCCC	United Nations Framework Convention on Climate Change
UPA	Urban and Peri-Urban Agriculture
US	United States (of America)
USA	United States of America
USAID	United States Agency for International Aid
USAID	United States Agency for International Development

USDA	United States Department of Agriculture
WB	World Bank
WHO	World Health Organization
WMC	World Muslim Congress
WOCAN	Women Organizing for Change in Agriculture and Natural Resource Management

List of Figures

List of Tables

CHAPTER 1

Tackling Regional Climate Change and Food Security Issues: An Introduction

The world population now stands at 7.8 billion and one in seven of these people is hungry. By 2050, the population is expected to reach 9.9 billion (IISD 2020; WFP 2011). What does that mean for food security and hunger? The number of hungry people in the world remains unacceptably high with over one billion people reported to be chronically undernourished. This situation is further exacerbated by the global COVID-19 pandemic that accentuated the plight of the underprivileged. Most of these people are ironically found in Asia (FAO et al. 2019; FAO 2012). From the regional impacts of the 2008 food crisis, it is clear that one central challenge for the Asia-Pacific region is how to "make progress in guaranteeing food security in a context where the production of food will be increasingly stressed in the face of decreasing resources pitched against continually expanding demand" (Mukherjee 2009: 1). The growing impacts of climate change have exacerbated this challenge even further (Economist Intelligence Unit 2014).

Despite Asia's unprecedented economic growth and advances in science and technology, there has been an increase in poverty and stagnation in average crop yields. The problem of food security remains a major challenge because of destabilizing factors such as competition for land, rural–urban migration, rapid urbanization, population growth, climate change, and the increasing shortages of energy and water. Currently, the

M. S. Islam and E. Kieu, *Climate Change and Food Security in Asia Pacific*, International Political Economy Series,
https://doi.org/10.1007/978-3-030-70753-8_1

region is home to two-thirds of the world's poor, with 947 million living on less than US$ 1.25 per day (Teng 2010: 6). To feed the growing population, the region may need to raise productivity by 70% by 2050. However, the attempt to increase food production has become a major food security challenge, which is now compounded by climate change. Similar to food security, climate change is a multidimensional issue. Therefore, the impacts of climate change on the four dimensions of food security, namely, availability, physical and economic access, and utilization, are complex as these impacts are also linked to other factors influencing the changing climate (*Public Forum* 2010; Rayfuse and Weisfelt 2012; Islam and Kieu 2020).

On the historical impacts of climate change on food production, scientific findings have shown that rising temperatures increasingly affect crops. It is projected that, based on a scenario of an increase of 2 degrees Celsius, without taking into account changes in rainfall patterns, production of major crops would decline. Climate change produces several challenges. First, there will be regional changes in available water and in rainfall patterns, causing changes in land productivity due to the reduced availability of both surface water and groundwater for irrigation in some regions as well as increased competition and demand. Second, the competition for land will intensify due to biofuel production and products for livestock. Third, elevated carbon dioxide (CO2) levels will have interactive impacts on temperature, rainfall, pollution, pests, diseases, and weeds especially for non-key cereal grains and for developing nations. Fourth, there is a lack of knowledge on available adaptation options, modes of resilience, and their costs and benefits. Although climate change is happening faster than anticipated, adaptation policies still lack clear directions. The incorporation of basic knowledge and science into adaptation measures for food production, which would likely provide a great return on investment, is still nascent. Finally, lack of regional and global initiatives to face these challenges will likely to generate "tragedy of the commons" (*Public Forum* 2010; Pearson 2012; Vyas 2005; Rayfuse and Weisfelt 2012; Tookey 2007). These compelling scenarios have given rise to a number of pressing questions: How can we address the complex issue of food security which is complicated by other issues such as climate change? Is solution lies in science and technological developments such as biotechnological (or gene) revolution as well as supply chain management? More production with fewer resources? More effective distributive mechanisms? How are individual countries addressing this pressing problem? What is regional cooperation doing in addressing this issue? Are country-specific initiatives enough while the problem is global in nature? These questions need a very thorough and robust investigation.

In the last one century, dietary patterns of the world shifted from traditional food to wheat-based diet (driven largely by the green revolution and American Public Law 480) to animal protein and other high-value foods such as meat, fruits, and vegetables (driven by biotechnology, retail power, and supermarket revolution) to different exotic foods (shark fins, wheal meat, etc.) for wealthy buyers (Islam 2013; McMichael 2008). Despite these food revolutions, food security remains a critical issue for many. While scholars have argued that an increase in food production to meet future demand is inevitable, we argue that in order to accelerate hunger reduction, economic growth needs to be accompanied by purposeful and decisive public action as well as participation of the poor in the growth process while reaping its benefits. Climate change is exacerbating a trajectory of widening inequality if the poor are unable to contribute and partake meaningfully in the process of policy formulation and implementation. Increased productivity is perhaps a part of the solution, but the real solution lies in "global food justice" (that includes creating access to food, finding alternative sources of food such as in oceans, changing food habits away from exotic to more environmentally friendly ones, global food bank for the impoverished ones, and global food governance). Regional initiatives can play vital roles.

Objectives and Central Themes

This interdisciplinary monograph has two initial related objectives. The first objective is to assess the regional initiatives on addressing climate change and food security issues. We have examined current cooperative mechanisms and modalities on tackling climate change and food security in order to identify best practices as well as gaps in those arrangements and to evaluate their likely impact on the future of food security in the Asia-Pacific region. We have focused on three important regions: the South Asian Association for Regional Cooperation (SAARC), the Association of Southeast Asian Nations (ASEAN), and the Pacific Island Forum (PIF). The second objective is to assess the current state of and the future prospects for mitigations and resilience with regard to climate change and food security issues of the Asia-Pacific region vis-à-vis other regions of the world. For this objective, we have tried to promote intellectual exchange on the climate change dynamics, security dimensions of food scarcity and adaptation mechanisms, as well as to deepen mutual understanding of the complexities of effective governance arrangements for food security. We have assessed the impacts of the climate change such as drought, loss of biodiversity, disaster vulnerabilities, new weather patterns, climate refugees, new diseases, etc. and their impacts on food productivity, food distribution, and food safety. Then we have also investigated whether climate change (increased temperature) can enhance food production, for example, in the colder regions of the world. While our focus remains on the Asia-Pacific region in the current stage, it has a wider implication for making a global analysis on the critical nexus of climate change and food security.

There are three inter-related central themes emanated out of our study: First, as the discourse of climate change is becoming powerful and its effects are becoming clearer, it generates a new kind of "resource war" that defines our future with an apparent polarizing trajectory: The "climate change haves" get more business opportunities, access to resources, and morally upstanding green products and services; the "climate change have-nots," on the other hand, languish in the smoke, fumes, toxic chemicals, and illnesses of the old pollution-based economy. This polarizing trajectory is becoming evident within a country and between countries. "Climate change is widening the world's gap between the haves and have-nots, worsening economic inequality between rich and poor countries…The difference between the economic output of the world's cool wealthy nations and hot struggling nations is 25% larger today than it would have been without global warming" (Krieger 2019). Second, climate change pushes for the national and regional actors to take numerous initiatives on, for example, food security. As these initiatives are largely driven not by a genuine intention to protect the environment, ensure food security, and address the need of the poor, but by protecting a "green image" and finding economic opportunities alone, the success is very little. While there are prospects for regional cooperation and opportunities, competing interests on power and resources further fragment the region. Third, economic growth is necessary but not sufficient to tackle climate change as well as to accelerate reduction of hunger and malnutrition unless it is accompanied by robust public policies and meaningful participations of the poor. Food security can be sufficiently solved by higher income and trade, with distribution/equality improvements. Since neoliberal logics (profits and power) largely dictate over social and environmental logics (equity and sustainability), the levels of consumption remain unsustainable, inequitable, and inaccessible to majority of humans in the Asia-Pacific region.

There are currently few relevant studies that focus on regional governance arrangement for food security in the context of climate change. The significance of the project lies in its relevance for policymakers and other communities of practice. While this is clearly an important issue for countries in the regions, it is only now that governments are beginning to realize the risks and threats posed by climate change and food insecurity. This project explores and examines the imminent threats of climate change and food insecurity from local, regional, and global contexts and therefore has profound policy implications for academic institutions, governments, corporations, and NGOs.

Conceptual Threads

The project has been framed by three conceptual threads—climate change, food security, and resilience. *Climate change* means a significant change in the measures of climate, such as temperature, rainfall, or wind, lasting for an extended period—decades or longer—resulting in increased air and ocean temperatures, drought, melting ice and snow, rising sea levels, increased rainfall, flooding and other influences (EPA 2013). Climate change is real, and human beings are responsible for a substantial part of it. It is putting our planet into peril, resulting in, among other far-reaching impacts, the loss of biodiversity, disaster vulnerabilities, and millions of climate refugees (Islam 2013; Islam and Kieu 2020). Currently, there are over 20 million climate refugees, and this number will increase to 50 million within the next few decades (McMichael 2008). The world was expecting a conclusive and successful climate deal to be sealed during the Copenhagen talks in December 2009. However, a lack of consensus over issues including the character of differentiated responsibilities, financial support, technology transfer, trade subsidies, and trade sanctions hindered the progress of a successful deal (Islam 2013). The World Food Program (WFP 2011) released an alarming report on seven facts about climate change and hunger a decade earlier:

- Climate change is expected to add another 10–20% to the total number of hungry people by the year 2050.

- By 2050, we can expect twenty-four million more malnourished children as a result of climate change. Almost half of this increase, ten million children, will be in Sub-Saharan Africa.
- Between 1980 and 2006, the number of climate-related disasters quadrupled.
- The number of people affected by climate-related disasters is expected to reach 375 million per year by 2015.
- In 2010, climate-related extreme events and disasters affected some 300 million people, most often in countries that have little capacity to cope.
- With climate change, two-thirds of the arable land in Africa could be lost by 2025, according to the UN Food and Agriculture Organization.
- By 2030, climate change could push food prices up 50–90% more than they would otherwise be expected to rise, according to a recent report by Oxfam.

The world's poor, women and children in particular, will bear the brunt of the effects of climate change. As rainfall becomes increasingly unpredictable, smallholder farmers will find it harder than ever to grow the food they need. The poor, who have no support structures to protect themselves, will most likely suffer from the severe hunger resulting from a potential increase in the frequency of natural disasters. More often than not, the people who suffer first and worst during climate disasters are not the main contributors to the problem. An analysis of 4040 climate-related disasters between 1980 and 2002 found that some poor nations had mortality and homelessness rates from climate disasters that were 200–300 times worse than in the United States (Roberts and Parks 2007). They have far less capacity to deal with and to recover from disasters. As the economy grows, and wealth increasingly concentrates from few to fewer hands, the woes of these marginalized masses are also constantly piling up (Islam 2013).

The World Food Summit of 1996 defined *food security* as existing "when all people at all times have access to sufficient, safe, nutritious food to maintain a healthy and active life" (Quoted in WHO 2013). Commonly, the concept of food security is defined as physical and economic access to food that meets people's dietary needs as well as their food preferences. Due to pressures from the global food supply chain, there is an inter-relationship between food supply and demand at the regional and global levels. Food security can be considered from the perspective of the individual, the family unit (households), the community (country), and the region as well.

Our conceptualization of "food security" includes the essential components such as *acceptability* (access to culturally acceptable food, which is produced and obtained in ways that do not compromise people's dignity, self-respect, or human rights), *availability* (providing a sufficient supply of food for all people at all times), *accessibility* (the equality of access to food), *adequacy* (adequate measures are in place at all levels of the food system to guarantee the sustainability of production, distribution, consumption, and waste management), and *agency* (Koc et al. 1999). Drawing on this conceptualization, along with transitory and chronic threats related to, for example, climate change, we will locate and examine four-dimensional threats related to food security:

a. Food availability: This involves issues of production, imports, and stockpiles;
b. Physical access to food: This involves access to markets and infrastructure;
c. Economic access to food: This involves issues such as employment, overseas remittances, foreign direct investment and trade; and
d. Food utilization: This involves issues of health and nutrition, sanitation or hygiene, storage and processing facilities as well as clean water.

The concept of *resilience* has its origins in the field of ecology (e.g., Hollings 1973) and in the works of early sociologists. In the past resilience as a general concept was understood as "how altered ecological conditions shaped changes in the organization of social groups and societies" (Smith et al. 2012: 381), it is now understood quite broadly such as community and urban resilience. Urban resilience generally refers to "the ability of a city or urban system to withstand a wide array of shocks and stresses" (Leichenko 2011: 164). With increasing threats posed by, for example, climate change and food insecurity, the term "resilience" is increasingly employed across various academic disciplines and policy debates. However, understanding resilience as the ability to withstand shocks and stresses may stagnate a nation's development and progress. "While a system ought to have a decent degree of robustness to withstand shocks, modernity is characterized by constant change; societies need to possess the ability to constantly transform itself in face of such changes. A focus on 'bouncing back' and building robustness into a system may unwittingly promote stagnation and stubborn resistance to change" (Islam and RiAn 2014: 207). Sovacool et al. (2012: 113) outlined three dimensions of urban resilience, formulated as adaptations to climate change:

a. *Infrastructural adaptation* refers to the assets, technologies, or "hardware" in place that could be disrupted by climate change, such as irrigation systems, roads, or electricity networks.
b. *Organizational adaptation* refers to the endurance of an institution or set of institutions, usually government ministries or departments, in charge of planning and policy.
c. *Social adaptation* refers to the cohesion of communities and the livelihoods of the people that compose them."

Approach and Methods

Climate change and food security issues are multi-faceted and transcend national boundaries. Regional organizations are therefore optimally positioned to address climate change and food security issues, while actively engaging global partners to slow down or reverse current trajectories (Islam and Kieu 2020; Beddington et al. 2012). We have therefore taken "regional initiatives" as an approach for our study to understanding the intra-regional environmental and social politics at the regional level as opposed to relying merely on anthropocentric activities affecting the natural environment. Because of the global nature of climate change and global food chains, we posit that regional organizations are key to effectively addressing current and future impacts. We can discern five main reasons why regional initiatives framework to address food security are vital (Table 1.1).

Regional initiatives to deal with critical issues like food insecurity and climate change are of paramount need for climate-related information exchange (Glantz 1994). They also provide wider scale arrangements that can be called on in periods of crisis, while purely local systems can be too shaky and vulnerable to disruptions from natural disasters and other crises (Wahlqvist et al. 2012). The global food crisis in 2007–08 taught us

Table 1.1 Critical functions of regional organizations

	Role of regional organizations	*Critical functions*
1.	Market regulation	Regional initiatives can regulate regional markets effectively by implementing controls over volatile global food markets. Such controls will ensure the stability and dependability of imports and exports of vital food resources.
2.	Internal supply chain	Regional initiatives can enhance food security internally by supplying essential food resources that are relevant to regional needs. Internal supply chains can act as a buffer from price volatility and the monopoly of major multinational corporations over global food supply and the commodity market.
3.	Cooperation and good governance	It is vital to encourage cooperation between stakeholders and ensure good security sector governance. Cooperation means that decision-making is objective and responsive to public needs and demands and provides a multi-level concept of security while promoting the transfer and sharing of knowledge.
4.	Need-based food production	It is necessary to increase food security by directing and managing food production in line with food consumption patterns, which could account for regional socio-economic shifts that are not bounded within nations. National development agendas that focus on industrialism otherwise lead to declining investments in agriculture, thus making nations reliant on food imports and subject to market fluctuations and possible shortfalls
5.	Protecting the marginal communities	Regional initiatives are vital to ensure food security for marginalized communities, which are often minorities that have been displaced and persecuted by their own governments. Hence, regional involvement could provide the necessary blanket of security for marginalized populations facing internal persecution

Source Islam and Kieu (2020); Islam and De Jesus (2012) [no copyright issue] that the reliance on the state or market mechanism alone is not sufficient to ensure regional food security at the time of crisis. National or state-centric approaches are sometimes important in stabilizing domestic food prices and in providing effective protection for some domestic consumers, producers, as well as the vulnerable segment of the population such as rural landless laborers, small-scale farmers, and the urban poor who suffer most from food insecurity, hunger, and malnutrition. However, the state-centric approaches to food security can benefit some countries to the detriment of others in the region. Regional cooperation is therefore vital and it plays a pivotal role in reassuring member states about food availability during crises and in discouraging them from pursuing detrimental trade restrictions and panicked hoarding. Trade facilitation and sharing information about food production and national reserves and various other cooperative measures during a crisis can enhance transparency, counter mistrust, and assist in stabilizing regional food markets (Belesky 2014).

Along with local as well as international reserves, regional food reserves can play an important role in alleviating food insecurity in times of crisis and emergency situations. Historically, stockpiling of agricultural commodities—particularly staple grains—has played an important role as a buffer to address the likely adverse impact of natural disasters, calamities, seasonal discrepancies, and market turbulences. Regional food reserves can also function as a safeguard mechanism to tackle after-effects of major production failures due to, for example, climate change, and global and local price upsurge and trade restrictions (Rahman et al. 2018).

With respect to the climate change issue, at least three features of regional organizations make them important: (a) their political influence, deriving from the consensus of several governments, acting in common self-interest, and often in non-traditional groupings based on shared impacts of climate change; (b) their ability to mobilize financial resources; and (c) their relatively narrow focus compared to global organizations (Glantz 1994). In an era of climate change with increasing frequencies and intensities of disasters, multilateral cooperation and maintaining a substantive regional food reserve is an increasingly important aspect of a regional strategy as well as a policy framework for ensuring regional food security. Since disasters and calamities induced and driven largely by climate change often transcend national boundaries, an effective response needs to be multilateral, relying on regional cooperation between countries that share the common geography, history, cultures, and increasingly interconnected economies (Belesky 2014).

For a robust and exhaustive investigation on the regional initiatives as well as mitigations and resilience with regard to climate change and food security issues in the Asia-Pacific region vis-à-vis other regions of the world, we employ a triangulation of methods: multi-sited ethnography, archival study, institutional collaboration, and professional workshop. While both multi-sited ethnography and archival study provided the bulk of data and information needed to address both objectives of this research, two additional approaches—institutional collaboration, and a professional workshop were used in the later stage in order to (a) promote intellectual exchange on the climate change dynamics, security dimensions of food scarcity, and adaptation mechanisms, (b) enhance mutual understanding of the complexities of effective governance arrangements for food security, and (c) make a final consistency check on the collected data.

Multi-sited Ethnography is the primary method used in this study that enables the researcher to grasp a holistic view of the world system (Marcus 1995). A multi-sited ethnography was useful for the study because the case is situated at the global level that requires multiple observations at different locations. To achieve the objectives of our study, we conducted a detailed research in the three countries: Australia, Singapore, and Bangladesh. We have chosen these three countries to represent the three regions of the Asia-Pacific region, namely the Pacific Island Forum (PIF), the Association of Southeast Asian Nations (ASEAN), and the South Asian Association for Regional Cooperation (SAARC). While we recognize the dynamics in these three regions of the Asia-Pacific, we were assertive in delving into both country-specific as well as regional initiatives on addressing climate change and food security challenges. To make a comparative study between the Asia-Pacific and other regions including the North America, we also made a field-visit in Canada, a country known for its various green initiatives in addressing the challenges of food security and global climate change.

The objective of doing fieldwork across different places and different contexts was to capture narratives, discourses, and knowledge circulated among food security and climate change experts and to analyze how these narratives, discourses, and knowledge potentially shift toward and translate into regional initiatives and adaptation mechanisms. During fieldwork, we collected first-hand data in three forms, namely (a) verbal accounts, (b) technical documents and archives, (c) images and videos. The fieldwork involved conducting in-depth interviews with scholars and policymakers, and attending academic seminars or meetings. Interview questions and the seminars aimed to get data and information that can be used to address both objectives of this research. Four categories of sites were visited during fieldwork: universities, research institutions/think-tanks, NGOs, and governmental offices. This multi-sited ethnography was employed to map out a broader picture dealing with, for example, food availability (issues of production, imports, and stockpiles), physical access to food (access to markets and infrastructure), economic access to food (issues such as employment, overseas remittances, foreign direct investment and trade), and food utilization (issues of health and nutrition, sanitation or hygiene, storage and processing facilities as well as clean water).

The goal of *archival study* was to collect data and information from printed sources such as government policy documents, technical papers, journal articles, meeting minutes, working papers, brochures, and notes. Thus, we visited libraries and public offices where related archives are placed. These materials were retrieved and catalogued. To complement the regional and country-specific data, we also drew on data collected through the information available on websites maintained by research organizations, industry and business organizations, food and climate change related institutions, NGOs, FAO, WHO, and other government agencies to map out climate change trajectories and their impacts on food security and sustainability initiatives. Difficulties emerged from the circumstances in which the sources of data were inaccessible due to sensitivity of the subject explored. It was caused in part by secrecy that generally shrouds security and vulnerability issues in which not all information related to disaster, risk, and scientific progress in food security and resilience are disclosed to the public. *Institutional collaboration* (with MIT's Abdul Latif Jameel Water and Food Systems Lab, University of Canberra, University of Nottingham Malaysia Campus, to name a few) and various *professional workshops* within and beyond Singapore were used to cope with these potential impediments.

Taken as a whole, methodological techniques used in this study are quite robust to understand the comprehensive dynamics of the Asia-Pacific region. The response and resilience focusing on the overall efficacy of regional initiatives for climate change and food security have been analyzed through five major factors: planning, implementation, cooperation, legal obligation, and international contribution.

The Prospectus

With this opening context and background, Chapter 2 unpacks further the complex relationship between climate change and food (in)security, focusing on how climate change is affecting food security and how the current food system exacerbates the problem of climate change. Chapters 3–5 then cover ASEAN, SAARC and PIF, respectively, providing background and history of the regions and their member states, examining the impacts of climate change and food security on the respective region and analyzing the regional initiatives and their effectiveness to mitigate regional risks of food security considering climate change impacts.

Within the Asia-Pacific region, China and India's economic development in recent decades brought both countries to the forefront as the two largest emitters today, facing threats from ecological degradation, food and water scarcity due to agricultural shifts from the impacts of climate change. Chapter 6 examines Chindia's (China and India) dilemma by looking at the challenges both countries face, examining economic developments thus far, the impacts of climate change on food security and the approaches both countries undertake to address the associated problems. Taking the cases of two Asian Tigers, Singapore and Hong Kong, Chapter 7 offers an understanding of how vulnerable highly dependent food-importing cities can survive in an increasingly urbanized, capitalistic, and environmentally eroding world. The chapter explains why and how cities in the world are vulnerable to food security despite economic prosperity, and examines broader responses to battle food insecurity for its growing inhabitants. Chapter 8 then returns to the cases of India and China again in their involvements in local and global land and water grabs.

Chapter 9 examines the food movements in Asia. Food security extends beyond the provision of relief from economic woes and environmental disasters, but rather, it should be designed in ways that enable the disadvantaged sections of the population to break out of a vicious cycle of poverty and insecurity. As such, food security echoes the need for sustainable and actionable ways where people from all walks of life have the means and ability to ensure both equitable and sustainable production and consumption of food—food justice and food sovereignty. This chapter highlights the importance of food sovereignty and food justice, and examines both top-down and bottom-up organized green movements within Asia, as well as the impact of green movements on food security. The closing chapter (Chapter 10) concludes the book by summarizing the findings, showing patterns and pitfalls across the regions, and pathways for a sustainable food system in Asia-Pacific.

References

Beddington, John R., Mohammed Asaduzzaman, Fernandez A. Bremauntz, Megan E. Clark, Marion Guillou, Molly M. Jahn, Lin Erda, Tekalign Mamo, Nguyen van Bo, and Carlos A. Nobre. 2012. *Achieving Food Security in the Face of Climate Change: Final Report from the Commission on Sustainable Agriculture and Climate Change*. The CGIAR Research Program on Climate Change, Agriculture and Food Security (CCAFS).

Belesky, Paul. 2014. Regional Governance, Food Security and Rice Reserves in East Asia. *Global Food Security* 3 (3–4): 167–73.

Economist Intelligence Unit. 2014. *Food Security in Focus: Asia & Pacific 2014*. The Economist Intelligence Unit.

EPA 2013. *What is Climate Change*. http://www.epa.ie/whatwedo/climate/communicatingclimatescience/whatisclimatechange/. Accessed 1 Apr 2013.

FAO (Food and Agricultural Organization of the United Nations). 2012. *The State of Food Insecurity in the World*. http://www.fao.org/docrep/016/i3027e/i3027e.pdf. Accessed 31 July 2013.

FAO, UNICEF, WFP, and WHO. 2019. *Placing Nutrition at the Centre of Social Protection: Asia and the Pacific Regional Overview of Food Security and Nutrition 2019*. Bangkok: FAO.

Glantz, Michael H. 1994. *The Role of Regional Organizations in the Context of Climate Change*. Berlin Heidelberg: Springer-Verlag.

Holling, C.S. 1973. Resilience and Stability in Ecological Systems. *Annual Review of Ecology and Systematics* 4: 1–23.

IISD (International Institute for Sustainable Development). 2020. *World Population to Reach 9.9 Billion by 2050*. http://sdg.iisd.org/news/world-population-to-reach-9-9-billion-by-2050/. Accessed 22 Oct 2020.

Islam, M.S., and Edson Kieu. 2020. Tackling Regional Climate Change Impacts and Food Security Issues: A Critical Analysis across ASEAN, PIF and SAARC. *Sustainability* 12 (883): 1–21.

Islam, M.S., and I.C. De Jesus, 2012. Regional Initiatives on Food Security. In *The Challenge of Food Security: International Policy and Regulatory Frameworks*, 1st ed. R. Rayfuse and N. Weisfelt, 255–274. Northampton, MA, USA: Edward Elgar Publishing Limited.

Islam, M.S., and Quek Ri An. 2014. Climate Change and Urban Resilience: The Singapore Story. In *Globalization, Development, and Security in Asia*, vol. IV, ed. Jieli Li, 205–220. New Jersey, NY, London: Ohio University and World Scientific Publishing.

Islam, Md Saidul. 2013. *Development, Power and the Environment: Neoliberal Paradox in the Age of Vulnerability*. London, New York, NY: Routledge.

Koc, M., R. McRae, L. Mougeot, and J. Welsh. 1999. Introduction: Food Security as a Global Concern. In *For Hunger Proof Cities: Sustainable Urban Food Systems*, ed. M. Koc et al., 1–7. Ottawa: International Development Research Centre.

Krieger, Lisa. 2019. How Climate Change Widens Gap Between Haves and Have-nots: New Stanford Study Shows a Warming Planet Worsens Global Economic Inequalities. *Enterprise-Record*, April 22.

Leichenko, R. 2011. Climate Change and Urban Resilience. *Current Opinion in Environmental Sustainability* 3: 164–168.

Marcus, G.E. 1995. Ethnography in/of the World System: The Emergence of Multi-Sited Ethnograohy. *Annual Review of Anthropology* 24: 95–117.

McMichael, Philip. 2008. *Development and Social Change: A Global Perspective*. Thousand Oaks, CA: Pine Forge Press.

Mukherjee, Amitava. 2009. *Securing Food Security in the Asia Pacific: A Partial Analysis*. Beijing: UN Asia Pacific Centre for Agricultural Engineering and Machine.

Pearson, Craig. 2012. A Fresh Look at the Roots of Food Insecurity. In *The Challenges of food Security: International Policy and Regulatory Frameworks*, ed. R. Rayfuse and N. Weisfelt, 19–43. Cheltenham, UK, and Northampton, MA: Edward Elgar.

Public Forum. 2010. The State of Food Security in the Asia-Pacific. RSIS, NTU

Rahman, Mustafizur, Estiaque Bari, and Sherajum Monira Farin. 2018. *Operationalizing the Saarc Food Bank: Issues and Solutions*. ESCAP South and South-West Asia Office.

Rayfuse, R., and N. Weisfelt, eds. 2012. *The Challenges of Food Security: International Policy and Regulatory Frameworks*. Cheltenham, UK, and Northampton, MA: Edward Elgar.

Roberts, J.Timmons, and Bradley C. Parks. 2007. *A Climate Inequality: Global Inequality, North-South Politics, and Climate Policy*. Cambridge, MA: MIT Press.

Smith, J.W., D.H. Anderson, and R.L. Moore. 2012. Social Capital, Place Meaning, and Perceived Resilience to Climate Change. *Rural Sociology* 77 (3): 380–407.

Sovacool, Benjamin K., Anthony Louis D'Agostino, Amireeta Rawlani, and Harsha Meenawat. 2012. Improving Climate Change Adaptation in Least Developed Asia. *Environmental Science & Policy* 21 (2012): 112–125.

Teng, Paul. 2010. The State of Food Security in the Asia-Pacific. *Public Forum*. RSIS, 6–9 October, NTU.

Tookey, Douglas L. 2007. The Environment, Security and Regional Cooperation in Central Asia. *Communist and Post-Communist Studies* 40 (2): 191–208.

Vyas, Vijay S. (ed.). 2005. *Food Security in Asian Countries in the Context of Millennium Goals*. New Delhi: Academic Foundation.

Wahlqvist, Mark L., John McKay, Ya-Chen Chang, and Ya-Wen Chiu. 2012. Rethinking the Food Security Debate in Asia: Some Missing Ecological and Health Dimensions and Solutions. *Food Security* 4 (4): 657–70.

WFP (World Food Programme). 2011. *Feeding 9 Billion People*. http://www.wfp.org/stories/feeding-7-billion-people-7-must-reads. Accessed 29 Mar 2013.

WHO. 2013. *Food Security*. http://www.who.int/trade/glossary/story028/en/. Accessed 25 Mar 2013.

CHAPTER 2

Climate Change and Food (In)Security Nexus

With Andrea Wong

Introduction

Climate change has been gaining a larger foothold in public discourse. In recent years, this issue has been given greater attention by international bodies, non-profit organizations, national bodies, corporations, and individuals. As warned by the 44th President of the United States, Mr. Barrack Obama, climate change is no longer a problem of the future but rather a challenge that "will define the contours of this century more dramatically than any other" (The Straits Times 2015). Climate change is defined as: "The change in the state of the climate that can be identified (e.g., using statistical tests) by changes in the mean and/or variability of its properties, and that persists for an extended period of time, typically decades or longer. It refers to any change in climate over time, whether due to variability or as a result of human activity" (IPCC 2007a).

Climate change has not only resulted in increasing global-averaged mean annual air temperatures but also the increased amount of atmospheric greenhouse gases (GHGs). It has been reported that the global mean temperature has increased by 0.74 degree Celsius during the last 100 years and that the Gangtori glacier, one of the Himalayas' largest

M. S. Islam and E. Kieu, *Climate Change and Food Security in Asia Pacific*, International Political Economy Series,
https://doi.org/10.1007/978-3-030-70753-8_2

glaciers, is rapidly disintegrating at 12–13 m a year (Misra 2014; Khandekar 2015). The impacts of climate change such as the depletion of water resources and the rise in average global temperature have created conditions for a decline in agricultural production. This in turn leads to escalated food inflation globally as well as food shortages in the developing countries where the poor suffer greatly as they are unable to pay the upmarket prices for food (Misra 2014).

According to the Food and Agricultural Organization of the United Nations (FAO), there are about 795 million people who are undernourished globally, with poor nutrition accounting for nearly 45% of deaths in children below the age of 5 annually. A further 13.5% of the population in developing countries are undernourished due to the lack of food availability; stability of food; and/or economic and physical access to food (FAO 2015). These findings are expected to be further exacerbated due to the rise in world population, projected by the United Nations to increase by 2.4 billion by 2050 (UNDESA 2015). The rise in population coupled with growing urbanization and increasing environmental problems such as pollution and deforestation, would have detrimental effects on food production, distribution, and consumption. In addition, the inability of food producers to meet the demands of the population would cause food prices to escalate. This, together with the increased occurrences of climate-related disasters and further climate changes worldwide, would worsen the problem of food security faced by the already-at-risk individuals/populations as well as the global community. Food security is thus understood as: "A situation that exists when all people, at all times, have physical, social and economic access to sufficient, safe and nutritious food that meets their dietary needs and food preferences for an active and healthy life" (FAO 2001).

With the recent signing of the climate agreement introduced in the Paris Climate Conference (COP 21) that seeks to limit global temperature rise to well below two degree Celsius, more attention has been turned toward greening movements and alternative forms of actions to reduce their greenhouse emissions (BBC News 2015). There has been a rise in alternative forms of eco-friendly food production processes such as the System of Rice Intensification (SRI), that can substantially reduce GHG emissions as compared to conventional forms of agriculture (Uphoff and Dazzo 2016). However, despite such alternative forms of food production, the FAO reported in 2014 that GHG emissions from agriculture, forestry, and fisheries have almost doubled over the past 50 years. This figure is expected to increase by an additional 30% by 2050 if nothing is done to reduce it (FAO 2014). As such, questions may arise about the gaps in our knowledge and therefore, this indicates the dire need to understand the complex processes between food production and the environment. The advances in our understanding can equip relevant stakeholders with the necessary tools to develop meaningful solutions to attain positive outcomes.

In efforts to advance our understanding on food security, it is essential to examine its mechanisms and interrelated processes. As such, this chapter focuses on understanding the dialectic relationship between climate change and food security: firstly, on the implications of climate change on food security and, secondly, on the impact of food production on climate change. This chaper aims to establish the links between soil, water, and crops to present a clearer understanding of processes related to food security and food production in the context of climate change.

How Climate Change Is Affecting Food Security

Climate change is an outcome of a multitude of factors but it is commonly accepted that the main cause for worsening climate conditions is the increase of greenhouse gas emissions in the atmosphere. The increased concentration of GHGs in the atmosphere is expected to trap more heat on Earth which in turn results in an increase in global mean temperatures (Thomas and López 2015). Climate change causes adverse impacts on both ecosystems and human societies as it increases the incidence of floods, droughts, and other climate-related disasters that have the potential to affect farmlands, livestock, and animal husbandry, which are essential for agricultural purposes (Gould and Lewis 2009). In order to better understand the effects of climate change on food security, this chapter will focus on three factors identified to have the most direct effects on food production: soil, water, and crops (Lal 2013). These three factors are crucial in understanding the effects that climate change has on food security as they are the most basic and essential components of food production.

Soil: Soil resources are limited, unequally distributed and susceptible to degradation by land misuse, mismanagement, and climate change (Lal 2013). Climate change, i.e., high-atmospheric carbon dioxide (CO_2) concentrations (400 ppm), along with increasing air temperatures (2–4°C or greater) that persist for an extended period of time, will significantly affect soil properties and fertility, food quantity and quality, and environmental quality (Qafoku 2015). This is because the atmospheric carbon cycle is dynamic and responsive to climate change (Lal 2013). In addition, accelerated weathering of the rocks and minerals in soils is exacerbated by high-atmospheric CO_2 concentrations (400 ppm), temperatures, intensive rainfalls, heat waves, and extended periods of drought (Qafoku 2015).

Weathering has the ability to decrease CO_2 concentration (through increasing the inorganic carbon pool in soils via carbonate mineral formation), but it can also disturb the balance between biotic and abiotic carbon cycles within soils (Qafoku 2015). This disturbance affects the distribution of carbon into "less stable soil pools; increasing containment mobilization that might significantly alter soil microbial activity, plant productivity, life in soils, and carbon and elemental cycling. . . [as well as] the elemental balances in rivers, lakes and oceans" (Qafoku 2015: 117). Changes in the CO_2 concentration in soil affect the organic matter content of soils and soil quality, resulting in soil degradation. Soil degradation reduces the output of agriculture and the efficiency of inputs. In addition, this decline in soil quality might increase land's vulnerability to degradation including "crusting, compaction, accelerated erosion and salinization" (Lal 2013: 10). Climate change thus leads to soil-related consequences that include "significant/dramatic changes in soil properties, surface water and groundwater quality, food (national) security, water supplies, human health, energy, agriculture, forests, and ecosystems" (Qafoku 2015: 117).

In addition, research has shown that climate change increases the likelihood of climate-related disasters such as droughts, floods and heatwaves which causes adverse impacts on food security through social, economic and agro-ecosystems. This affects the drying–rewetting cycles of the land, which in turn, directly affects the "microbial nitrogen turnover rates in soil by changing the water content and the oxygen partial pressure" (Gschwendtner et al. 2014: 1). These changes might increase the likelihood of nitrification that will lead to nitrate formation, and depending on the soil type, nitrates might enter groundwater streams and significantly reduce the availability of nitrogen pools in soil (Gschwendtner et al. 2014). The impoverished soil affects food security as it causes a reduction in quality and quantity of crops, thereby lowering the availability of food for the population. Changes in the nitrogen content in the soil have the potential to affect soil nutrient levels that get taken up by plants, and this can result in yields having low-tissue concentrations of trace elements (St. Clair and Lynch 2010). The resulting effect may cause populations to suffer from micronutrient deficiencies if they lack alternative dietary choices to compensate for the lack of nutrient intake from these crops.

Another critical factor for food security is soil quality. Extensive damage to soil is irreversible which becomes a serious problem particularly when soil is an important non-renewable resource that plays a irreplaceable role in food production. Arguably, damaged soil might be a more imminent and immediate problem to society than the depletion of fossil fuels, primarily because it affects food production, emission of greenhouse gases and the quality as well as quantity of water (Shahid and Ahmed 2014). Damaged soil is also brought about by climate change as it alters the carbon concentration and nutrients in the soil that results in the negative impact on the quality and quantity of crop production. Such implications impact food security in very fundamental ways which illustrates the role of soil quality.

Water: Similar to soil resources, water resources are also scarce and susceptible to pollution, contamination, eutrophication, and changes in climate (Lal 2013). In 2014, the United Nations Department of Economic and Social Affairs (UNDESA) reports that existing climate change scenarios will result in almost half the world's population living in areas of high water stress by 2030 (UNDESA 2014a). The changing precipitation is altering the hydrological systems, affecting water quality and quantity (Lal 2013). Water availability is being threatened by climate change as it has the potential to decrease or cause fluctuations in temperature and precipitation in some regions of the world (Kang et al. 2009). Fluctuations in rainfall and temperature can potentially cause crop failure especially for crops that require high temperature and rainfall conditions such as rice.

As exemplified, climate change affects the drying–rewetting cycles of the land, thereby changing the nitrogen content in soils. This in turn affects water resources when nitrates from the soil seep into groundwater systems and alter the nutrient concentration of water bodies. The increased nitrogen concentration in water bodies may lead to the process of eutrophication. Eutrophication is a process whereby nutrient overloads in the water body lead to an increase in floating plant communities and plankton (Feuchtmayr et al. 2009). In addition, increased production of floating plant communities is also facilitated by warmer water bodies, due to climate change that encourages and prolongs the growing period. The increased growth in floating plant communities will have an adverse effect on submerged plant communities, as sunlight needed for these plants to photosynthesize is blocked and absorbed by the plants floating on the surface. In order to grow, these floating plant communities compete with submerged plants and other marine animals for nutrients present in the water bodies.

The inability of submerged plant communities to photosynthesize, respire, and absorb the necessary nutrients might eventually lead to its death. The deaths of submerged plant communities will alter the chemical balance in water bodies due to the increase in oxygen content in water bodies, as the plants are no longer able to take in oxygen and convert it to CO_2 via the process of respiration. Such cascading processes upsets the aquatic biodiversity as marine animals reliant on these plants for food are also affected by changes in the food chain. Animals that are not able to switch to alternative forms of food might either die or have nutritional deficiencies due to the changes in nutrition uptake. Thus, increased nitrogen content in water bodies and warmer water conditions have led to the increase in floating plant communities at the expense of submerged aquatic plant diversity.

In addition, the high concentration of GHGs in the atmosphere together with the irresponsible disposal of chemicals into water bodies has altered water concentration, leading to ocean acidification and hypoxia that will influence the distribution and productivity of fisheries and aquaculture in many places (Porter et al. 2014). The rising global temperature has also led to the rise in the temperature of water bodies, and marine animals that are unable to acclimatize or migrate to cooler water bodies will thus be affected. Studies have indicated that even a small rise of 1 degree Celcius in water temperature could greatly impact the mortality of fishes, breeding, geographical distributions, and harvests (Mahapatra 2014).

It has also been postulated that rising temperatures in water bodies have led to smaller body sizes of fishes such as herring and haddock (Baudron et al. 2014). This is because warmer water conditions increases anabolic oxygen demands while simultaneously reducing oxygen solubility necessary for the survival of marine life (Baudron et al. 2014). Thus, in order to adapt to the change in oxygen content underwater, fish species have evolved to have smaller bodies so that they have a larger surface area to volume ratio to balance their oxygen demand and uptake (Baudron et al. 2014). This biological change in fishes is worrying as it not only represents a decrease in per capita reproductive rates and decreased resilience against predators and altered ecosystems but also threatens food security (Baudron et al. 2014). With reduced per capita reproductive rates, the fish species population will be significantly reduced. Warmer water conditions thus threaten food security, as these warmer conditions result in the reduction of food availability and stability—decreased fish species populations and smaller body-sized fishes.

Furthermore, rising global temperatures resulted in water bodies drying up, leading to the phenomenon of desertification. Desertification causes the loss of arable land as the lack of water causes the land to harden and make it unsuitable for crop production or livestock rearing. Climate change impacts water in a number of ways by altering the physical conditions (e.g., temperature and land conditions), chemical environment (e.g., acidity and oxygen content) in water bodies and, the biological environment (e.g., the decline in aquatic life and the shift in marine species distribution and abundance) (Cheung et al. 2015). These changes reduces agricultural output and worsen food security.

Crops: Climate change brought about an increase in the frequency of climate-related disasters such as floods and droughts. Both have direct adverse impacts on crop production and food security. Global temperature rise has resulted in floods due to increasing sea levels caused by the melting of glaciers and the expansion of oceans (Kibria 2016). Sea-level rise (SLR) affects food security and food production as the rise in sea level can lead to increased flooding and saltwater intrusion into soil, groundwater, and freshwater bodies (Kibria 2016). SLR can result in crop failure when the crops become submerged by the floodwaters that prevent aeration of the soil. Saltwater intrusion can also result in salinization and water-logging which causes land degradation, thereby making affected land unsuitable for the cultivation of crops. It has been discovered that an SLR of 1.5 m in Bangladesh may flood about 16% of the country's land area and make it unsuitable for rice production (Kibria 2016). Droughts caused by climate change, can result in crop failure as the lack of water available for agricultural production causes crops to die. This is evident in the significant drop in crop yields, i.e., maize yields in Italy and France dropped 36% and 30%, respectively, during the severe heat season in Europe in 2003 (Farmar-Bowers 2013: 225). Droughts also affect soil quality leading to a decline in plant-available water capacity, thereby making the land unsuitable for crop production.

In addition, the rise in global temperatures as an implication of climate change might result in an increase in the growth of weeds and as a consequence, increases in the usage of pesticides (Keating 2013). With rising temperatures, crops are faced with more intense attacks from pests and are more susceptible to diseases that threaten to wipe out the harvest (Santra et al. 2014). This is because rising temperatures create optimal conditions for disease-causing organisms and pests, which adversely affect the quality and quantity of crops (Santra et al. 2014). Researchers from the Indian Agricultural Research Institute highlights that there would be a "loss of 4–5 million tonnes in wheat production with every 1 degree Celsius rise in temperature throughout the growing period" (Mahapatra 2014: 219). Climate change thus affects food security, as increasing temperatures and conditions detrimental to crop production affect the quality and quantity of crops.

Climate change affects crop production through the change in atmospheric conditions such as the rise in GHGs—rising CO_2 levels. It has been postulated that CO_2 concentrations will rise from current atmospheric levels of about 385 ppm to about 500–1000 ppm by 2100 (Taub 2010). Elevated levels of atmospheric CO_2 are said by some to be beneficial to the physiology, growth, and chemistry of the plant. It has been postulated that "a twofold increase in CO_2 will lead to a 10–15% increase in dry matter production provided that all other factors remain constant" (Santra et al. 2014: 363). This is because increased CO_2 allows for an increased rate of photosynthesis, thus allowing for an increased production of products (e.g., water, glucose, and oxygen). However, it is important to note that the benefits of increased CO_2 levels, are only possible if they are independent of any effects of climate change, i.e., rising global temperature and changes to nitrogen content in the soil. Researchers at Stanford University have discovered that elevated concentrations of CO_2 in the presence of other effects of climate change will lead to a reduction in plant growth and nutrients (Shwartz 2012).

Nitrogen changes in soil coupled with increased atmospheric CO_2 have the effect of making changes in plant tissue nitrogen and this can in turn affect the protein concentrations of plants. There is a lack of surface area for crops to take up other nutrients and minerals, as elevated levels of CO_2 encourage higher levels of photosynthetic activity that leads to the formation of more nonstructural carbohydrates. This in turn takes up the space needed for the uptake of other minerals and nutrients such as calcium, magnesium, nitrogen, and phosphorous (Taub 2010).

Furthermore, rising global temperatures can cause heat injury and physiological disorders in crops, thus affecting the quality and quantity of crops produced (Santra et al. 2014). Climate change consequences affect CO_2 levels, as seen with the increased nitrogen concentrations in soils and rising global temperatures. It is evident that the effects of rising CO_2 levels are in fact detrimental to crop production. Crops are adversely affected by climate change due to the altered weather conditions and seasons (due to increased global mean temperature) that are critical elements to grow specific crops, for instance, the growing of rice during the monsoon period. However, there are two sides to the effects of climate change on crop production. One critical aspect is the process where climate change reduces the growing period of crops allowing for more production cycles, thereby increasing production output (Kang et al. 2009). However, shorter crop rotation periods are not always beneficial. Certain crops like rice require conditions that are more rigid than other crops. With the onset of shorter crop rotation periods, the overall productivity of rice production could be stymied. As such, the effects of shortened crop rotation periods are largely dependent on the type of crop and the necessary conditions that enable certain crops to either flourish or flounder.

How All Three Factors Affect Food Security

The impact of soil, water, and crops on food security will be measured using four components: food availability, economic and physical access to food, food utilization, and the stability of food supply. Food availability refers to the physical presence of food available for consumption; economic and physical access to food refers to having the ability and resources to acquire food; food utilization refers to having the "appropriate nutritional content of food and the ability of the body to use it effectively;" and stability of food supply refers to the ability to ensure that there is sufficient food for individuals all the time (Burke and Lobell 2010: 14).

Food Availability

If the soil lacks nutrients or is unable to support the growth of crops, there would be a lack of supply that has dire consequences for food availability. Likewise, if the water is contaminated due to its high-acidic concentration, crops would die as the acidity of the water would kill the crops. In addition, the rise of natural disasters such as floods and droughts affect food security. Drought prevents the growing of crops and leads to crop failure or the delay of crop production, while floods cause crops to die or the land to be unsuitable for agricultural purposes due to the lack of fertile soil. Crops are sensitive to changes in temperature and precipitation, and a rise in global mean temperatures by 2 degree Celcius can destabilize agricultural practices and crop production periods (Kang et al. 2009). In addition, food availability is further threatened as climate change leading to climate fluctuations has the potential to lead to the loss of local diversity and translate to a lower variety of resources for both current and future generations (Úbeda et al. 2013).

As mentioned, climate change has the potential to alter the geographical distribution of some marine animals due to increased temperatures in water bodies. Increases in temperatures may create conditions that are unsuitable for the continued survival of certain marine species. Nevertheless, migration may not always be negative as it can increase the number of fisheries in certain regions that may increase employment opportunities and food production capabilities. However, those originally dependent on such marine life will be greatly affected because of this migratory process. Fisheries and local fishermen would notice a substantial drop in catch as fishes that are unable to adapt to changing water conditions shift to other water bodies. The decline in catch would result in a decrease in food availability, employment, and a rise in prices. This would in turn affect food security as these affected regions will have reduced availability and access to these resources.

Economic and Physical Access to Food

When crops fail due to climate-related disasters, farmers are unable to sell their crops to support their families. Between 2003 and 2013, these disasters affected more than 1.9 billion people in developing countries and resulted in about half a trillion US dollars in estimated damages (FAO 2015). FAO estimates that the "agricultural sector absorbs approximately 22% of the total economic impact of these disasters" which in turn affects its capability to support food security (FAO 2015). Evidently the effects of climate change are unequal. Developing countries as compared to developed ones are more likely to be affected by climate change due to: (1) greater dependency on agriculture, (2) lacking the knowledge and skills to mitigate climate-related threats and, (3) the lack of stockpiling practices to ensure consistent supply and access to critical resources.

In addition, farmers in developing countries often live from one harvest to another. The failure of one harvest might cause farmers to lose much of their savings and financial safety nets. As such, they may not have the financial means to purchase necessities nor remain self-sufficient from their harvest. Farmers resing in developing countries are more vulnerable due to the general lack of governmental support and resources to aid them in times of crises. It is postulated that with increased climate change, rice production in the Philippines might decrease as much as 75% by 2100 (Singh 2014). This decline might result in many Filipinos having to settle for meals with little or no rice due to the rice shortage as well as the lack of economic access to food. This problem can however be lessened if the government intervenes and implements climate adaptation programs, i.e., increased use of technology for agricultural purposes, to help prevent such significant losses in rice production (Singh 2014).

Climate change aggravates the problem of food security due to the increases in the frequency and intensity of climate-related disasters. Disasters bring about bad weather patterns that destroy productivity of livestock and crop production, disrupt the viability of trade and affect the price stability of essential commodities. Climate-related disasters also cause infrastructural damages, effectively trapping certain populations in areas where they have limited or no physical access to food because of distrupitions of critical supply chains. The inability of food imports to reach the intended market will exacerbate food insecurity faced by marginalized communities who do not have, (1) the means to address infrastructural damages and deal with supply disruptions and, (2) afford the increased prices brought about by global and regional shortages of essential commodities.

Food Utilization

Climate change affects the availability and access to food with high nutritional value for people facing disruptions in the quality of crops produced. As highlighted, climate change alters the nutritional value of the crops produced as it changes the nutrient levels in the soil. Individuals whose main diet consists of crops produced under impoverished soil conditions are susceptible to malnutrition and nutrient deficiencies due to decreased nutrient content in the foods they are consuming. Therefore, the full nutritional value of food cannot be fully absorbed if climate change causes changes in food production factors, i.e., soil and water, that decrease the nutritional value found in food yields. Food utilization is thus negatively affected, as nutritional content of food is insufficient for the body to use it effectively to meet the dietary needs for a healthy lifestyle (Gschwendtner et al. 2014; St. Clair and Lynch 2010).

In addition, climate change affects food safety, if crops are grown from contaminated water resulting in potentially harmful produce. Climate-related disasters such as flooding could cause harmful substances to enter water sources that are used for hydration and agricultural purposes. Flooding might also lead to large pools of stagnant water in communities that can increase the chances of vector-borne (e.g., malaria and dengue) and water-borne (e.g., cholera) diseases that affect the health of individuals and their ability to utilize food properly (IPCC 2007). During times of climate-related disasters, people might not have the luxury to pick foods that are rich in nutrients due to the shortage in food availability. As a result, people affected by disasters might turn to rationing consumption to prioritize calorie-rich but nutrient-poor foods. These behaviours will lead to a decrease in dietary quality, resulting in the loss of health, productivity capacity and low incomes (Porter et al. 2014). Hence, climate-related disasters are equally consequential in terms of quality and quantity of food for affected populations.

Stability of Food Supply

Climate change affects the stability of food due to the changing anthropogenic conditions, drying–rewetting cycles and global mean temperatures, that will affect livestock rearing and crop production. Joint efforts between governments and farmers have turned to potential use of technological advances and developments to mitigate the effects of climate change on food stability. However, technological advances used to mitigate the effects of climate change might further exacerbate the issue of food security and climate change. The effects society's anthropogenic use of the environment and its resources to fulfil the demands of technology involves many unexplored variables and therefore, our understanding of the potential pros and cons of newer technologies are still nascent. It remains to be seen if the technological advancements incorporated into food production systems will indeed creates the necessary buffers against the effects of climate change effects and increase food stability. As many of these advances are still in their infancy period, more research and time are needed to gain a better understanding of these advances.

The stability of food supply is not only affected by climate change but also by other factors such as food distribution and transportation. Reports suggests that climate change increases the frequency and intensity of climate-related disasters, and this in turn affects the stability of food supply as food trade. Disasters can hinder flight and shipping routes due to poor visibility as a result of harsh weather conditions or infrastructural damages.

The instability of food supply is more predominantly felt in developing countries that do not practice stockpiling. Often, these countries lack the technical expertise and financial resources to engage experts and engineers in establishing food storage facilities that have the appropriate capabilities to store food supplies for an extended period and withstand the impact of natural disasters. Without proper stockpiling, the instability of food supply is amplified when major infrastructure and transportation hubs such as airports and ports are closed. In addition, developing countries do not have the technological capabilities nor tools necessary to mitigate crises such as the acidification of oceans and salinization of the soil which are essential to ensure a constant production and supply of food. Therefore, based on the components of food security—food availability, economic and physical access, utilization and the stability of food, it is imperative to recognize that climate change has both a direct and indirect impact on food security. The inability of people to get their hands-on nutritious food to meet their dietary needs and food preferences for an active and healthy life goes against the very definition of food security. The examples given have shown the current and future challenges that climate change will bring to agricultural and livestock-rearing methods that are used to meet the food demands of the population.

Numerous research studies on the effects of climate change on food production have led to many governments or farmers incorporating various adaptation methods to their agricultural practices so as to reduce the effects of climate change on yields. However, researchers may neglect the connection between food production systems and climate change, e.g., "rice farming is responsible for approximately 10% of the methane released" into the atmosphere (Singh 2014: 189). In order to gain a better understanding of the issue of food (in)security, it is essential that both systems be examined without prejudice. As such, this chapter would now examine the impact of food production systems on climate change in hopes of providing a more balanced view of the issues of food (in)security and a greater understanding of the issue of climate change and food (in)security.

Food production systems cannot be disregarded when examining food security because the latter is the by-product of the former. Without food production systems, there would not be a concept of food security that enables for all people, at all times, to have physical, social, and economic access to sufficient, safe, and nutritious food (FAO 2001).

How Food Production Systems Are Affecting Climate Change

The world's population in 1990 was 5.3 billion people, and over the span of 15 years this figure increased by 7 billion (US Consensus Bureau, n.d.). The projected population growth for 2050 is said to be 9.4 billion according to a report released by the US Census Bureau in 2015. In order to keep up with the growing population, it is necessary that food production be increased manifold. There are many components of food production systems, however, for the purposes of this paper, food production will be defined as the system which encompasses the growing, processing, distribution, and consumption of food products.

The increased demand for agricultural products has led to many food producers turning to artificial means such as the use of fertilizers (e.g., the input of inorganic and organic nitrogen in agro-ecosystems) in efforts to improve soil fertility for crop cultivation. Due to the increased demands for higher yields, farmers are unwilling to allow the land to rest and fallow between crop rotation and harvests. According to studies, agriculture sectors have been identified as being responsible for 13.5% of the global GHG emissions, and one factor apart from deforestation that plays a significant role in these relatively high-GHG emissions in the atmosphere is the excessive use of synthetic fertilizers, pesticides, and insecticides (Shahid and Ahmed 2014). Although the use of fertilizers, pesticides, and insecticides reduces the amount of crops lost to pests and diseases and increased the overall yield of crops, there are exemplifications of negative repercussions. Excessive mismanagement of land and the use of certain chemicals and can lead to soil degeneration that reduces the efficiency of crops to take up nitrogen. As a result, these interacting mechanisms in turn leads to an increase in N_2O (and NOx) emissions in the atmosphere (Lal 2015).

The use of nitrogen fertilizer for agricultural purposes has led to "emissions of N_2O from food systems account[ing] for 77% of total anthropogenic emissions" (Lal 2015: 474). In addition, the production of nitrogen fertilizers leads to the release of GHGs such as methane, CO_2, and nitrous oxide, thus increasing the concentration and percentage of GHGs in the atmosphere (Carlsson-Kanyama and González 2014). N_2O exacerbates climate problems as it depletes the stratospheric ozone, increases anthropogenic discharges into the atmosphere, and causes the global mean temperature to increase (Lal 2015). In addition, changes in the global mean temperatures lead to rising sea levels due to the melting of polar caps and alteration of weather cycles, which results in climate-related disasters.

In order to increase the amount of food to meet the ever-growing demands of the world's 7.3 billion people, large conglomerates have been buying out small, family-owned agricultural businesses to convert them into huge food production enterprises. This results in large amounts of forest area being deforested to increase arable land for crop production and livestock rearing. As of 2012, cattle ranchers, loggers, and soya farmers had stripped 17% of the Amazon forests in Brazil, and at the peak of clearance, 10,723 square miles were deforested in a year (Watts 2012). The effects of deforestation have a huge impact on climate change. Trees are natural air purifiers of the Earth—a tree takes in CO_2 for photosynthesis and releases oxygen back into the atmosphere; it also stores carbon within its leaves, thereby reducing the carbon concentration in the environment that contributes to GHGs. In addition, a tree's transpiration and canopy reduce temperature, as it affects "radiation absorption and heat storage, wind speed, relative humidity, turbulence" (Nowak 2002). Thus, when trees are cleared to increase food production, the Earth loses its natural air purifiers and natural air-conditioners, which results in large amounts of CO_2 being released into the atmosphere. This increases GHG concentrations exponentially through the rise in global mean temperatures.

Deforestation also increases the likelihood of salinization, soil erosion, acidification, and desertification as it alters the natural landscape and the normal functionalities of the systems. For example, deforestation removes tree roots that would otherwise hold the soil together and prevent it from being washed away during heavy rainfall. When the topsoil is washed away, the nutrients and minerals that make the soil fertile for cultivation are also removed. The introduction of synthetic means of increasing soil fertility and productivity through the use of fertilizers with high levels of inorganic or organic nitrogen might alter chemical compositions in water bodies as these fertilizers are washed into rivers and lakes. The introduction of these natural and artificial nutrients as well as minerals can lead to water pollution (i.e., acidification and eutrophication) and the death of aqua flora and fauna that are unable to adapt to this change. Studies have also shown that the effects of deforestation (e.g., salinization, acidification, desertification, and soil erosion) and the excessive use of artificial fertilizers have rendered once productive arable crop land into infertile, unusable land (Lawrence et al. 2013). Thus, it can be seen that food production systems, the effects of climate change, and food security are all closely linked and integrated, as changes to one system can lead to substantial effects on the other systems.

Food production systems are heavily dependent on fossil fuels for transportation, creation of artificial fertilizers and pesticides and the running of various machineries needed for packaging, producing, and distributing food (Lawrence et al. 2013). It has been discovered that the production of nitrogen fertilizers uses large amounts of fossil fuels such as coal that "can account for more than 50% of total energy use in commercial agriculture" and 1.2% of all anthropogenic GHG emissions (Woods et al. 2010). A life-cycle study in the United States found that "agricultural transport as a whole contributes 11% of all agricultural GHG emissions from agriculture" (Lin et al. 2011: 5). However, the actual contribution of agricultural transport emissions is higher than the stated figure as it fails to include emissions from agricultural inputs.

Agriculture is heavily reliant on transportation as the produce from this sector are voluminous and perishable. The total distance food travels from the original production site to its place of consumption is termed as "food miles" (Lin et al. 2011). For most cases, higher food miles would equate to greater GHG emissions as more fossil fuels are required to be combusted for transportation purposes. Thus, food supplies that are transported overseas via air freight often account for a high amount of GHG emissions. The estimates of the various forms of transportation are as follows: air transport contributes 1.093 CO_2 equivalent/t/km, truck transport contributes 0.15 CO_2 equivalent/t/km, and rail transport at 0.01 CO_2 equivalent/t/km (Lin et al. 2011).

The World Urbanization Prospects: The 2014 Revision published by the UNDESA (2014b), reported that 54% of the world is now urbanized. This means that there is less land available for agricultural purposes or that more land needs to be cleared in order to meet the agricultural demands of the ever-growing population. Countries like Singapore which lack land area for food production are thus reliant on other countries for food import. Singapore imports more than 90% of their food, e.g., 73% of eggs are imported from Malaysia, and 63% of frozen chickens are imported, of which 84% are imported from Brazil (RSIS 2010). The importing of food contributes to climate change as transportation of food from one place to another requires energy that is usually generated by the burning of fossil fuels. With a rising world population and an approximation of two-thirds of the world being urbanized by 2050, the carbon footprint associated with the transportation of food will certainly increase from the current rate of 11% (UNDESA 2014b; Wakeland et al. 2012).

This reliance on fossil fuel has a direct impact on climate change as the burning of fossil fuels for energy not only releases toxic substances into the atmosphere but also leads to land degradation as more ores are extracted from the ground. The combustion of fossil fuels will increase anthropogenic conditions that will further exacerbate the issue of climate change and its consequences, i.e., food security (Adebisi-Adelani and Oyesola 2014). This is because elevated levels of CO_2 can cause "protein content [in grain quality to decrease] by 10–14% in non-leguminous grain crops and concentrations of minerals, such as iron and zinc [to] decrease by 15–30%" (Anisworth and McGrath 2010: 109). Changes in food nutritional properties will affect the quality of food produced and its utilization. Hence, food production and food processing contribute to GHG emissions that are detrimental to the environment and in itself becomes a factor that worsen climate change.

Another factor of food production that affects climate change is the food we are producing. The increasing affluence of middle-class consumers and the rising urban population have led to changes in food preferences toward more meat-based diets. Global meat consumption has increased 325% from 1961 to 2011 (National Geographic, n.d.). This increase in meat consumption is accompanied by increases in livestock-rearing producers and meat-based processing systems that seek to maximize profit through catering to the growing population's changing food preferences. However, the rise in global meat consumption has led to increased climate change effects, as it can take 10–20 times more energy and greenhouse gas emissions to produce certain meat-based foods than grains and vegetables (Lal 2013).

According to the FAO (2015), the livestock sector emits about "7.1 gigatonnes of CO_2 equivalent per year, representing 14.5 percent of all human-induced emissions." This significant amount of GHGs being emitted into the air has negative effects on climate change as it raises the global air temperature and affects the compositions of the atmosphere, which results in the increased occurrences of natural disasters. Thus, changing food consumption patterns plays a significant role in influencing climate change. In addition, land area required for livestock rearing is more significant than for crop producing. This is because "an area of 200 m^2 can produce 142 kg of wheat or 9.6 kg of beef. The number of persons which can be fed in one day is 210 for the vegetarian diet and 13 for the beef diet" (Lal 2013: 14). By comparisons, the figures highlight that crop production are more effective in providing food security for the greater masses than livestock rearing when input demands and corresponding efficiencies are considered. However, due to rising affluence and the growing middle-class brings about changing consumption patterns that favors meat-based diets created new markets incentivizes suppliers to shift production toward high-inout meat production instead of low-input crops. These demand-led factors results in an accelerated process of suppliers converting natural ecosystems into agro-ecosystems to support new demands.

Livestock rearing can also lead to soil erosion and desertification due to overgrazing. As mentioned, the effects of soil erosion would affect the soil health affecting the quality and quantity of produce. Soil erosion and desertification affect the soil carbon sequestration and reduces the soil's ability to remove atmospheric CO_2 that helps mitigate climate change. Carbon sequestration according to United Nations Convention to Combat Desertification (UNCCD, n.d.) is "the process by which CO_2 sinks (both natural and artificial) remove CO_2 from the atmosphere, primarily as plant organic matter in soils" (UNCCD N.d.: 1). Soil plays an important role in mitigating climate change as, after all, it holds more organic carbon than atmospheric CO_2 and vegetation combined (National Geographic, n.d.). Poor soil health correspondingly afffects the ability of soil to act as a sink to remove atmospheric carbon and thus results in higher levels of CO_2 concentration in the atmosphere, exacerbating climate change. Based on the examples highlighted above, it can be seen that food production systems have a direct and indirect influence on climate change. The increased release of environmentally harmful gases into the atmosphere due to human activites increases the concentration of GHGs and the rate of warming in the atmosphere. In addition, food production and food security face threats from land damages due to soil leaching, deforestation, and salinization that converts previously fertile land into one that is unsuitable for both crop and livestock production.

Conclusion

In sum, food security, food production, and climate change are interlinked and intertwined. Changes in one factor have corresponding implications on a variety of other interrelated environmental, economic and social systems. As exemplified in this chapter, the attempts to address food security concerns and food demands subsequently brought about actions increased food production. In turn, increases in food production and the need to support growing production systems brought about land clearing and burning of fossil fuels which are one of the main causes for our climatic woes. Hence, this chapter critically highlights the interrelated mechanisms between food security, food production and climate change. The acknowledgement of how these processes interact will enhance our ability to address strategic tradeoffs without neglecting and isolating either processes through policies and actions.

With a projected increase of 2.4 billion people by 2050, it is vital that current food production systems should adopt an environmentally friendly system so that Malthus' prophesy of geometric growth of population and arithmetic growth of food production leading to inevitable food insecurity does not come true. The wider adoption of environmentally friendly food production systems would allow for sustainable development and progress for current and future generations to come and a higher chance of achieving both food security and better management of climate change. This is because, with more environmentally friendly food production systems and the introduction of environmental certification regimes, the current levels of GHG emissions can be reduced or maintained at levels where we are still able to seek solutions to mitigate and adapt to this phenomenon and address the problems in the other systems. The reduction of climate change effects will help to improve the food security problem as it reduces the likelihood of crop failure or the deaths of livestock due to natural disasters and climate change. It is also important to note that the factors identified for causing climate change and the lack of food security in this report are limited and there remains a huge range of other factors that can or are contributing to climate change and threatening food security such as political instability and economic interests.

Acknowledgements An earlier version of this chapter was published in *Environments* 2017, 4 (2): 38; https://doi.org/10.3390/environments4020038 (by Md Saidul Islam, and Andrea Wong). The authors have the copyright and permission to reproduce as a chapter here.

References

Adebisi-Adelani, O., and O. B. Oyesola. 2014. Adaptation Strategies of Citrus and Tomato Farmers Towards the Effect of Climate Change in Nigeria. In *Vulnerability of Agriculture, Water and Fisheries to Climate Change*, ed. M. Behnassi, G.R.V. Prasar, K. N. Shelat, and M. S. Muteng'e, 157–165. Dordrecht, The Netherlands: Springer.

Ainsworth, Elizabeth A., and Justin M. McGrath. 2010. Direct Effects of Rising Atmospheric Carbon Dioxide and Ozone on Crop Yields. In *Climate Change and Food Security: Adopting Agriculture to a Warmer World*, ed. D. Lobell and M. Burke. Rotterdam, 109–130. The Netherlands: Springer.

Baudron, Alan R., Coby L. Needle, Adriaan D. Rijnsdorp, and C. Tara Marshall. 2014. Warming Temperatures and Smaller Body Sizes: Synchronous Changes in Growth of North Sea Fishes. *Global Change Biology* 20 (4): 1023–1031. https://doi.org/10.1111/gcb.12514.

Burke, Marshall, and David Lobell. 2010. Climate Effects on Food Security: An Overview. In *Climate Change and Food Security*, ed. D. Lobell, and M. Burke. Rotterdam, 13–30. The Netherlands: Springer.

Carlsson-Kanyama, Annika, and Alejandro D. González. 2014. Potential Contributions of Food Consumption Patterns to Climate Change. *The American Journal of Clinical Nutrition* 89 (5): 1704S–1709S. https://doi.org/10.3945/ajcn.2009.26736AA.

Cheung, William W.L., Richard D. Brodeur, Thomas A. Okey, and Daniel Pauly. 2015. Projecting Future Changes in Distributions of Pelagic Fish Species of Northeast Pacific Shelf Seas. *Progress in Oceanography* 130: 19–31. https://doi.org/10.1016/j.pocean.2014.09.003.

Clair, Samuel B. St., and Jonathan P. Lynch. 2010. The Opening of Pandora's Box: Climate Change Impacts on Soil Fertility and Crop Nutrition in Developing Countries. *Plant and Soil* 335 (1–2): 101–115. https://doi.org/10.1007/s11104-010-0328-z.

COP21 Climate Change Summit Reaches Deal in Paris. 2015. *BBC News*, December 13. Retrieved June 14, 2016 (http://www.bbc.com/news/science-environment-35084374).

Farmar-Bowers, Quentin. 2013. Framing the Research Needs for Food Security in Australia. In *Food Security in Australia*, 219–233. New York, NY: Springer US.

Feuchtmayr, Heidrun, Rebecca Moran, Keith Hatton, Les Connor, Tom Heyes, Brian Moss, Ian Harvey, and David Atkinson. 2009. Global Warming and Eutrophication: Effects on Water Chemistry and Autotrophic Communities in Experimental Hypertrophic Shallow Lake Mesocosms. *Journal of Applied Ecology* 46 (3): 713–723. https://doi.org/10.1111/j.1365-2664.2009.01644.x.

Food and Argriculture Organization. 2001. *The State of Food Insecurity in the World 2001*. Rome: Italy. United Nations. Retrieved September 26, 2015. (http://www.fao.org/docrep/003/y1500e/y1500e00.htm).

Food and Argriculture Organization. 2014. *Agriculture's Greenhouse Gas Emissions on the Rise*. Food and Argriculture Organization, 11 April. Retrieved May 23, 2016. http://www.fao.org/news/story/en/item/216137/icode/.

Food and Argriculture Organization. 2015. *The Impact of Natural Hazards and Disasters on Agriculture and Food and Nutrition Security: A Call for Action to Build Resilient Livelihoods*. Rome: Italy. United Nations. Retrieved September 21, 2015 (http://www.fao.org/3/a-i4434e.pdf).

Food and Argriculture Organization, International Fund For Agricultural Development, and World Food Programme. 2015. *The State of Food Insecurity in the World. Meeting the 2015 International Hunger Targets: Taking Stock of Uneven Progress*. Rome, Italy: United Nations. Retrieved September 26, 2015 (http://www.fao.org/3/a-i4646e.pdf).

Gschwendtner, Silvia, Javier Tejedor, Carolin Bimueller, Michael Dannenmann, Ingrid Kögel Knabner, and Michael Schloter. 2014. Climate Change Induces Shifts in Abundance and Activity Pattern of Bacteria and Archaea Catalyzing Major Transformation Steps in Nitrogen Turnover in a Soil from a Mid-European Beech Forest. *PLoS ONE* 9 (12): e114278. https://doi.org/10.1371/journal.pone.0114278.

Gould, Kenneth Alan, and Tammy L. Lewis. 2009. An Introduction to Environmental Sociology. In *Twenty Lessons in Environmental Sociology*, ed. K.A. Gould, and T.L. Lewis, 1–8. New York, NY: Oxford University Press.

Intergovernmental Pancel On Climate Change. 2007a. *Climate Change 2007: Synthesis Report*. Contribution of Working Groups I, II and III to the Fourth Assessment Report. Geneva: Switzerland. Retrieved August 27, 2015. https://www.ipcc.ch/publications_and_data/ar4/syr/en/mains1.html.

Intergovernmental Pancel On Climate Change. 2007b. *Food Security and Vulnerability*. IPCC Fourth Assessment Report: Climate Change 2007. Geneva: Switzerland. Retrieved June 12, 2016. https://www.ipcc.ch/publications_and_data/ar4/wg2/en/ch5s5-6-5.html.

Islam, Md Saidul. 2013. *Development, Power, and the Environment: Neoliberal Paradox in the Age of Vulnerability*, vol. 34. New York, NY and London, UK: Routledge.

Kang, Yinhong, Shahbaz Khan, and Xiaoyi Ma. 2009. Climate Change Impacts on Crop Yield, Crop Water Productivity and Food Security–A Review. *Progress in Natural Science* 19 (12): 1665–1674. https://doi.org/10.1016/j.pnsc.2009.08.001.

Keating, Adriana. 2013. Food Security in Australia: The Logistics of Vulnerability. In *Food Security in Australia: Challenges and Prospects for the Future*, ed. Q. Farmar-Bowers, V. Higgins, J. Millar, 21–34. New York, NY: Springer.

Kibria, Golam. 2016. *Sea-Level-Rise and its Impact on Wetlands, Water, Agriculture, Fisheries, Aquaculture, Migration, Public Health, Infrastructure and Adaptation*, 6. Retrieved March 30, 2016. https://www.researchgate.net/profile/Golam_Kibria7/publication/266794121_Sea-level_rise_and_its_impact_on_wetlands_water_agriculture_fisheries_aquaculture_public_health_displacement_infrastructure_and_adaptation/links/57ea21e708aeb34bc0909409.pdf.

Khandekar, Nivedita. 2015. Too Few Scientists Track Loss of Himalayan glaciers. *Responding to Climate Change*, July 13. Retrieved September 7, 2015. http://www.rtcc.org/2015/07/13/too-few-scientists-track-loss-of-himalayan-glaciers/.

Lal, Rattan. 2013. Food Security in a Changing Climate. *Ecohydrology & Hydrobiology* 13 (1): 8–21. https://doi.org/10.1016/j.ecohyd.2013.03.006.

Lal, Rattan. 2015. Climate Change and Agriculture. In *Climate Change Observed Impacts on Planet Earth*, 2nd ed., 465–489. https://doi.org/10.1016/B978-0-444-63524-2.00028-2.

Lawrence, Geoffrey, Carol Richards, and David Burch. 2013. The Impacts of Climate Change on Australia's Food Production and Export. In *Food Security in Australia*, ed. Q. Farmar-Bowers, V. Higgins, and J. Millar, 173–186. New York, NY: Springer US.

Lin, Brenda B., M. Jahi Chappell, John Vandermeer, Gerald Smith, Eileen Quintero, Rachel Bezner-Kerr, Daniel M. Griffith, Stuart Ketcham, Steven C. Latta, Philip McMichael, Krista McGuire, Ron Nigh, Dianne Rocheleau, John Soluri, and Ivette Perfecto. 2011. Effects of Industrial Agriculture on Climate Change and the Mitigation Potential on Small-Scale Agro-Ecological Farms. *Animal Science Reviews* 2011(69): 1–18. http://dx.doi.org/10.1079/PAVSNNR20116020.

Mahapatra, Samarendra. 2014. Impact of Climate Change on Indian Agriculture. In *Climate Change Effect on Crop Productivity*, ed. R.S. Sengar, and K. Sengar, 213–228. Boca Raton, FL: CRC Press.

Misra, Anil Kumar. 2014. Climate Change and Challenges of Water and Food Security. *International Journal of Sustainable Built Environment* 3 (1): 153–165. https://doi.org/10.1016/j.ijsbe.2014.04.006.

National Geographic. n.d. *What the World Eats*. Retrieved December 11, 2015. http://www.nationalgeographic.com/what-the-world-eats/.

Nowak, David J. 2002. *The Effects of Urban Trees on Air Quality*. Sycrause: NY: USDA Forest Service. Retrieved September 28, 2015. (http://www.nrs.fs.fed.us/units/urban/local-resources/downloads/Tree_Air_Qual.pdf).

Obama Says World Must Speed up Climate Change Fight. 2015. *The Straits Times*, September 1. Retrieved September 7, 2015 (http://www.straitstimes.com/world/united-states/obama-says-world-must-reach-climate-deal-in-paris-while-we-still-can).

Porter, J.R., L. Xie, A.J. Challinor, K. Cochrane, S.M. Howden, M.M. Iqbal. D. Lobell, and M.I. Travasso. 2014. Food Security and Food Production Systems. In *Climate Change 2014: Impacts, Adaptation, and Vulnerability. Part A: Global and Sectoral Aspects*, 485–533. Contribution of Working Group II to the Fifth Assessment Report of the Intergovernmental Panel on Climate Change. Cambridge, UK: Cambridge University Press; New York, NY, USA.

Qafoku, Nikolla P. 2015. Chapter Two-Climate-Change Effects on Soils: Accelerated Weathering, Soil Carbon, and Elemental Cycling. *Advances in Agronomy* 131: 111–172. https://doi.org/10.1016/bs.agron.2014.12.004.

Santra, Subhas Chandra, Anusaya Mallick, and Alok Chandra Samal. 2014. Global Warming Impact on Crop Productivity. In *Climate Change Effect on Crop Productivity*, ed. R.S. Sengar, K. Sengar, 357–384. Boca Raton, FL: CRC Press.

Shahid, Shabbir A., and Mushtaque Ahmed, ed. 2014. *Environmental Cost and Face of Agriculture in the Gulf Cooperation Council Countries: Fostering Agriculture in the Context of Climate Change*. Berlin, Germany: Springer.

Shwartz, Mark. 2012. Climate Change Surprise: High Carbon Dioxide Levels can Retard Plant Growth Study Reveals. *Stanford News Service*, 12 May. Retrieved June 10, 2016. https://news.stanford.edu/pr/02/jasperplots124.html.

Singh, Devendra Pal. 2014. Global Warming Impact on Rice Crop Productivity. In *Climate Change Effect on Crop Productivity*, ed. R.S. Sengar, and K. Sengar, 187–196. Boca Raton, FL: CRC Press.

Taub, Daniel R. 2010. Effects of Rising Atmospheric Concentrations of Carbon Dioxide on Plants. *Nature Education Knowledge* 3 (10): 21.

The RSIS Centre for Non-Traditional (NTS) Studies. 2010. *Food Security Expert Group Meeting on 'Food First: Ensuring food and Nutrition for Urbanites'*. The National Security Coordination Secretariat. Singapore: S. Rajaratnam School of International Studies. Retrieved December 11, 2015. https://www.rsis.edu.sg/wp-content/uploads/2014/07/ER100805_Food_First.pdf.

Thomas, Vinod, and Ramón López. 2015. Global Increase in Climate-Related Disasters. Asian Development Bank Economics Working Paper Series, Asian Development Bank, Manila, Phillippines. Retrieved May 28, 2016. http://www.adb.org/sites/default/files/publication/176899/ewp-466.pdf.

Úbeda, Bárbara, Adrian S. Di Giacomo, Juan Jose Neiff, Steven A. Loiselle, Alicia S. Guadalupe, Jose Angel Poi, Silvina Casco Galvez, and Andres Cozar. 2013. Potential Effects of Climate Change on the Water Level, Flora and Macro-Fauna of a Large Neotropical Wetland. *PLoS ONE* 8 (7): e67787.

United Nations Convention to Combat Desertification. n.d. *Climate Change and Desertification*. Bonn, Germany: United Nations. Retrieved Devember 11, 2015. http://www.unccd.int/Lists/SiteDocumentLibrary/Publications/Desertificationsandclimatechange.pdf).

United Nations Department of Economic and Social Affairs. 2014a. *Water Stress versus Water Scarcity*. Retrieved 9 December, 2015. Available online http://www.un.org/waterforlifedecade/scarcity.shtml.

United Nations Department of Economic and Social Affairs. 2014b. *World Urbanization Prospects: The 2014 Revision*. New York, NY: United Nations. Retrieved December 11, 2015. (http://esa.un.org/unpd/wup/FinalReport/WUP2014-Report.pdf).

United Nations Department of Economic and Social Affairs. 2015. *World Population Projected to Reach 9.7 Billion by 2050*. New York, NY: United Nations. Retrieved December 11, 2015. https://www.un.org/development/desa/en/news/population/2015-report.html.

United States Consensus Bureau. n.d. *World Population*. Retrieved September 28, 2015. http://www.census.gov/population/international/data/worldpop/table_population.php.

Uphoff, Norman, and Frank B. Dazzo. 2016. Making Rice Production More Environmentally-Friendly. *Environments* 3 (2): 12. https://doi.org/10.3390/environments3020012.

Wakeland, Wayne, Susan Cholette, and Kumar Venkat. 2012. Food Transportation Issues and Reducing Carbon Footprint. In *Green Technologies in Food Production and Processing*, 211–236. New York, NY: Springer. Retrieved September 28, 2015. http://www.cleanmetrics.com/pages/Ch9_0923.pdf.

Watts, Jonathan. 2012. Brazil's Amazon Rangers Battle Farmers' Burning Business Logic. *The Guardian*, November 14. Retrieved September 28, 2015 http://www.theguardian.com/environment/2012/nov/14/brazil-amazon-rangers-farmers-burning.

Woods, Jeremy, Adrian Williams, John K. Hughes, Mairi Black, and Richard Murphy. 2010. Energy and the food system. *Philosophical Transactions of the Royal Society of London B: Biological Sciences* 365 (1554): 2991–3006. https://doi.org/10.1098/rstb.2010.0172.

CHAPTER 3

Climate Change and Food Security in ASEAN

This chapter will provide: (1) the historical background to ASEAN and its member states, (2) highlight the impacts of climate change on food security in the region, and (3) provide an analysis of the efficacy of the regional initiatives to mitigate regional-level risks of food security considering the impact of climate change. The chapter aims to inquire and assess the current state of action within the region. The regional case study examines regional policies, notwithstanding that individual member states may have national-level policies and programs to mitigate climate change and food security risks. Secondly, policies specific to food security and climate change in tandem will only be presented here as considerations for climate change and food security as separate issues may be beyond the scope and aims of this chapter.

Background and History of ASEAN

ASEAN was established on the 8th of August 1967 by its founding nations, Indonesia, Malaysia, Philippines, Singapore, and Thailand with the signing of the ASEAN Declaration. The objectives and resolutions of ASEAN as inscribed in the ASEAN Declaration (ASEAN 2017) are:

M. S. Islam and E. Kieu, *Climate Change and Food Security in Asia Pacific*, International Political Economy Series,
https://doi.org/10.1007/978-3-030-70753-8_3

1. To accelerate the economic growth, social progress, and cultural development in the region through joint endeavors in the spirit of equality and partnership in order to strengthen the foundation for a prosperous and peaceful community of Southeast Asian Nations;
2. To promote regional peace and stability through abiding respect for justice and the rule of law in the relationship among countries of the region and adherence to the principles of the United Nations Charter;
3. To promote active collaboration and mutual assistance on matters of common interest in the economic, social, cultural, technical, scientific, and administrative fields;
4. To provide assistance to each other in the form of training and research facilities in the educational, professional, technical, and administrative spheres;
5. To collaborate more effectively for the greater utilization of their agriculture and industries, the expansion of their trade, including the study of the problems of international commodity trade, the improvement of their transportation and communications facilities and the raising of the living standards of their peoples;
6. To promote Southeast Asian studies; and
7. To maintain close and beneficial cooperation with existing international and regional organizations with similar aims and purposes, and explore all avenues for even closer cooperation among themselves.

In addition, ASEAN Member States have adopted the following fundamental principles, in accordance to the Treaty of Amity and Cooperation in Southeast Asia (TAC) of 1976 (ASEAN 2017). The TAC of 1976 is a critical aspect of ASEAN as it has a vast impact on regional cooperation and conflict resolution which respects member nation's national sovereignty above regional imperatives. The TAC's fundamental principles state the following: (a) Mutual respect for the independence, sovereignty, equality, territorial integrity, and national identity of all nations; (b) The right of every State to lead its national existence free from external interference, subversion, or coercion; (c) Non-interference in the internal affairs of one another; (d) Settlement of differences or disputes by peaceful manner; (e) Renunciation of the threat or use of force; and (f) Effective cooperation among themselves.

Since ASEAN's formation in 1967, ASEAN member states expanded in the following years with Brunei Darussalam joining on the 7th of January

1984, Viet Nam on the 28th of July 1995, Lao PDR and Myanmar on the 23rd of July 1997 and finally Cambodia on the 30th of April 1999. These ten nations form ASEAN as we know it today (ASEAN 2017).

ASEAN countries have experienced remarkable growth over the last several decades. However, ASEAN nations and their successes have not been entirely smooth sailing as some countries have experienced radical and severe social, political, and economic setbacks. The total land area for ASEAN is 4.46 million square kilometers or 3% of the world's total and its coastline stretches a vast 173,000 km. While only occupying 3% of the world's total land area, the region is rich in biological heritage with Indonesia, Malaysia, and Philippines accounting for 80% of global biological diversity (ASEAN Cooperation on Environment 2015). The ASEAN region is also endowed with rich natural resources such as metals, oil, gas, and coal. Economic activities are supported by the mineral resources, oil industries, fisheries, tourism, and additionally, the strategic location of ASEAN has provided it numerous economic advantages as it is located at the crossroads of international shipping and foreign trade. It is often seen as a hinterland that is highly capable of supporting essential life regionally and globally with the vast array of renewable and nonrenewable resources at its disposal (Letchumanan 2010). Overall Gross Domestic Product per capita has been steadily increasing, with some fluctuations, over the last few years (Table 3.1).

ASEAN is highly populated with the total population of ASEAN member states in the mid-2008 was about 580 million, which accounts for 8.7% global population (Letchumanan 2010). Six ASEAN nations are among the top 50 highest populated countries in the world, namely; Indonesia, Philippines, Vietnam, Thailand, Myanmar, and Malaysia. Brunei Darussalam has the smallest population of approximately 418,000 and highest with Indonesia 258,124,000 in 2017. The total population of ASEAN stands at approximately 634,611,000 as at 2017 (United Nations Department of Economic and Social Affairs 2017) and is expected to increase to 650 million by 2020 (ASEAN Cooperation on Environment 2015). With the continuous increase in population, rapid economic growth and existing inter and intra social inequalities, ASEAN nations have exerted tremendous pressures on its natural resources which exacerbates environmental troubles and unsustainable development. It is notable that the high population and economic activities centered around its natural resources make the region particularly vulnerable to climate change impacts. Although ASEAN nations are abundant in resources, the

Table 3.1 Gross domestic product per capita in ASEAN, at current prices (nominal), in US dollars (as of August 2016)

Country	*2010*	*2011*	*2012*	*2013*	*2014*	*2015*
Brunei Darussalam	12,401.9	16,691.4	16,969.7	18,100.4	17,096.0	12,909.0
Cambodia	11,229.3	12,803.9	14,027.0	15,221.4	16,771.4	18,463.0
Indonesia	710,069.3	846,522.6	874,638.9	904,691.9	889,057.8	857,603.3
Lao PDR	6752.0	8060.6	9398.3	10,771.3	11,853.1	12,639.3
Malaysia	250,772.9	298,141.8	314,895.1	322,224.5	337,497.1	294,389.6
Myanmar	41,003.6	56,502.0	60,281.7	61,863.8	65,750.4	65,391.8
Philippines	199,975.9	224,107.8	250,603.0	268,883.1	285,108.3	289,502.8
Singapore	236,421.8	275,198.9	289,274.2	300,288.5	305,777.5	291,937.6
Thailand	341,338.5	370,722.0	397,494.8	420,156.8	404,280.3	395,726.3
Viet Nam	116,299.9	135,541.1	155,820.0	171,219.3	186,223.6	193,406.7
ASEAN	1,926,264.2	2,244,292.1	2,383,402.7	2,493,421.0	2,519,415.6	2,431,969.5
*ASEAN 6	1,750,979.3	2,031,384.5	2,143,875.7	2,234,345.2	2,238,817.0	2,142,068.7
^CLMV	175,284.9	212,907.6	239,527.0	259,075.8	280,598.6	289,900.8

Source ASEAN Secretariat Database (complied/computed from data submission, and/or websites of ASEAN member states' national statistics offices and relevant government agencies as well as the International Monetary Fund World Economic Outlook Database since April 2016) [no copyright issue]

*ASEAN 6 consists of Brunei Darussalam, Indonesia, Malaysia, Philippines, Singapore, and Thailand

^CLMV comprises of Cambodia, Lao PDR, Myanmar, and Viet Nam

growing needs from development and the inbound impacts from climate change will nevertheless be a challenge for the region (Dixon 1990; Mat and Othman 2014; Teng and Oliveros 2015).

Climate Change Impact on Food Security on ASEAN Member States

Impact on Land and Agricultural Productivity

The ASEAN region is also vulnerable to climate change and its impacts. There are numerous studies that highlighted the ways in which ASEAN nations will be affected. Due to the increased temperatures, studies on regional precipitation have shown that there will be statistically significant precipitation changes which could lead to ASEAN region being more vulnerable to intense and extreme heat and rainfall patterns (Mahlstein et al. 2012; Shiu et al. 2012; Teng and Oliveros 2015; Golan and Kohli 2013). These changing weather patterns can lead to lowered food and agricultural production as temperature changes can indirectly affect habitat structure, food supply, and resource availability (Williams and Middleton 2008; Siepielski et al. 2009; Reynolds 2010). The projected Sea-level rise will be expected to accelerate and thereby increase the inundation of agricultural lands. Adverse impacts of climate change will be intensified due to the large proportion of economic activity and population settlements being concentrated along the coasts. Furthermore, ASEAN as a region is heavily reliant on agriculture and for livelihoods and even greater dependency on natural resources. These climate-related impacts in combination with the level of extreme poverty which continues to plague the region may cause great economic and social setbacks (ASEAN Cooperation on Environment 2015; Bello 2005; Escaler et al. 2010; Lassa et al. 2015).

Rice is the main staple food source which is under threat. Rice plays a nutritional importance to ASEAN nations and its vital role permeates across political and economic spheres. ASEAN nations such as Thailand, Vietnam, and Cambodia are major exporters of rice to the global markets while on the other hand; Indonesia and Philippines are the biggest importers of rice (RSIS NTS 2013; Lassa et al. 2015). Due to the importance of rice and the impending impacts on its production, regional policy responses are necessary to mitigate the adverse impacts from climate change. Research has been progressing our understanding about heat stresses on rice production and highlighted that heat stresses changes gestation periods which will cause pollen sterility and decrease overall rice yield (Saseendran et al. 2000; Felkner et al. 2009; Vasanta 2013). Studies have shown significant results about temperature, rainfall, farm size educational knowledge, land area, and value of labor have brought about impacts on rice yield per hectare and reveals Malaysian vulnerability particularly during off seasons (Masud et al. 2014; Mat and Othman 2014; Teng and Oliveros 2015).

The location of rice plantations matter particularly for those in the deltas. Deltas are most vulnerable to the increase in water salinity as a resultant effect from storms and typhoons. Higher sea levels are associated with salinity because it brings saline water further inland and expose crops and there will be negative impact on rice yield because rice is only moderately tolerant of salt and higher levels of salinity reduces the rate of photosynthesis (Sultana, Ikeda and Kashem 2002; Bello 2005; Vasanta 2013). Projections of economic losses include a decline up to 50% of rice yield potential and a loss of 6.7% of combined GDP each year by 2100 (ASEAN Cooperation on Environment 2015). Although the impacts on rice may seem overly negative, there have been research that reported positive results. These disagreements highlight that climate stresses have differing consequences for different geographical regions. Experts have acknowledged that there must be assessment on the small and specific spatial and temporal scale for more targeted adaptation strategies due to the varying effects of climate changes. With greater knowledge about plausible impacts and its consequences, better guides and mitigation strategies can be employed more effectively to protect and develop resistant and resilient rice strains (RSIS NTS 2013; Bello 2005; Teng and Oliveros 2015).

Food security is not solely related to the availability of food but it is also vital to consider the nutritional value of food. Social ills due to malnutrition are a prominent problem among ASEAN nations and is the "hidden hunger." Commonly highlighted issues are vitamin A and iron deficiencies which can affect cognitive ability, work performance, and quality of life due to the resultant heath detriments that affect disproportionately those communities that are least developed and these remain a daily reality and concern for many ASEAN communities (RSIS NTS 2013). Vegetables can be seen as part of the solution to mitigate the risks of malnutrition. However, the production and cultivation of vegetables are likewise under threat from climate change due to higher temperatures, precipitation pattern changes, and saltwater intrusion. Despite these environmental changes, there are ongoing efforts to produce more resistant strains to combat the projected impacts so that vegetable yields can be enhanced. Collaborative efforts and research like that can drive positive results by adapting agricultural production to address food security problems by mitigating present and future risks.

Impact on Marine Ecosystems, Fisheries, and Aquaculture

Marine environment plays an intricate role among ASEAN nations and therefore, impacts affecting these marine environments from climate change can threaten overall food security as well as the survival and livelihoods of ASEAN communities. A starting point for examining the impact of climate change is to consider the increasing temperatures of oceans. Just a 1-degree Celsius water temperature increase can cause coral bleaching and additionally, increased sea levels increase the distance between organisms and the sun's energy damaging corals and threaten fish stocks, thereby destroying key habitats (Donner et al. 2007; Lesser 2007). A warmer climate will lead to saltwater intrusion and erosion for coastal areas and changes of weather patterns such as the increased intensity of storms (IPCC 2007).

The aforementioned issues will significantly affect communities ill-equipped to handle these changes. Experts noted the relevance of marine environments that extends beyond coastlines wherein outmigration of fishes can have a significant impact on fisher folk's livelihoods which can have tumulus implications with the subsequent outmigration of fisher folks toward inland towns and cities (RSIS NTS 2013). Smaller fisher folks are particularly vulnerable as fish stocks will be harder for them to access and they will lose out to corporate trawlers which threatens their stability and food security. Furthermore, a rise in sea level would result in major difficulties for many ASEAN cities such as Jakarta, Bangkok, and Manila which is situated along the coasts, therefore, millions will be affected and resettled. Resettlements can cause massive expenditures to protect and mitigate the threat facing these coastal cities (ASEAN Cooperation on Environment 2015). As such, both physical and social manifestations due to climate change impacts on marine systems and habitats must be considered dutifully to prevent its potential deterioration beyond its ability to sustain marine lifeforms, ecosystems and, the livelihood of coastal communities who depend on it.

Future Policy Implications

Despite these impacts, there have been notable positive signs of adaptation to these new threats from climate change. Positive adaptations include the use of innovative preemptive responses from the local and individual levels (RSIS NTS 2013). Nevertheless, these land and sea impacts highlighted will affect the region's vital need for important food sources and affect overall food security and threaten the survival and livelihoods of the ASEAN community should there be a lack of adaptation and mitigation strategies which can be beneficial for the region-at-large and for the local communities.

Implications and impacts on climate change have been a source of controversy due to the nature of its elusive information and its inconclusive projections. There has been much debate especially on policy formulation to mitigate future impacts. The difficulty for many decision-makers today is mainly because climate change affects a multitude of variables across social and environmental spheres. Two main methods dictate policy formulation today: (1) utilizing climate models and (2) immediate policy action. Policymakers utilizing climate models will develop appropriate policies based on the assembly of multiple climate models and focuses on the possible implications to mitigate the risks and progress scientific inquiry. The second method of pursuing immediate policy action involves recognizing overall climate change trends and impacts while providing guidance and responsive policies (RSIS NTS 2013). Notably, these policy methods for addressing climate change are not mutually exclusive but are useful to show how policies can be developed despite the contentious nature of information regarding climate change.

ASEAN as a Regional Forum for Climate Change and Food Security Initiatives

ASEAN cooperation on food security is guided by the 1979 Agreement on the ASEAN Food Security Reserve, the Vientiane Action Program (2004–2010), ASEAN Economic Community Blueprint, and the most recently adopted ASEAN Socio-Cultural Community Blueprint (ASEAN Sustainable Agrifood Systems, 2014). These regional initiatives aim to ensure that ASEAN remains resilient as a regional organization which coordinates cohesive efforts by providing a balance between economic and social development in a manner that does not affect food security and development in negative ways. Furthermore, there must be ASEAN cooperation and commitment between its member nations for the actualization of sustainable food production and trade which could boost food security in the region (Islam and Kieu 2020).

ASEAN Institutional Framework for Environmental Cooperation

The ASEAN Institutional Framework for Environmental Cooperation embraces interdisciplinary and cross-sectoral aspects of environmental issues. According to the ASEAN Cooperation on Environment, activities have been coordinated accordingly to the relevant sectoral bodies of ASEAN with regional and international institutions and all environmental considerations have incorporated into the development plans of other sectors which aim to ensure that environmentally sound and sustainable development within ASEAN has been attained (ASEAN Cooperation on Environment 2015; Islam and Kieu 2020).

ASEAN joint statements on climate change involve ASEAN Heads of State and various governments seeking to address climate change and the global community. The ASEAN joint statements released in 2007, 2009, 2010, 2011, and 2014 anchored sentiments of an "aspiration towards a global solution to the challenge of climate change and their resolve to achieve an ASEAN community resilient to climate change through national and regional actions" (ASEAN Cooperation on Environment 2015). The ASEAN community can be broadly segmented into three pillars, namely, political and security community, economic community, and the sociocultural community during the Declaration of the ASEAN Concord II in 2003 (Islam and Kieu 2020).

The first mention about climate change originated from the ASEAN Economic Community (AEC). Within the context of infrastructure development, the AEC emphasized the importance of ensuring the region's sustainable development through the establishment of an ASEAN community by 2015. These sustainable development issues reflected environmental problems such as greenhouse emissions as well as the instability of global prices of vital resources. Due to the threats, the AEC supports investment for climate change mitigation and as a collective effort, the ASEAN member states have responded to climate change by establishing the ASEAN Socio-Cultural Community (ASCC) blueprint 2009–2015. In addition, the ASEAN Working Group on Climate Change (AWGCC) was established in 2009 to oversee strategic implementation and action for the ASCC blueprint. Notably, due to the cross-sectoral nature of climate issues, climate change addressed is only relegated to AWGCC but across differing working groups which focus on environmental sectors and beyond; namely, agriculture, forestry, energy, transportation, science, and technology (ASEAN Cooperation on Environment 2015; Islam and Kieu 2020). A structural summary of the ASCC on climatic issues can be seen in Fig. 3.1.

The purpose of the ASCC stated to "contribute to realising an ASEAN Community that is people-centered and socially responsible with a view to achieving enduring solidarity and unity among the nations and peoples of ASEAN by forging a common identity and building a caring and sharing society which is inclusive and harmonious where the well-being, livelihood, and welfare of the peoples are enhanced" (ASEAN Secretariat 2009a: 67). The ASCC Blueprint for cooperation focuses on ten areas for 2009–2015 (ASEAN Secretariat 2009b). The ACSS Blueprint

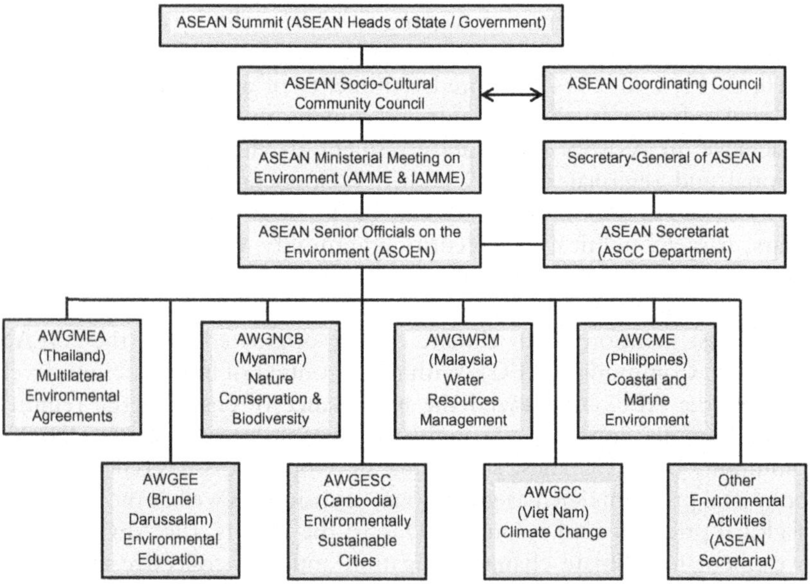

Fig. 3.1 Environmental cooperation institutional framework for ASEAN (*Source* ASEAN Cooperation on Environment (2015) [public document; no copyright issue])

examines transnational boundaries for sustainable development which is inclusive of climate change and a multitude of other environmental issues. The cooperation examines avenues to enhance regional and international cooperation to mitigate the impacts from climate change on socioeconomic and environmental development of ASEAN nations. These strategies, policies, and programs should be based on the principles of "equity, flexibility and effectiveness and common but differentiated responsibility" (ASEAN Secretariat 2009b: 14). Under Section D of the "ASEAN Socio-Cultural Community Blueprint" titled "Ensuring Environmental Sustainability" highlights the ten areas of environmental focus which can be seen in Excerpt 3.1:

Excerpt 3.1 *ASEAN Socio-Cultural Community (ASCC Blueprint)*

ASEAN shall work toward achieving sustainable development as well as promoting clean and green environment by protecting the natural resource base for economic and social development including the sustainable management and conservation of soil, water, mineral, energy, biodiversity, forest, coastal, and marine resources as well as the improvement in water and air quality for the ASEAN region. ASEAN will actively participate in global efforts toward addressing global environmental challenges, including climate change and the ozone layer protection, as well as developing and adapting environmentally sound technology for development needs and environmental sustainability

D.1. Addressing global environmental issues
D.2. Managing and preventing transboundary environmental pollution (transboundary haze pollution and transboundary movement of hazardous wastes)
D.3. Promoting sustainable development through environmental education and public participation
D.4. Promoting environmentally sound technology
D.5. Promoting quality living standards in ASEAN cities/urban areas
D.6. Harmonizing environmental policies and databases
D.7. Promoting the sustainable use of coastal and marine environment
D.8. Promoting sustainable management of natural resources and biodiversity
D.9. Promoting the sustainability of freshwater resources
D.10. Responding to climate change and addressing its impacts
D.11. Promoting sustainable forest management

Source ASEAN Secretariat (2009b) [public document; no copyright issue]

Under Subsection D10 "Responding to Climate Change and Addressing its Impacts," its strategic objective is stated as follows, "Enhance regional and international cooperation to address the issue of climate change and its impacts on socio-economic development, health and the environment, in ASEAN Member States through implementation of mitigation and adaptation measures, based on the principles of equity, flexibility, effectiveness, common but differentiated responsibilities, respective capabilities, as well as reflecting on different social and economic conditions" (ASEAN Secretariat 2009b). The foundations for cooperation are laid out in 11 points (refer to Excerpt 3.2):

Excerpt 3.2 *Section D10: Responding to climate change and addressing its impacts; points of action*

1. Encourage ASEAN common understanding on climate change issues and where possible, engage in joint efforts and common positions in addressing these issues
2. Encourage the efforts to develop an ASEAN Climate Change Initiative (ACCI)
3. Promote and facilitate the exchange of information/knowledge on scientific research and development (R&D), deployment and transfer of technology and best practices on adaptation and mitigation measures, and enhance human resource development
4. Encourage the international community to participate in and contribute to ASEAN's efforts in afforestation and reforestation, as well as to reduce deforestation and forest degradation
5. Develop regional strategies to enhance capacity for adaptation, low-carbon economy, and promote public awareness to address effects of climate change
6. Enhance collaboration among ASEAN Member States and relevant partners to address climate-related hazards, and scenarios for climate change
7. Develop regional systematic observation system to monitor the impact of climate change on vulnerable ecosystems in ASEAN
8. Conduct regional policy, scientific and related studies, to facilitate the implementation of climate change convention and related conventions
9. Promote public awareness and advocacy to raise community participation on protecting human health from the potential impact of climate change
10. Encourage the participation of local government, private sector, non-governmental organizations, and community to address the impacts of climate change; and
11. Promote strategies to ensure that climate change initiatives lead to economically vibrant and environment-friendly ASEAN Community taking into account win-win synergy between climate change and the economic development

Source ASEAN Secretariat (2009b) [public document; no copyright issue]

ASEAN Regional Cooperation Architecture for Food Security

In direct relation to food security, Vichitlekarn (2011), the Head of Agriculture Industries and Natural Resource Division within the ASEAN Secretariat highlights that ASEAN's policy and framework for cooperation revolves around four main aspects; (1) the provision for a political platform and commitment to it; (2) joint advocacy, development approach, and actions; (3) sharing of information, knowledge, and expertise and finally; (4) resource mobilization. ASEAN as a regional organization does not simply operation alone but also engages with external nations as part of its regional cooperation architecture for food security. Details can be seen in Fig. 3.2.

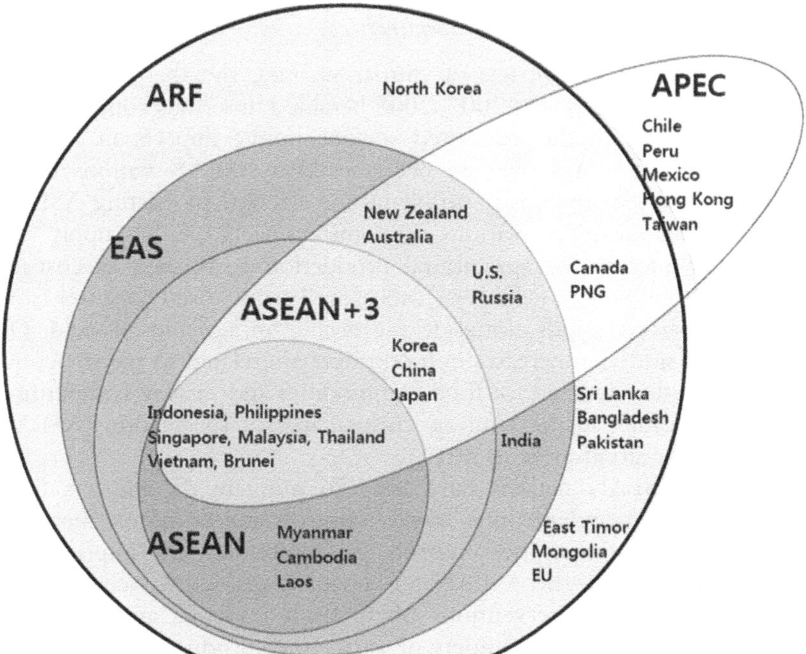

Fig. 3.2 ASEAN regional cooperation architecture (*Credit* Vichitlekarn (2011) [public document; no copyright issue])

As seen from Fig. 3.2, food security is acknowledged as a long-standing agenda for ASEAN and external ASEAN relations. Notwithstanding, food security is also widely accepted as an issue which involves cross-sectoral cooperation and evolves with time. Hence, mitigation strategies for food security in light of climate change require a multi-sectoral framework which employs coordination with various stakeholders. In the following sections, we will examine some imperative regional policy and frameworks addressing food security and climate change in ASEAN, notably ASEAN Plus Three which include two initiatives; (1) ASEAN Plus Three Emergency Rice Reserve (APTERR) and, (2) ASEAN Food Security Information System (AFSIS).

ASEAN Multi-sectoral Framework on Climate Change and Food Security

Notwithstanding the impacts of climate change, the sharp increase in international food prices in 2007–2008 heralded in serious concerns over food shortages and the associated socioeconomic impacts of ASEAN nations. Hence, it was deemed necessary that ASEAN nations cooperate to address food security problems and strengthen existing ASEAN initiatives and measures. Various economic impacts on the supply side include the increase of agricultural production costs such as cost-led increases in fuel oil and fertilizers costs as well as increased expenses from storing perishable goods alongside the decline in agricultural yield. On the demand side, the increases in food prices are related to the structural change of global demand for food commodities and varying competition as well as biofuels market and agricultural market speculation (ASEAN Sustainable Agrifood Systems 2014).

Notably, ASEAN nations have tried to mitigate the impacts from market prices by implementing market controls and economic measures like export restrictions, price controls, price subsidies, and import facilitation. However, as the ASEAN Sustainable Agrifood Systems (2014) notes, such market interventions often result tradeoffs and asymmetrical assistance toward consumers or agriculture producers. Due to the volatility of food security, ASEAN nations began discussions for future and long-term strategies for food security in the region. As such, concrete plans were discussed by the Special Senior Officials Meeting of the 29th Meeting of the ASEAN Ministers on Agriculture and Forestry (Special SOM-29th AMAF) in August 2008 which discussed the concept note of the ASEAN Integrated Food Security (AIFS) Framework (ASEAN Sustainable Agrifood Systems 2014). A work plan was also solidified with the Strategic Plan of Action on Food Security for the ASEAN Region (SPA-FS) for consideration and endorsement at the AMAF meeting during the ASEAN Summit in 2008 (ASEAN Sustainable Agrifood Systems 2014). The SPA-FS serves as a support to the AIFS framework (Islam and Kieu 2020).

ASEAN Integrated Food Security (AIFS) Framework: The Plan

The AIFS and SPA-FS is an attempt to systematize an approach to food security. The AIFS framework is a regional umbrella for food security-related initiatives which includes bioenergy and climate change and the goal are to ensure the long-term food security and to improve the livelihoods of farmers in the ASEAN region. There are four main initial components to the AIFS framework as seen in Fig. 3.3.

To concretize the AIFS framework, the SPA-FS was implemented over the period of 2009–2013 which is further elaborated into Action Programs and Activities. ASEAN Ministers of Agriculture and Forestry

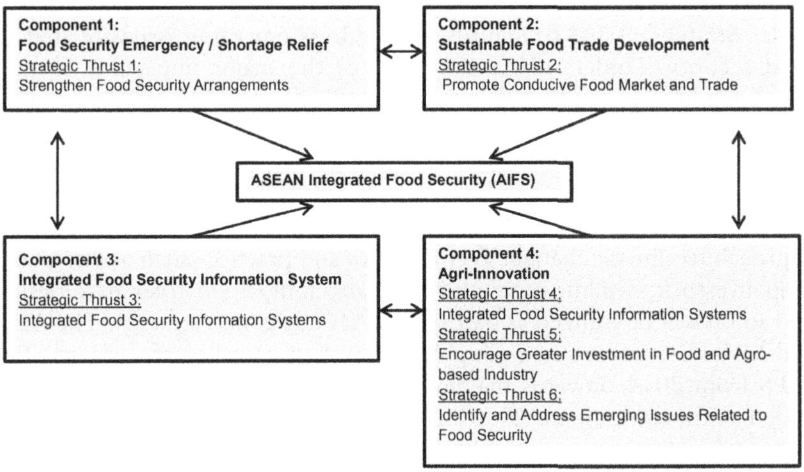

Fig. 3.3 The AIFS framework and its components (*Source* ASEAN (2009) [public document; no copyright issue])

has the primary responsibility to implement the AIFS and SPA-FS frameworks which is supported by ASEAN Secretariat and the ASCC. Some of the key achievements of the SPA-FS for its mid-term review as highlighted by the 35th Senior Officials Meeting—ASEAN Ministers of Agriculture and Forestry (ASEAN Sustainable Agrifood Systems 2014: Islam and Kieu 2020):

1. Launch of ASEAN Plus Three Emergency Rice Reserve (APTERR) Agreement and the APTERR secretariat as a permanent scheme since March 2013.
2. Initiatives that support the strengthening of ASEAN Food Security Reserve Board (AFSRB).
3. Planned for a self-sustained ASEAN Food Security Information System (AFSIS).
4. Strengthened cooperation with international institutions and developed food security support and capacity-building initiatives with the Food and Agriculture Organization and Asian Development Bank.
5. Launched ASEAN-US MARKET (Maximizing Agriculture Revenue through Knowledge Enterprise and Trade) cooperation project.

Under the AIFS and SPA-FS most strongly tied to climate issues is under Strategic Trust 6: identify and address emerging issues related to food security. Under this section, one of the major impacts is Output 6.2: introducing climate-smart agriculture with ASEAN Member States. Climate-smart agriculture is the new approach to ensure food security and adequate nutrition by increases in agricultural productivity and income while building resilience to climate change. Climate-smart agriculture has begun pilot testing as part of the eventual goal of ASEAN agriculture approach to climate change. Technologies and practices such as integrated crop–livestock, organic agriculture and drought/flood tolerant varieties, and so on will be utilized as part of ASEAN mitigation strategy. The AIFS and SPA-FS continue to be highly relevant in coordinating efforts. The AIFS from 2014 onwards maintained the original four components and added a fifth component "Nutrition-enhancing agricultural development" which is further supported by three strategic thrusts (ASEAN Sustainable Agrifood Systems 2014) seen in Excerpt 3.3:

Excerpt 3.3	*Fifth Component "Nutrition-Enhancing Agricultural Development"*
Strategic Thrust 7	Utilize nutrition Information to support evidence-based food security and agriculture policies
Strategic Thrust 8	Identify policies, institutional, and governance mechanisms for nutrition-enhancing agriculture development in the ASEAN Member States
Strategic Thrust 9	Develop and strengthen nutrition-enhancing food, agriculture, and forestry policies/programs and build capacity for their implementation, monitoring, and evaluation

[public document; no copyright issue]

The AIFS and SPA-FS continue to be a vital mechanism for food security, policy formulation and coordination, managing trade, information, and stakeholder engagements. The facilitation of dialogues and coordinated decision-making to address the multi-varied issues that face ASEAN continues its relevance well into the future.

ASEAN Climate Change Initiative (ACCI)

The ACCI indicated under the ASCC is a comprehensive and cross-sectoral platform for coordination and cooperation, designed to respond specifically to climate change and its impacts. The ACCI will provide the platform for various sectors such as energy, forestry, agriculture, disaster management to address climate change impacts. As part of ASEAN endeavors for climate change, the ASEAN Action Plan on Joint Response to Climate Change highlights several key areas that ASEAN will engage in by leveraging from the ACCI. As adopted by the 12th ASEAN Ministerial Meeting (AMME) 2012, one of the key areas is (i) *Adaptation*: sharing of information on food security, agricultural management and productivity, water resource sustainability, ongoing efforts in urban, rural, and coastal areas as well as enhancing existing ASEAN climate/meteorological/oceanographical networks. (ii) *Mitigation*: sharing best practices to mitigate greenhouse gas emissions, promoting a common understanding through workshops on Nationally Appropriate Mitigation Actions (NAMAs) and Measurement, Reporting and Verification (MRV), sharing information on promoting, developing, and enhancing Clean Development Mechanisms (CDM) and exploring the ability to impose a carbon cap and trade system within the region. (iii) *Finance and Investment*: promote common understanding on accessing multilateral funds. (iv) *Technology Transfer*: facilitate support internationally for technological transfer to ASEAN which could aid needs assessment, mitigation, and adaptation, share information and experience on science and policy as well as development strategic alliances to promote research and development with private sectors. (v) *Capacity Building*: facilitate regional as well as international support in capacity-building for ASEAN and long-term regional cooperation integrating various experiences of strengthening adaptive capacities of communities. (vi) *Other Matters of Regional Cooperation*: encourage collaboration with other existing regional institutions and to promote better collaboration of climate change related issues (12th ASEAN Ministerial Meeting 2012).

Agriculture, Fisheries, and Forestry Toward Food Security (AFCC)

AFCC is an initiative under the AIFS Framework and it provides inputs to the ACCI. Its main goal is "to contribute to food security through sustainable and efficient use of land and water resources by minimizing the impacts of and the contributions to climate change" (Vichitlekarn 2011). There is an emphasis by the AFCC to cooperate, coordinate, and implement integrated adaptation and mitigation strategies. To attain these objectives, the AFCC has laid down four driving components (Vichitlekarn 2011): (i) the integration of climate change mitigation and adaptation strategies into economic and social development policy framework, (ii) implementation of adaptation and mitigation measures, (iii) strengthening of regional information, communication and networking on climate change and food security, (iv) developing a more comprehensive multi-sectoral strategic framework and a roadmap for implementation.

ASEAN Plus Three Initiatives: Mechanism and Capacity-Building for Food Security

The APTERR (ASEAN Plus Three Emergency Rice Reserve) serves as a mechanism for the ASEAN region as an emergency food reserve with three additional members; Japan, China, and South Korea. The food crisis in 2008 which saw export bans and increased import orders led to uncertainty in the rice market which because a springboard for APTERR. Under APTERR the rice will be available for consumption through a triple-tiered system of commercial contracts, emergency grants, and delivery in times of acute emergency. Total rice commitments were 787,000 tons based on the APTERR rice reserves in 2011 (ASEAN 2011; Islam and Kieu 2020) (refer to Table 3.2). The APTERR can potentially increase transparency in the regional rice market through the mutual exchange of information, and build trust and confidence in the regional rice economy by ensuring availability and supply of food during emergencies, reducing regional volatility and instability (Belesky 2014).

As Desker et al. (2013) puts into perspective, the total reserves of 787,000 tons will only be worth two days of regional consumption which numbers 542,000 tons a day. In addition, the corresponding contribution and commitment of each ASEAN nation is its domestic consumption for a single day. These figures pale in its regional efforts to provide reserves that could last for one to two weeks of domestic consumptions. There is therefore a need for ASEAN nations to show greater levels of commitment to APTERR's operational capacity. Some critique by Desker et al. (2013) highlights that non-utilization of APTERR reserves is further related to its inefficient request and delivery procedures. Other issues are related to the differentiation in various nations' capacity in APTERR responsibilities, issues related to financial sustainability, and the trade-offs between food security and storage costs.

Table 3.2 2011 ASEAN Plus 3 Emergency Rice Reserve

Countries	*Earmarked Quantity (in tons)*
Brunei Darussalam	3000
Cambodia	3000
Indonesia	12,000
Lao PDR	3000
Malaysia	6000
Myanmar	14,000
Philippines	5000
Singapore	5000
Thailand	15,000
Viet Nam	14,000
ASEAN	87,000

Source ASEAN (2011) [public document; no copyright issue]

The effects of the APTERR, however, are short-lived. The regional reserves are too small to significantly offset domestic market movements on an annual basis (Briones et al. 2012). In order to improve the effectiveness of APTERR, Belesky (2014) suggests, there needs to be more transparency through greater regional cooperation and information sharing in rice markets. More effective integration of AFSIS with the APTERR council and secretariat could build trust and confidence in the regional rice economy through the mutual exchange of more accurate data on rice production and national reserves and stockpiles. Enhance cooperation between AFSIS and other multilateral information systems, such as the G20's initiative on the Agricultural Market Information System (AMIS) is important too.

ASEAN Food Security Information System (AFSIS)

A second agreement between ASEAN Plus Three is the AFSIS carried out between 2003 and 2012 which aims to build future capacity for the systematic collection, analysis, and dissemination of food-related information. The AFSIS enabled human resource, knowledge sharing, and technical cooperation for the management of early warning systems and management of food policy programs. Assessments conducted will enable the region to identify areas whereby for food insecurity is likely to take place (Desker et al. 2013). Despite acknowledging the significant progress in operationalizing AFSIS, Desker et al. (2013) claim that the quality of data and the reliability remains a concern. It is suggested that the data quality can be improved through periodic analysis of food supply and demands. Some form of technology across nations with technical capacity could help with those without such established methods for data production. By establishing links across various stakeholders and the improvement of informational quality and dissemination, it will help boost AFSIS to greater potential (Islam and Kieu 2020).

Analysis of the Initiatives and Programmes

We have thus far examined the various programs that will implicate ASEAN's future food security in light of the threats it faces from climate change. As presented, climate change is a multi-sectoral issue which cannot be encompassed in a single framework or initiative. With ASEAN's acknowledgment that food security and climate change are vital concerns

Table 3.3 Evaluation criteria for ASEAN initiatives and programs

	Factor	*Justification*
1.	Planning	This criterion examines the overarching frame of the programs and initiatives. It is mainly concerned with the goals and objectives of the initiatives
2.	Implementation	This criterion scrutinizes the nature of the programs and initiatives laid out. It is concerned with the execution of the related initiatives
3.	Cooperation	The criterion observes the state of relations and the commitment levels between ASEAN nations. This will highlight the level of commitment and cooperation ASEAN has garnered among its member states for its programs
4.	Legal obligation	This criterion reviews the enforcement and legality of various agreements, treaties, and initiatives. Legal obligations will review the enforcement rights of ASEAN as a regional organization to ensure its member nations comply with the various initiatives
5.	International contribution	This criterion assesses how the region has contributed or impacted climate change and food security globally

Source Authors' own analysis

for the future, it has undertaken numerous initiatives to address matters related to climate change and food security as seen in the preceding sections. Beyond providing an overview of the current initiatives that exist under ASEAN, we will further examine the efficacy of these initiatives in this section. Some of the factors utilized to evaluate ASEAN initiatives and programs are highlighted in Table 3.3.

Planning

While it is without doubt that ASEAN has taken climate issues and its threat to food security seriously. Most of the issues raised and strategies discussed revolved around mitigating climate change and food security impacts within the region. However, ASEAN falls short on its ability to tackle long-term measures in climate change policymaking at the international level. ASEAN face similar dilemma as many other regions with the inability to ascertain the impacts of climate change. Yet, there have been attempts by ASEAN at coordinating responses. Notably ASEAN's detailed plans of the ASCC, AIF, and others, highlight that ASEAN has not been overwhelmed by political passivity and divisions in addressing its climate change vulnerabilities. ASEAN has thorough frameworks such as the ASEAN Institutional Framework for Environmental Cooperation and the ASCC Blueprint that facilitates cooperative relationships across its member states. The varied frameworks have addressed the needs for a multinational, multi-sectoral and multidisciplinary approach to be filtered through its organizational networks (Islam and Kieu 2020). The scope of ASEAN initiatives addressed pertinent environmental issues from land and agricultural resources to coastal and marine environments, without overlooking the impacts of these physical environments have on the social and economic stability of the region.

ASEAN also notes that sustainable development must be attained in conjunction with national development goals. In terms of food security, ASEAN have been forward-looking by addressing regional food security with external partnerships such as the establishment of APTEER and AFSIS while at the same time taking long-term measures to establish food trade development, information systems, and agri innovation under the AIFS framework. ASEAN as a regional body has indeed been active to promote formal avenues for collaboration between its member states to enhance regional strategies for knowledge and capacity development to address climate change and food security issues. Hence, in terms of planning, ASEAN has a clear foundational strategy for collaboration and avenues to facilitate discussions on mitigation and adaptation measures (Islam and Kieu 2020). However, the current frameworks that ASEAN has undertaken diverges from a human-rights approach as it does not address the needs of those suffering from climate change effects or specific measures undertaken for these vulnerable groups. If we examine the various Excerpts 1–3, we are able to note the lack of attention to vulnerable populations which should be considered as another dimension for consideration.

Implementation

Although ASEAN has proven to be proactive in the development of adaptation-related programs, the implementations of such programs have been by and large limited. Sahraie (2011) highlights that while there has been a combination of both reactive and proactive adaptation and mitigation measures, most were seen as merely reactive, noting that ineffective mechanisms and problems such as monitoring, reporting, sanctions, and the associated non-compliance have constrained ASEAN's efforts to address impacts of climate change. These issues mentioned are regional-specific and should be likewise be tackled regionally. Hence, despite having ASEAN declarations, action plans and strategic trusts have been laid out extensively; there have been little progress in furthering those goals. Much of the current plans have yet to be translated to implemented programs and actions that will decisively and effectively aid ASEAN in their long-term goals as a region (Islam and Kieu 2020).

In addition, ASEAN regional initiatives have largely been focused on top-down approaches, revolving around top politicians and experts, with minimal inputs from local communities. Although Section D10 subpoint 9 and 10 of the ASCC blueprinting stating that ASEAN should "promote public awareness and advocacy to raise community participation" and "encourage the participation of local government, private sector, non-governmental organizations and community to address the impacts of climate change," there is very little evidence of ASEAN having done so.

Cooperation

ASEAN's ability to gather support for its programs are performative at best. Cooperation among its member nations for programs can be evidently seen from the efforts made to further the agenda with APTEER. While it does consider securing some safety net for food security, the insignificant amount pledged by each country coupled with the bureaucratic obstacles to utilize the rice reserves brings forth questions related to its efficacy in dealing with food crises. There are also other aspects of cooperation which could be better developed, namely, capacity building, information, market and economic priories, and the position of each member country. These highlight the gaps and disparities between nations which results in a differentiation of priorities and goals. National development and economic needs are still prioritized above the long-term sustainable needs for the region (Islam and Kieu 2020).

Legal Obligation

ASEAN member states are not legal bound by agreements and declarations set forth by ASEAN. This notion or phenomenon is termed as the "ASEAN way" which is reflective of the Treaty of Amity and Cooperation (TAC) of 1976, emphasizing "non-interference" and the sanctity of each nation's sovereignty (see Goh 2003). As such, this has brought about the restriction of regional cooperation and adaptation due to the avoidance of any action that may be interpreted as an infringement of national sovereignty. The drawback of the non-legally binding agreements is seen to be more disadvantageous for ASEAN because climate change impacts and its methods to mitigate the effects are neither tangible nor concrete at this moment. Due to the underlying consensus of respecting national sovereignty, various cross-boundary programs may be unnecessarily withheld from any progress (Islam and Kieu 2020).

As evidence of the lack of legality to ASEAN agreements, we must analyze the relationship and extent of cooperation ASEAN garners between its member nations. A pertinent example is to examine ASEAN's actions to prevent annual transboundary haze originating from Indonesia. The haze is brought about by the slash and burn techniques of commercial and private landowners. The extensive deforestation due to burning causes massive haze with Indonesia's neighbors; namely Singapore and Malaysia. However, despite the seemingly concrete actions by the 1997 Regional Haze Action Plan and the following 2003 ASEAN Agreement on Transboundary Haze Pollution framework is non-legally binding, resulting in clashes due to the haze problem between Indonesia and those nations affected were not resolved. Indonesia had claimed that the haze problem is a domestic issue and other ASEAN member nations should not interfere. Hence, this is indicative of the weak executive and legislative powers of ASEAN as an associating for coordinating and implementing programs across its member nations.

International Contribution

It is seen that although climate change is a pertinent issue within Southeast Asia, the role in which ASEAN has adopted within the international community remains minimal. Sahraie (2011) highlights that ASEAN's ability to support regional climate change is often dependent on external agencies and secondly, there is no financial commitment from the national governments to support the programs laid out. In addition, the effectiveness and willingness of ASEAN cooperation is dependent on the impacts programs have on the nation's development trajectory. Compounding this issue is that ASEAN consists of a diverse group of countries with varying levels of development (seen in Table 3.1), with some countries lacking in the available financial resources, experts, and technology leads to very limited accurate information about climate change and food security situation. As such, capacity to gain knowledge and mitigate the risks in question are largely contingent on the efforts of the developed nations within ASEAN and internationally. While ASEAN may facilitate regional cooperation and coordination, it ultimately has to depend on individual national governments to act upon the relevant measures and support systems for better future climate change adaptations. Yet due to the abovementioned limitations and barriers, the development of institutional policy frameworks and programs may be far from being optimally effective.

Taken together, the following Table 3.4 summarizes the overall efficacy of ASEAN regional initiatives for climate change and food security.

Table 3.4 Summary table for ASEAN initiatives efficacy

	Factor	*Summary conclusion*
1.	Planning	ASEAN has extensive frameworks to coordinate initiatives and programs regionally
2.	Implementation	While active in planning both reactive and proactive mitigation measures, there has been little progress due to the ineffective mechanisms in place
3.	Cooperation	Support for the programs has been cursory and lacks actual effectiveness for its cause
4.	Legal obligation	Not legally binding due to TAC and the notion of non-interference due to respect for national sovereignty
5.	International contribution	Role within the international community is minimal and there is still dependence on international and external agencies

Source Authors' own investigation

Conclusion

This chapter examined closely the various initiatives for climate change and food security implemented by ASEAN as a regional organization. While is it hardly deniable that ASEAN has been progressive in its attempts to coordinate efforts between its member states for a collective regional response, these initiatives have not been translated to programs that can effectively attain the goals set out in its agenda. The lack of ability to fulfil its agenda is largely due to reactive adaptation measures, weak and ineffective mechanisms such as monitoring, reporting, non-compliance as well as the lack of cooperation between member states coupled with the scarcity of legally binding agreements due to the "ASEAN way."

Despite this criticism, ASEAN has nevertheless been fervently bringing for issues of concerns for the region. It should, however, much further on the agendas and gain member states' commitment to pursue proactive collaborations and implement programs on the ground. With current facilitative avenues already in place, ASEAN's potential to adequately address climate change and food security issues are boundless. With climate change becoming an increasing concern, ASEAN should address its weaknesses and utilize its strength to further regional long-term interests.

References

ASEAN. 2009. Components and Strategic Thrusts of ASEAN Integrated Food Security (AIFS) Framework. Retrieved 28 August 2017. https://cil.nus.edu.sg/rp/pdf/2009%20AIFS%20Framework%20and%20Strategic%20Plan%20of%20Action%20on%20Food%20Security%20in%20the%20ASEAN%20Region-pdf.pdf.

ASEAN. 2011. ASEAN Plus Three Emergency Rice Reserve Agreement, 2011. Retrieved 29 August 2017. http://cil.nus.edu.sg/rp/pdf/2011%20ASEAN%20Plus%20Three%20Emergency%20Rice%20Reserve%20Agreement-pdf.pdf.

ASEAN. 2017. Overview. Retrieved 28 August 2017. http://www.asean.org/asean/about-asean.

ASEAN Cooperation on Climate Change. 2015. ASEAN Cooperation on Climate Change. Retrieved 29 August 2017. http://environment.asean.org/asean-working-group-on-climate-change/.

ASEAN Cooperation on Environment. 2015. Overview of ASEAN Cooperation on Environment. Retrieved 29 August 2017. http://environment.asean.org/about-us-2/.

ASEAN Ministerial meeting (AMME). 2012. ASEAN Action Plan on Joint Response to Climate Change. ASEAN. Retrieved 30 August 2017. http://environment.asean.org/wp-content/uploads/2015/06/ANNEX-8-Lead-Countries-for-ASEAN-Action-Plan-on-Joint-Response-to-Climate-Change-27-March-2013.pdf.

ASEAN Secretariat. 2009a. Roadmap for an ASEAN Community 2009–2015. Retrieved 29 August 2017. http://www.asean.org/storage/images/ASEAN_RTK_2014/2_Roadmap_for_ASEAN_Community_20092015.pdf.

ASEAN Secretariat. 2009b. ASEAN Socio-Cultural Community Blueprint. Retrieved 28 August 2017. http://asean.org/wp-content/uploads/archive/5187-19.pdf.

ASEAN Sustainable Agrifood Systems. 2014. ASEAN Integrated Food Security (AIFS) Framework and Strategic Plan of Action on Food Security in the ASEAN Region (SPA_FS 2015–2020). Retrieved 26 August 2017. http://asean-agrifood.org/?wpfb_dl=58.

Belesky, Paul. 2014. Regional Governance, Food Security and Rice Reserves in East Asia. *Global Food Security* 3 (3–4): 167–173.

Bello, Amelia L. 2005. Ensuring Food Security—A Case for ASEAN Integration. *Asian Journal of Agriculture and Development* 2 (1&2): 87–108.

Briones, Roehlano, Alvaro Durand-Morat, Eric Wailes, and Eddie Chavez. 2012. Climate Change and Price Volatility: Can We Count on the ASEAN Plus Three Emergency Rice Reserve? ADB Sustainable Development Working Paper Series. Asian Development Bank.

Desker, B., M. Caballero-Anthony, and P. Teng. 2013. Thought/Issues Paper on ASEAN Food Security: Towards a More Comprehensive Framework. ERIA Discussion Paper Series, RSIS. Retrieved 30 August 2017. http://www.eria.org/ERIA-DP-2013-20.pdf.

Dixon, J.A. 1990. Environment and Economic Growth: The Political Economy of Resource Management in ASEAN. *ASEAN Economic Bulletin* 7 (2): 159–172.

Donner, S.D., T.R. Knutson, and M. Oppenhelmer. 2007. Model-based Assessment of the Role of Human-Induced Climate Change in the 2005 Caribbean Coral Bleaching Event. *Proceedings of the National Academy of Sciences* 104 (13): 5483–5488.

Escaler, Margarita, Paul Teng, and Mely Caballero-Anthony. 2010. Ensuring Urban Food Security in ASEAN (Association of South East Asian Nations): Summary of the Findings of the Food Security Expert Group Meeting Held in Singapore 4–5 August 2010. *Food Security* 2 (4): 407–411.

Felkner, J., K. Tazhibayeva, and R. Townsend. 2009. Impact of Climate Change on Rice Production in Thailand. *American Economic Review: Papers and Proceedings* 99 (2): 205–210.

Goh, Gillian. 2003. The 'ASEAN Way'; Non-intervention and ASEAN's Role in Conflict Management. *Stanford Journal of East Asian Affairs* 2 (1): 113.

Golan, Amnon, and Harinder Kohli. 2013. ASEAN Dynamism: Agricultural Transformation and Food Security. *Global Journal of Emerging Market Economies* 5 (1): 3–21.

IPCC (Intergovernmental Panel on Climate Change). 2007. Climate Change 2007 Synthesis Report: Projected Climate Change and Its Impacts. Retrieved 29 August 2017. https://www.ipcc.ch/publications_and_data/ar4/syr/en/spms3.html.

Islam, M.S. and Edson Kieu. 2020. Tackling Regional Climate Change Impacts and Food Security Issues: A Critical Analysis across ASEAN, PIF and SAARC. *Sustainability* 12 (883): 1–21.

Lassa, Jonatan A., Allen Yu-Hung Lai, and Tian Goh. 2015. Climate Extremes: An Observation and Projection of Its Impacts on Food Production in ASEAN. *Natural Hazards* 84 (S1): 19–33.

Lesser, M.P. 2007. Coral Reef Bleaching and Global Climate Change: Can Corals Survive the Next Century? *Proceedings of the National Academy of Sciences* 104 (13): 5259–5260.

Letchumanan, R. 2010. Is Here an ASEAN Policy on Climate Change? Climate Change: Is Southeast Asia Up to the Challenge? *LSE Ideas*: 50–62.

Mahlstein, I., R.W. Portmann, J.S. Daniel, S. Solomon, and R. Knutti. 2012. Perceptible Changes in Regional Precipitation in a Future Climate. *Geophysical Research Letters* 39 (5): N/a.

Masud, M.M., M.S. Rahman, A.Q. Al-Amin, F. Kari, and W.L. Filho. 2014. Impact of Climate Change: An Empirical Investigation of Malaysian Rice Production. *Econpapers* 19 (4): 431–444.

Mat, Bakri, and Zarina Othman. 2014. Regional Cooperation in Addressing Food Security Issues in Southeast Asia: Malaysian Perspectives. *Malaysian Journal of Society and Space* 10 (6): 37–47.

Reynolds, M.P. 2010. *Climate Change and Crop Production*. UK: CABI.

RSIS NTS (Rajaratnam School of International Studies Centre for Non-Traditional Security Studies). 2013. Expert Group Meeting on the Impact of Climate Change on ASEAN Food Security. Retrieved 16 August 2017. https://www.rsis.edu.sg/wp-content/uploads/2014/07/ER130607_Impact_of_Climate_Change_on_ASEAN.pdf.

Sahraie, M. 2011. The ASEAN Actions on Climate Change: Recognizing or Pro-Actively Addressing the Issue? International Development Law organization: IDLO Sustainable Development Law on Climate Change Working Paper Series No. 5. Retrieved 25 August 2017. http://cisdl.org/public/docs/news/5._Melodie_Sahraie_2.pdf.

Saseendran, S.A., K.K. Singh, L.S. Rathore, S.V. Singh, and S.K. Sinha. 2000. Effects of Climate Change on Rice Production in the Tropical Humid Climate of Kerala, India. *Climate Change* 44 (4): 495–514.

Shiu, C.J., S.C. Lui, C. Fu, A. Dai, and Y. Sun. 2012. How Much Do Precipitation Extremes Change in a Warming Climate? *Geophysical Research Letters* 39 (17): N/a.

Siepielski, A.M., J.D. DiBattista, and S.M. Carlson. 2009. It's About Time: The Temporal Dynamics of Phenotypic Selection in the Wild. *Ecology Letters* 12 (11): 1261–1276.

Sultana, N., T. Ikeda, and M.A. Kashem. 2002. Effect of Seawater on Photosynthesis and Dry Matter Accumulation in Development Rice Grains. *Photosynthetica* 40 (1): 115–119.

Teng, Paul P.S., and Jurise Oliveros. 2015. Challenges and Responses to Asian Food Security. *Cosmos: Journal of the Singapore National Academy of Science* 11: 1–18.

United Nations Department of Economic and Social Affairs. 2017. 2017 Revision of World Population Prospects. Retrieved 19 August 2017. http://esa.un.org/unpd/wpp/.

Vasanta, K. 2013. Impact of Climate Change on Wheat and Rice Production: An analysis. *Economic Affairs* 58 (2): 89–95.

Vichitlekarn, S. 2011. ASEAN Multi Sectoral Framework on Climate Change: Agriculture, Fisheries and Forestry Towards Food Security (AFCC). Regional Workshop on Climate Change and Food Security in ASEAN Plus Three Countries.

Williams, S.E., and J. Middleton. 2008. Climatic Seasonality, Resource Bottlenecks, and Abundance of Rainforest Birds: Implications for Global Climate Change. *Diversity and Distributions* 14: 69–77.

CHAPTER 4

Climate Change and Food Security in SAARC

Nearly 35% of the world's poor population lives in South Asia (Cai et al. 2016). Agriculture plays a crucial role in South Asian economies. Over 70% of people in the region live in rural areas depending on agriculture, making up around 75% of the poor in the region. Agriculture, forestry and fishing contributes about 16.3% of the region's GDP and provides employment for a large section of the population (World Bank 2021). Despite enormous natural resources, poverty and hunger are quite pervasive in South Asia. The region is home to about 40% of the world's undernourished people (Kaur and Kaur 2016), and the level of hunger in South Asia is the second highest in the world (Cai et al. 2016). Climate change has exacerbated the regional vulnerabilities even further.

This chapter synthesizes the impact of climate change and food security on the South Asian region by (1) outlining the background and history of the South Asian Association for Regional Cooperation (SAARC) and its member states, (2) highlighting the impacts of climate change and food security on SAARC, and (3) providing an analysis of its regional initiatives and their effectiveness in mitigating the impact of climate change on regional risks to food security. The chapter examines the efficacy of SAARC's adaptive and mitigating measures on issues of food security and climate change. Similar to the previous case study on ASEAN, the

M. S. Islam and E. Kieu, *Climate Change and Food Security in Asia Pacific*, International Political Economy Series,
https://doi.org/10.1007/978-3-030-70753-8_4

SAARC case study specifically examines regional policies, while noting that individual member states do possess their own domestic approaches to mitigating impacts from climate change and addressing food security. Secondly, only policies that address food security and climate change in tandem are presented here.

Background and History of SAARC

SAARC was established on December 8, 1985 by Bangladesh, Bhutan, India, Maldives, Nepal, Pakistan, and Sri Lanka (SAARC 2009a). Afghanistan became the eighth member of SAARC in April 2007 during the 14th SAARC Summit in Delhi. The objectives and resolutions of SAARC are inscribed in Article I of the SAARC Charter (SAARC 2009a):

1. to promote the welfare of the peoples of SOUTH ASIA and to improve their quality of life;
2. to accelerate economic growth, social progress, and cultural development in the region and to provide all individuals the opportunity to live in dignity and to realize their full potentials;
3. to promote and strengthen collective self-reliance among the countries of SOUTH ASIA;
4. to contribute to mutual trust, understanding, and appreciation of one another's problems;
5. to promote active collaboration and mutual assistance in the economic, social, cultural, technical, and scientific fields;
6. to strengthen cooperation with other developing countries;
7. to strengthen cooperation among themselves in international forums on matters of common interests; and
8. to cooperate with international and regional organizations with similar aims and purposes.

In addition, SAARC Member States have adopted the following fundamental principles, in accordance with Article II of the SAARC Charter (SAARC 2009a): (a) Cooperation within the framework of the ASSOCIATION shall be based on respect for the principles of sovereign equality, territorial integrity, political independence, non-interference in the internal affairs of other States and mutual benefit. (b) Such cooperation shall not be a substitute for bilateral and multilateral cooperation but shall complement them. (c) Such cooperation shall not be inconsistent with bilateral and multilateral obligations.

The SAARC region is home to about 2 billion people, one-fourth of the world's population. However, its regional share of global resources is vastly lower than its population, as it represents only 3.95% of the world's landmass (SAARC 2009b). Many SAARC member states are still poorly developed and suffer from multiple social problems, ranging from a lack of basic necessities such as food and housing to criminality and weak governance. The region's economic activities are diverse; notable exports include information technology, tourism, and garments. Many SAARC nations have a vast amount of land dedicated to agricultural use, ranging from 40 to 70% of their total land area; the exception is Bhutan, where only 13% of land is devoted to agricultural use (CIA 2014). The region also has a very high concentration of poverty and hunger, with an estimated 451 million people living below their country's poverty line (Chand 2010). Afghanistan has the highest poverty rate (36% below the poverty line), while Sri Lanka has the lowest (8.9%). The poverty rates for Maldives, Bhutan, Nepal, India, Pakistan, and Bangladesh are 16, 13.3, 25.2, 21.9, 29.5, and 31.5%, respectively (CIA 2017).[1] Nevertheless, South Asia has been growing steadily over the past decade, as is shown in Table 4.1.

South Asia is also the least integrated region in the world, with regional trade at 4%; this figure is very low compared to the European Union, North American Free Trade Agreement (NAFTA), Association of Southeast Asian Nations (ASEAN), Common Market for Eastern and Southern Africa, Gulf Cooperation Council, and Latin America and the Caribbean at 67, 62, 26, 22, 8, and 22%, respectively (Kher 2012; World Bank 2007). As a region, it is distinct from other regions due to its security issues, interstate problems, and untapped economic potential (Kher 2012).

The SAARC region is densely populated. India has the largest population, with an estimated 1.2 billion people, and Maldives has the smallest, 300,000. Due to the ongoing economic restructuring and expansion of SAARC nations, there will be increased environmental pressures, which may exacerbate environmental troubles if sustainable development and

[1] Information provided by the CIA (Central Intelligence Agency) *World Factbook*. Data are based on varied year estimates: 2008, 2012, 2011, 2011, 2013, and 2010 for Maldives, Bhutan, Nepal, India, Pakistan, and Bangladesh, respectively.

Table 4.1 GDP of SAARC nations, in US dollars (2007–2011)

GDP in constant prices											
Country	*2005 US dollars per capita*					*% change per capita per annum*					*% change*
	2007	*2008*	*2009*	*2010*	*2011*	*2007*	*2008*	*2009*	*2010*	*2011*	*2005–2010*
Afghanistan	803.8	823.3	873.8	937.1	984.9	7.5	2.4	6.1	7.2	5	6.8
Bangladesh	318	318	363	366	378	16.1	2.3	17.2	3.2	5.7	7.5
Bhutan	447	469	491	515	543	6.4	6.2	5.7	6.1	6.7	5.5
Maldives	1519	1560	1636	1797	1870	17.9	4.7	6.7	11.8	5.9	8.5
India	4257	4691	4387	4552	4800	10.6	12.2	−4.7	5.7	7.5	7.2
Nepal	867	889	949	1027	1083	9.8	3.9	8.2	9.6	6.9	7.6
Pakistan	341	358	370	384	394	3.4	6.1	4.5	4.8	3.9	3.4
Sri Lanka	748	746	758	771	781	5.7	1.6	3.6	3.5	3	2.3
SAARC	1382	1454	1494	1602	1720	6.8	6	3.5	8	8.3	6.1

Source SAARC Group on Statistics (2009) [no copyright issue]

environmentally friendly practices are not pursued. Furthermore, finding resources for future development and dealing with future impacts from climate change will be an additional challenge for the region (CIA 2017).

Climate Change Impact on Food Security in SAARC Member States

South Asia is one of the regions in the world most vulnerable to climate change. Extreme weather events such as heatwaves, cyclones, droughts, floods often plague South Asia (Cai et al. 2016; Bandara and Cai 2014). Altered rainfall patterns with lower average seasonal rainfall and greater variability over the decades, increased frequency of deficit monsoons, and heavy precipitation events are among the general trends. Sea-level rise, on the top of these, can potentially affect livelihoods and push migration both at national and subnational levels in the region (Kaur and Kaur 2016). Cold waves in South Asia cause significant damage to crop yields such as mustard, mango, guava, papaya, brinjal, tomato, and potato in northern India, Nepal, Afghanistan, and Pakistan (Aggarwal and Sivakumar 2010).

South Asia is highly vulnerable to natural disasters, which are likely to have increased frequency and intensity with climate change (Kaur and

Kaur 2016; Islam and Si Hui 2015). From 1990 to 2008, for example, more than 750 million people—50% of South Asia's population—were affected by at least one type of disaster, resulting in almost 2,30,000 deaths and about US$45 billion in damages. Droughts are increasingly becoming more frequent, intense, and prolonged in the arid and semi-arid areas of Bangladesh, and India. Landslides and glacial lake outburst floods, on the other hand, are becoming more frequent in the mountain regions of Bhutan and Nepal (Kaur and Kaur 2016). Low-lying coastal areas such as Bangladesh, parts of India, and Sri Lanka are prone to frequent natural disasters like cyclones, Sea-level rise, and floods. Glacier melt is happening in the mountain ecosystems of Bhutan, Nepal, India, and Pakistan. Heat and drought stress are frequently experienced by the semiarid and arid areas of India, Afghanistan, Pakistan, and Bangladesh. These climatic extremes have serious threat to food security as they negatively impact agricultural production, and farmers' livelihoods (Aggarwal and Sivakumar 2010).

Taken together, the region's mountains, coasts, forests, deltas, and deserts expose it to threats such as glacial melts, rising sea levels, extreme heat waves, droughts, desertification, floods, storms, and loss of farmlands, grasslands, biodiversity, and marine ecosystems (Kaur and Kaur 2016). Several global studies indicate a probability of 10–40% loss in crop production in India with increases in temperature by 2080–2100 (Aggarwal and Sivakumar 2010). For almost all crops regardless of the climate change scenario, South Asia experiences the greatest yield decline (Nelson et al. 2009). The impacts of climate change on food security in the South Asian region are outlined below.

Impact on Land and Agricultural Productivity

Agriculture is the predominant sector of economic activity in SAARC nations, and a vast majority of the inhabitants are dependent on agriculture for their livelihood and sustenance. Because of the region's strong dependence on agriculture, the future trajectory of the agricultural sector holds the key to livelihood security. However, as in many parts of the world, natural resources within SAARC nations are showing signs of degradation, which will adversely impact future growth and sustainability. Some major events that have impacted global agriculture, as highlighted in earlier chapters, have similarly affected SAARC regional agricultural productivity. Two major developments have huge impacts on agricultural productivity: (1) an increase in temperatures, and (2) changes in precipitation patterns (IPCC 2007). Both temperature and precipitation changes can have disastrous consequences if they are not managed effectively (Chand 2010). The agricultural profile of SAARC nations have some distinct disadvantages. Firstly, with the exception of Pakistan, the agricultural sector in South Asia is generally dominated by small farm owners; the average farm holding is below half a hectare, accounting for more than 60% of all farms. Compounding the problems associated with small farm sizes, one hectare of arable land typically supports more than one worker; in countries like Bangladesh and Nepal, one hectare supports an average of five workers. Secondly, another disadvantage faced by farmers is the heavy dependence on rain due to the lack of irrigation. The percentage of arable land under irrigation ranges from about 90% for Pakistan to only 33% for India, the lowest for the region (Chand 2010).

Cereals, wheat, and rice are staples in South Asia, yet the region's agricultural productivity for these essentials is generally lower than in the rest of the world. Agricultural productivity for rice among SAARC countries are lower than the world's average, ranging from 2.15 tons/hectare for Afghanistan to 3.85 tons/hectare for Bangladesh. However, the annual growth rates for rice productivity are higher than in the rest of the world. The scenario for wheat production is similar to rice, in that productivity is lower than the world average but its rate of growth is higher, with the exception of Bangladesh. For cereals as a general category, productivity ranged from 1.65 tons in Afghanistan to 3.77 tons in Bangladesh; the productivity of Bangladesh, Sri Lanka, and Maldives is seen to be higher than the world average (Chand 2010). Given the future impacts of climate change on temperature and precipitation patterns and the current state of agricultural productivity among SAARC nations, South Asia as a region might face an uphill battle in terms of food security. According to Lal (2011), there may not be significant impacts on food production in South Asia up to 2020, with a less than 2 degrees Celsius change, provided that farms receive adequate irrigation and crop pests are kept under control. However, Lal (2011) and Mirza (2011) indicate that the main concern for food security is the frequency of droughts and floods. These potential impacts on agricultural productivity, coupled with the region's population growth and growth in per capita income compound the intensity of impact. According to Paroda and Kumar (2000), regional demand is expected to grow across all products in both low- and high-income growth estimates.

Apart from climate change impacts, SAARC (2009b) highlights other challenges the region faces in agricultural productivity: (1) increasing and sustaining agricultural growth, (2) reducing inequalities in income and disparities between agriculture and other economic sectors, which adversely affect investment in the agricultural sector, (3) reducing poverty, hunger, and malnutrition and increasing food access and affordability, (4) reducing natural resource degradation and ecosystem fatigue, (5) dealing with energy demands and the diversion of crops for biofuel, and (6) addressing biosafety and biosecurity issues, as plants and animals become more vulnerable to diseases and pests. The many threats South Asian nations face and the need to boost agricultural productivity mean that the attainment of food security for the region is an urgent task for the future.

Impact on Marine Ecosystems and Fisheries

The SAARC region can be separated into coastal states such as Bangladesh, India, Maldives, Sri Lanka, and Pakistan, and landlocked states such as Nepal and Bhutan. Bangladesh borders the Indian Ocean and Pakistan is adjacent to the Arabian Sea, while India is a big landmass with numerous small islands. Maldives and Sri Lanka are both island states; the former is made up of 1190 islands, and the latter is a single island (Sivasubramaniam 2009). Afghanistan, Bhutan, and Nepal are landlocked states that lie north of the Indian mainland. The coastal and marine areas are important national assets to SAARC countries, and they are where most socioeconomic activities are concentrated (Amjad et al. 2013). In South Asia, aquaculture production comes largely from traditional freshwater farming, and demands for it have been increasing (FAO 1995). Shrimps are also mainly produced in South Asia for export, and the main producers are India, Sri Lanka, and Bangladesh (Subasinghe 1997; Islam 2014). Some of the products of South Asia's coastal/aquatic ecosystems are listed in Table 4.2.

As Table 4.3 shows, there are many ways in which coastal and aquatic ecosystems support human and nonhuman populations. They play a major role in South Asia by providing essential services for socioeconomic activities (Sivasubramaniam 2009). However, current projections indicate that climate change may have adverse impact on these activities. Climate change can impact sea levels, temperature variability, groundwater levels, salinity, wave and current patterns, sedimentation, weather events, and

Table 4.2 Products of coastal/aquatic ecosystems in South Asia

	Products and output	*Activities*
1.	Products of Direct Economic Activities	Food sources, hydrocarbons, minerals, desalinated water provision
2.	Products of Natural System	Rich nutrients that support the productivity, nursery, and breeding of fish and shellfish
3.	Coast-Dependent Activities	Ports, harbors, shipping and transportation, and coastal aquaculture
4.	Coastal and Wetland Services	Real estate, housing business, industries
5.	Coastal Linked Activities	Fish processing, agricultural activities along wetlands, marine industries, shipbuilding
6.	Regulatory Services	Habitats, ecosystems, and natural resources. Maintains biodiversity for organisms and aquatic plants
7.	Livelihood of Coastal Communities	Variety of agricultural and livestock species, which provide a livelihood for coastal communities

Source Amjad et al. (2013) [public document; no copyright issue]

Table 4.3 SAARC improvements in non-climate change areas to be addressed

	Areas to be addressed		
1.	Producers and Production Base	10.	Food Prices
2.	Output Growth Acceleration	11.	Food Safety and Food Standards
3.	Technology	12.	Biodiversity, Intellectual Properties (IPs)
4.	Seed and Other Inputs	13.	Biosafety, Biosecurity
5.	Food Requirements	14.	Infrastructure, Research & Development (R&D)
6.	Sustainable Use/Management of Natural Resources	15.	Technology Delivery System
7.	Farm Structure	16.	Capacity Building
8.	Biotechnology	17.	Regional Complementarities and Collaborations
9.	Energy Prices		

Source SAARC (2015) [public document; no copyright issue]

erosion, all of which will alter the environment and ecology. The ecological destabilization of species and of the established communities that depend on these environments could threaten their survival.

Future Policy Implications

Agricultural, aquacultural, and marine-related production must be increased to ensure food security for the region. SAARC has noted that climate change is a global challenge, and the region will need a concerted effort to collaborate on and promote strategies to mitigate threats from climate change. Due to the demands on agriculture, aquaculture, and marine fisheries, there must be a set of responses that address the specific needs of each industry. Such protective and regulatory policies should ensure that food production is in line with the region's needs. SAARC (2009b: 8) further declares that adaptive actions require a "degree of confidence" about the impacts of climate change, and should be accompanied by coping mechanisms and the necessary investments. SAARC (2009b) has highlighted ways to improve food production among its member states as part of its Agriculture Vision 2020. Other areas for improvement identified in Agriculture Vision 2020 are presented in Table 4.3.

The vast array of issues to be addressed is cross-sectoral and thus requires the coordination and cooperation of various stakeholders. SAARC (2009b) highlights the need to operationalize regional cooperation and partnerships to realize the goal of boosting food productivity. There is a huge potential for SAARC member states to cooperate and collaborate to further regional food security goals and mitigate climate change impacts. In the next section, we will review the initiatives SAARC has undertaken to boost regional food productivity and security.

SAARC on Climate Change and Food Security

SAARC first began documenting intergovernmental initiatives concerning the environment as early as 1982, with reports such as "Causes and Consequences of Natural Disasters and the Protection and Preservation of the Environment" and "Greenhouse Effect and Its Impact on the Region" (Mittal 2011). Officially, SAARC only began expressing deeper concerns over climate change during the Fourteenth SAARC

Summit in New Delhi in 2007. These concerns saw SAARC undertaking initiatives to address the challenges posed. Follow-ups on climate change were added to the official agenda during the Dhaka Declaration, which translated to initiatives and activities to promote advocacy programs, cooperation for capacity building, and the exchange of best practices, research, and mitigation adaptation measures (SAARC 2009c). From 2009 to 2011, the SAARC Action Plan on climate change was realized, which addressed seven themes and areas for cooperation. In 2009, SAARC member nations also signed the Delhi Statement on Cooperation in Environment, which reaffirmed their commitment to cooperation. In 2010, the Thimphu Statement on Climate Change was outlined to ensure the strengthening and facilitation of regional cooperation to address the adverse impacts of climate change (SAARC 2009c). In relation to food security, the 1987 SAARC Agreement on Establishing the SAARC Food Security Reserve is the only binding agreement among the member states that addresses food security (SAARC 1987; Khadka 1990). While noting that food security reserves do not specifically address future climate change impacts, we will nonetheless separately examine both aspects and initiatives undertaken by the regional organization (Islam and Kieu 2020).

SAARC Regional Initiatives

Back in 1982, the intergovernmental initiative "South Asia Cooperative Environment Programme" engaged in transboundary environmental issues and provided a crucial forum for promoting regional cooperative activities related to the environment (South Asia Cooperative Environment Programme 2015). One of its aims was to address climate change by taking relevant action and solving transboundary environmental issues like pollution. While these aims may not seem directly related to food security, attempts to address climate change may nonetheless alleviate climate change impacts on food security. Later, in 1992, the SAARC member nations set up a Technical Committee on Environment, which aimed to make recommendations on issues relevant to food production levels such as conservation of natural resources, biological diversity, alternative fuels, impacts on greenhouse emissions, rising sea levels, increased water salinity, and changes in rainfall patterns. The committee has reportedly met numerous times over the last two decades to assess the progress and plans of SAARC to ensure environmental sustainability (Islam and Kieu 2020).

The next watershed was the Ministerial Meeting on Climate Change, which was held in Dhaka in 2008 and led to the "Dhaka Declaration and SAARC Action Plan on Climate Change." The Dhaka Declaration requires member states to build capacity, exchange information, promote advocacy programs and mass awareness on climate change, provide incentives for the reduction of greenhouse gases, and undertake mitigation and adaptation measures for climate change. The SAARC Action Plan on Climate Change was another result of the same Ministerial Meeting, which identified six thematic areas for cooperation among the member states (see Table 4.4).

The SAARC Action Plan on Climate Change themes point to areas with room for capacity-building: Clean Development Mechanisms projects, informational exchange on climate change impacts, and engaging in international negotiations (SAARC 2009c). Under the SAARC Action Plan, the Technical Committee on Environment and Forestry was created to enhance South–South cooperation on climate change and to generate support and action plans on the national and regional levels. One crucial aspect of the SAARC Action Plan is the agricultural focus, which will address the assessment of and adaptive measures to climate change (Mittal 2011). The commitment of SAARC members to the Action Plan is clear, as it was reiterated by the Thimphu Statement on Climate Change.

In 2009 and 2010, there were two additional statements: the Delhi Statement on Cooperation in Environment and the Thimphu Statement on Climate Change (SAARC 2009c). The Delhi Statement on Cooperation in Environment 2009 identifies and reaffirms the commitment of all member states to regional cooperation regarding climate change. The Thimphu Statement on Climate Change established during the Sixteenth Summit outlined initiatives at the national and regional levels (see Table 4.5). The Thimphu Statement also saw the formation of the Inter-governmental Expert Group on Climate Change (IGEG.CC). The IGEG.CC's role is to monitor, review progress, and make recommendations to the SAARC Environment Ministers to eventually facilitate the implementation of the Thimphu Statement.

To further support food security, SAARC members have come together as a region to ensure food security by establishing a food reserve . This will serve to (1) "act as a regional food security reserve for

Table 4.4 Six thematic areas for the SAARC action plan on climate change

	Theme	*Details*
1.	Adaptation to Climate Change	• Adaptation to climate change impacts and risks in vulnerable communities, locations, and ecosystems • Adaptation in sectors (e.g., water, agriculture, fisheries, health, and biodiversity) • Adaptation to extreme climate events (e.g., flood, cyclone, glacial lake outburst, droughts, and heat and cold waves) • Adaptation to climate change impact (e.g., Sea-level rise, salinity intrusion, glacial melt and coastal and soil erosion) • Adaptation suited to urban settlements, coastal structures, and mountain terrain
2.	Policies and Actions for Climate Change Mitigation	• Sharing of best practices on nationally appropriate mitigation actions (e.g., energy, waste management, and transport) • Capacity-building for developing CDM projects including DNA and stakeholders • Sharing of best practices on sustainable forest management based on experiences
3.	Policies and Actions for Technology Transfer	• Technology needs assessment including R&D and capacity development • Assessing barriers to technology development for adaptation and mitigation options

	Theme	Details
4.	Finance and Investment	• Methods for assessing financing needs to deal with climate change in the short, medium, and long term • Climate change projects should be given priority and be financed as per SAARC norms • Determine the quantum of additional funding required to implement the action plans as identified under various thematic areas
5.	Education and Awareness—New Delhi Work Program	• Development of a toolkit for mass awareness-raising on climate change • Incorporating climate change awareness in educational curricula
6.	Management of Impacts and Risks Due to Climate Change	• Climate risk modeling and capacity-building in the region for impact assessment of climate change • Sharing of information and capacity-building in the management of climate change impacts and risks through cooperation among SAARC member states in early forecasting, warning, and adaptation measures • Cooperation among the SAARC member states in exchange for information on climate change and its impacts (e.g., Sea-level rise, glacial melts, droughts, floods) • Cooperation and sharing of good practices in disaster management

Source SAARC (2008) [public document; no copyright issue]

Table 4.5 The Thimphu Statement on Climate Change endorses and agrees to undertake the following points

	Agenda
1.	Review the implementation of the Dhaka Declaration and SAARC Action Plan on Climate Change and ensure its timely implementation
2.	Agree to establish an Inter-governmental Expert Group on Climate Change to develop clear policy direction and guidance for regional cooperation as envisaged in the SAARC Plan of Action on Climate Change
3.	Direct the Secretary-General to commission a study for presentation to the Seventeenth SAARC Summit on "Climate Risks in the Region: ways to comprehensively address the related social, economic and environmental challenges"
4.	Undertake advocacy and awareness programs on climate change, among others, to promote the use of green technology and best practices to promote low-carbon sustainable and inclusive development of the region
5.	Commission a study to explore the feasibility of establishing a SAARC mechanism which would provide capital for projects that promote low-carbon technology and renewable energy; and a Low-carbon Research and Development Institute in South Asian University
6.	Incorporate science-based materials in educational curricula to promote better understanding of the science and adverse effects of climate change
7.	Plant ten million trees over the next five years (2010–2015) as part of a regional afforestation and reforestation campaign, in accordance with national priorities and programs of Member States
8.	Evolve national plans, and where appropriate regional projects, on protecting and safeguarding the archaeological and historical infrastructure of South Asia from the adverse effects of Climate Change
9.	Establish institutional linkages among national institutions in the region to, among others, facilitate sharing of knowledge, information, and capacity-building programs in climate change related areas
10.	Commission a SAARC Inter-governmental Marine Initiative to strengthen the understanding of shared oceans and water bodies in the region and the critical roles they play in sustainable living to be supported by the SAARC Coastal Zone Management Center
11.	Stress the imperative of conservation of biodiversity and natural resources and monitoring of mountain ecology covering the mountains in the region
12.	Commission a SAARC Inter-governmental Mountain Initiative on mountain ecosystems, particularly glaciers and their contribution to sustainable development and livelihoods to be supported by SAARC Forestry Center
13.	Commission a SAARC Inter-governmental Monsoon Initiative on the evolving pattern of monsoons to assess vulnerability due to climate change to be supported by SAARC Meteorological Research Center

(continued)

Table 4.5 (continued)

	Agenda
14.	Commission a SAARC Inter-governmental Climate-related Disasters Initiative on the integration of Climate Change Adaptation (CCA) with Disaster Risk Reduction (DRR) to be supported by SAARC Disaster Management Center
15.	Complete the ratification process for the SAARC Convention on Cooperation on Environment at an early date to enable its entry into force
16.	The Inter-governmental Expert Group on Climate Change shall meet at least twice a year to periodically monitor and review the implementation of this Statement and make recommendations to facilitate its implementation and submit its report through the Senior Officials of SAARC to the SAARC Environment Ministers

Source SAARC (2010), Islam and Kieu (2020) [no copyright issue]

the SAARC Member Countries during normal time food shortages and emergencies" and (2) "to provide regional support to national food security efforts; foster intercountry partnerships and regional integration and solve regional food shortages through collective action" (SAARC 2007). Under this agreement, the SAARC Food Bank will hold in reserve the following food grains (see Table 4.6).

As can be seen, SAARC has been undertaking incremental and substantial steps in mitigating climate change impacts and addressing current food insecurity regionally through its various declarations, statements, and commissions.

Table 4.6 Assessed shares of food grains for the SAARC food reserve

	Country	*Quantity (Metric Tons)*
1.	Afghanistan*	--------*
2.	Bangladesh	40,000
3.	Bhutan	180
4.	India	153,200
5.	Maldives	200
6.	Nepal	4000
7.	Pakistan	40,000
8.	Sri Lanka	4000
Total		241,580*

Source SAARC (2007) [public document; no copyright issue]
*According to the 2007 agreement, the assessed share of Afghanistan will be decided during the First Meeting of the SAARC Food Bank Board

Other Bilateral and Multilateral Initiatives of South Asia

Apart from internal initiatives within SAARC member states or by SAARC as a regional organization, South Asian nations likewise engage with international partners for food security. A variety of bilateral and multilateral initiatives that target South Asian member states originate beyond the region, but play a substantial role in its ability to mitigate potential crisis from climate change and the resultant impact on regional food security.

(a) *Cereal Systems Initiative for South Asia*: The Cereal Systems Initiative for South Asia (CSISA) is an initiative established in 2009 that involves Bangladesh, India, and Nepal in collaboration with the United States Agency for International Aid (USAID) and the Bill and Melinda Gates Foundation. CSISA's main goal is to improve cereal production, food security, and the income of farmers in South Asia in a sustainable manner. The CSISA "complements regional and national efforts and involves public, civil society and private sector partners in the development and dissemination of improved cropping systems, resource-conserving management technologies, new cereal varieties and hybrids, livestock feeding strategies and feed value chains, aquaculture systems and policies and markets. CSISA supports women farmers by ensuring their access and exposure to modern and improved technological innovations, knowledge and entrepreneurial skills that can help them become informed and recognized decision makers in agriculture" (CSISA 2015). In attaining its objectives, CSISA develops and disseminates technologies and management practices across various facets of cereal production: resource conservation, labor and cost saving, crop–livestock and aquaculture management, nutrient management, and policy, partnership, and capacity-building. With this initiative, farmers will be better equipped to face possible threats from climate change, and South Asia may be better able to solve food insecurity through technological and management advances.

(b) *US-South Asia Agricultural Cooperation*: The United States Department of Agriculture (USDA) and the Indian Ministry of Agriculture has plans to renew their expired Memorandum of Understanding (MOU). The MOU will be expanded to engage a broader scope of topics. Both governments will also renew the Agricultural Dialogue, which will enable a broad scope of cooperation on food and agricultural regulations and policies (US Department of State 2015). Some areas for cooperation include technology transfer, agricultural practice, irrigation, and water management techniques (Mittal 2011).

The US has already been provided agricultural assistance to Afghanistan and Pakistan under the "Food for Progress Programme" (Mittal 2011). The principal US agency USAID has numerous agricultural projects in both countries. In Afghanistan, US assistance focuses on capacity-building by creating jobs, income, and productivity, which in turn enhances food security. According to USAID, since 2002, USAID has supported numerous endeavors in Afghanistan, such as distribution of seeds, fertilizers, tools, and technology to jumpstart the country's agricultural sector (USAID 2015a). Based on USAID estimates, USAID interventions have "generated more than $306 million in sales and services for farmers and agribusinesses. USAID has trained more than 1.5 million people, and provided more than 24,600 households with access to credit, while providing financing to agribusinesses that has generated 2913 jobs (direct and indirect). In total, USAID investments in agriculture have helped create over 358,968 new agricultural jobs" (USAID 2015a). Under USAID's Economic Growth and Agriculture (EGA) program, Pakistan similarly receives aid to stimulate growth and productivity in its economy and agricultural sector in hope of developing future relations that extend beyond aid toward trade. USAID terms the programs laid out in Pakistan "farm to fork." According to USAID, "USAID programs are collaborating with the U.S. Department of Agriculture to support R&D in the agricultural sciences to develop cutting edge seed technologies and management practices to support Pakistan's rapidly growing population" (USAID 2015b). USAID programs have helped to strengthen agricultural value and modernize commercial agribusiness and capacity-building in the agricultural sector (USAID 2015b).

(c) *Europe–South Asia Agricultural Cooperation*: There are two notable cooperation and development plans: (1) the European Union–Pakistan Five Year Engagement Plan, beginning in 2009/2010, and (2) the Country Strategy for Development Cooperation between Finland and Nepal, from 2013 to 2016. The European Union-Pakistan Five Year Engagement Plan involves a multitude of sectors, including trade, energy, security, and governance. One point on agriculture states that the aim is to "[e]nhance cooperation in agriculture through specific projects, including modernization of agro-based industry, expansion of storage facilities, research and development" (European Commission 2015). The Country Strategy for Development Cooperation between Finland and

Nepal highlights that the agriculture sector could be a major vehicle for development in Nepal. The countries' governments aim to cooperate and discuss development strategies as part of bilateral cooperation (Ministry of Foreign Affairs of Finland 2014).

(d) *South-Asia Multilateral Initiatives*: There are currently numerous multilateral initiatives in place under international organizations such as the United Nations (UN), the Food and Agriculture Organization of the UN (FAO), the World Bank (WB), and the Global Environment Facility (GEF). These international organizations coordinate efforts to enhance climate change adaptation and reduce scenarios where food insecurity is a problem through networks between governments, non-governmental organizations, local organizations, and companies. These international organizations are the source of billions of US dollars in financial support for many projects undertaken to date.

South Asia is a beneficiary of many of these funds and programs. The FAO's and WB's contributions are especially notable, and they have been directly involved in development efforts. Broadly speaking, the FAO and WB have been large contributors to regional efforts on many facets of food security and climate change. The FAO is a pivotal organization that pays attention to developing nations and contributes significantly by disseminating information and knowledge about agricultural practices. In South Asia, the FAO implemented programs related to disaster management and preparedness in Bangladesh and Nepal, capacities for climate change threat mitigation in Nepal, gender-sensitive strategies for adaptation to climate change, and assessment of food security concerns in all SAARC member states. Similarly, the WB has devised packages and interventions that aim to reduce climate change impacts in the region by introducing better irrigation practices, forecasting natural disasters, and promoting better management of water resources. These projects and multilateral cooperation have been another source of aid that could help the South Asian region cushion climate change impacts on food security.

Analysis of Initiatives and Programs

We have thus far examined various programs that will implicate SAARC's future food security given the threats it faces from climate change. Climate change is a multi-sectoral, multistakeholder issue that cannot be encompassed in a single framework or initiative. SAARC has acknowledged that food security and climate change are vital concerns for the

Table 4.7 Evaluation criteria for SAARC initiatives and programs

	Factor	*Justification*
1.	Planning	This criterion involves the overarching frame of the programs and initiatives. It is mainly concerned with their goals and objectives
2.	Implementation	This criterion concerns the nature of the programs and initiatives laid out, and the execution of the initiatives
3.	Cooperation	The criterion concerns the state of relations between SAARC nations and their relative commitment levels. It will highlight the level of commitment and cooperation SAARC has fostered among its member states for its programs
4.	Legal obligation	This criterion concerns the enforcement and legality of various agreements, treaties, and initiatives. Legal obligation involves the enforcement rights of SAARC as a regional organization to ensure its member nations comply with various initiatives
5.	International contribution	This criterion assesses how the region has contributed to or impacted global climate change and food security

Source Authors' own analysis

future, and undertaken numerous initiatives to address climate change and food security. Having provided an overview of current initiatives under SAARC, we will now briefly examine their efficacy. Some of the factors utilized to evaluate SAARC initiatives and programs are highlighted in Table 4.7.

Planning

SAARC acknowledges deep concerns over climate change impacts, and its regional efforts have been rhetorically addressed. However, the lack of political will among member states regarding regional initiatives means that they have mainly focused on preliminary approaches such as endorsements, agreements, and opening cooperative avenues to monitor and share practices regionally. Nevertheless, the seven thematic areas highlighted under the SAARC Action Plan on Climate Change and the scope of the Technical Committee on Environment show the vast potential for cooperation among SAARC nations. The themes for environmental cooperation are comprehensive, addressing policies, actions, finances, education and awareness, adaptation measures, management, and capacity-building. However, SAARC still lacks engagement with vulnerable populations and local communities, which is crucial for effectively dealing with climate change and food security threats. Notwithstanding, the Delhi and Thimphu Declarations have been endorsed over the years as a commitment to regional cooperation.

Implementation

SAARC has been undeniably quick to recognize climate change and its impacts, beginning in the 1980s. A crucial forum, the South Asia Cooperative Environment Programme, was formed to engage in transboundary environmental issues, and SAARC member states have endorsed thematic areas for cooperation under the SAARC Action Plan on Climate Change. While SAARC has fervently acknowledged regional threats, there has been little direct action to address future regional needs, despite plans, statements, and declarations such as the Dhaka Declaration and SAARC Action Plan on Climate Change, the Delhi Statement on Cooperation in Environment, and the Thimphu Statement on Climate Change. These approaches and discussions over food security and climate change are regional in focus, and fail to tackle long-term issues beyond the region by actively pursuing changes in international policy. Notably, SAARC falls short in its active role as the main organization to ensure South Asian nations' adaptive capacities; instead, bilateral initiatives between South Asian nations and external international partners are more vibrant.

Cooperation

SAARC has been highly vocal in its attempts to work on regional initiatives and cooperate on matters laid out by SAARC initiatives. However, as Sharma (2011) has highlighted, the limits of regional cooperation under SAARC can be exemplified by the July/August 2011 floods in Pakistan. The floods impacted Pakistan tremendously, damaging infrastructure and affecting millions of people. While there was a pledge of US$32 million, there were no additional supports from SAARC member nations to Pakistan during this time of crisis. As Sharma (2011) further highlights, these floods came only months after the Silver Jubilee SAARC Summit, which took Climate for its theme.

In addition, the South Asian sociopolitical scene has been hampered by conflicts due to its plural sociocultural background. Security issues include violence, terrorism, ethnic conflicts (in Kashmir, among Sri Lanka's Tamil and Sinhala populations, among Karachi's Mohajirs, and between Sind and Baluchistan), the instability of Nepal's Communist Party, and political unrest in Bangladesh. Many SAARC nations thus face internal struggles which are an impediment to regional cooperation. In addition, Afghanistan and Pakistan face external armed confrontations with fundamentalist forces and United States–NATO interference, severely undermining political security in the South Asian region.

Bilateral disputes between India and other SAARC member states have been an impediment to SAARC initiatives. India's posturing as a regional power and distrust of Pakistan create cross-border tensions, which result in proxy conflicts, breeding doubts over India's regional objectives among its SAARC neighbors. Although the SAARC has weathered many events and conflicts, there has been little progress in furthering regional goals and objectives (Sharma 2011), and the relevance of SAARC as an intermediary platform has been called into question due to its lack of relevance as a regional governing body. Hence, SAARC's initiatives and attempts to address regional issues have been largely overshadowed by its failures.

Legal Obligation

SAARC has developed multiple treaties due to ongoing security threats and violence. SAARC has vocally reiterated its support for the UN Charter, international law, and international conventions. However, the legality of declarations regarding environmental and food security is still uncertain because cross-boundary initiatives have been merely discussed and only nominally implemented. Nonetheless, issues regarding food security and climate change are still subject to the political will and commitment of individual states to abide by SAARC aims and goals, with little or no legal ramifications.

International Contribution

While climate change will undeniably impact food security in South Asia, the role of SAARC in the international community remains nominal. In addition, SAARC as a regional organization has undeveloped potential, and its member nations have been more active in engaging external agencies. SAARC member nations still prioritize national goals and ambitions over regional interests, and they have not dealt with long-standing tensions between and within national borders. While SAARC may facilitate regional cooperation as a platform for sharing and working toward future regional goals, weak institutional frameworks mean that overt declarations, agreements, and plans are often ineffective despite its vast potential to engage its members, and it has little success in its dealings with the international community. Taken together, the following Table 4.8 summarizes the overall efficacy of SAARC regional initiatives for climate change and food security.

Table 4.8 Summary table for SAARC initiatives' efficacy

	Factor	*Summary conclusion*
1.	Planning	SAARC has made progress in acknowledging the impacts of the climate change crisis on food security and has set up avenues for cooperation
2.	Implementation	SAARC is mostly reactive in mitigating the threats of climate change and has made minimal progress toward regional cooperation to mitigate its impacts. External bilateral collaborations have been more vibrant than SAARC's main regional body
3.	Cooperation	Ongoing disputes within and between national borders have created a climate of tension and suspicion between SAARC member states
4.	Legal obligation	Initiatives related to climate change and food security are based on the goodwill of member states, and there is no evidence that failure to adhere to past declarations will inherently lead to ramifications
5.	International contribution	Role within the international community is minimal and there is still dependence on international and external agencies

Source Authors' own analysis

Conclusion

Although South Asian countries have opened up their economies significantly over the past years, the intra-regional trade of the SAARC countries has remained at very low levels, at about 6.2% of their global trade. In case of food grain production and trade in South Asia, for example, we can discern at least five patterns: (a) status of South Asian countries vary with regard to the correspondence between demand and supply; (b) surplus/deficit status tends to change in view of production performance in particular periods; (c) bottlenecks in the movement of food grains between origin and destination involves significant delays; (d) both tariff and non-tariff barriers inform the nature of trade in food grains; and (e) a price of the food grains that tend to evolve through regional trade could serve as a reference point for price fixation in operationalizing the SAARC Food Bank (Rahman et al. 2017, 2018).

While SAARC has been progressive in its acknowledgment of climate change impacts on the region, attempts to coordinate efforts have not been effectively translated into programs that can curtail future problems related to food security and climate change. The inability to fulfill its agenda can be largely attributed to lack of political will and ongoing conflicts and tension, which impede translating agendas into active adaptive measures. Despite these criticisms, SAARC has been able to highlight issues of concern and areas for cooperation in the region. However, it has been unable to fulfill its potential as a driving force for climate change mitigation and improved food security in the region, and its vast potential remains mainly untapped. SAARC may have other more pressing issues to deal with regionally, which is an obstacle to ensuring cooperation among member states and gaining support for non-traditional security and environmental issues.

References

Aggarwal, P.K., and Mannava V.K. Sivakumar. 2010. Global Climate Change and Food Security in South Asia: An Adaptation and Mitigation Framework. In *Climate Change and Food Security in South Asia*, ed. R. Lal, M.V.K. Sivakumar, S.M.A. Faiz, and K.R. Islam. London: Springer.

Amjad, S., Q. Chaudhry, I. Ismail, M.I. Tariq, Z.U. Islam, and A.M. Qaimkhani. 2013. Workshop Report: Climate Change Impacts on Coastal and Aquatic Resources. SAARC Coastal Zone Management Centre Male,

Maldives Ministry of Climate Change, Climate Change Division, Government of Pakistan.

Bandara, Jayatilleke S., and Yiyong Cai. 2014. The Impact of Climate Change on Food Crop Productivity, Food Prices and Food Security in South Asia. *Economic Analysis and Policy* 44 (4): 451–465.

Cai, Yiyong, Jayatilleke S. Bandara, and David Newth. 2016. A Framework for Integrated Assessment of Food Production Economics in South Asia under Climate Change. *Environmental Modelling and Software* 75: 459–497.

Chand, R. 2010. SAARC Agricultural Vision 2020. *Agricultural Economics Research Review* 23: 197–208.

CIA. 2014. The World Factbook. Retrieved September 13, 2015. https://www.cia.gov/library/publications/the-world-factbook/index.html.

CIA (Central Intelligence Agency). 2017. The World Factbook. Retrieved 1 August 2017. https://www.cia.gov/library/publications/the-world-factbook/index.html.

CSISA (Cereal Systems Initiative for South Asia). 2015. Overview. Retrieved 12 August 2017. http://csisa.org/about-csisa/overview/.

European Commission. 2015. EU-Pakistan 5-Year Engagement Plan. Retrieved 10 August 2017. https://eeas.europa.eu/sites/eeas/files/eu-pakistan_five-year_engagement_plan.pdf.

FAO (Food and Agriculture Organization of the United Nations). 1995. Regional Study and Workshop on the Environmental Assessment and Management of Aquaculture Development. (TCP/RAS/2253) NACA Environment and Aquaculture Development Series No. 1. Bangkok, Network of Aquaculture Centres in Asia-Pacific.

IPCC (Intergovernmental Panel on Climate Change). 2007. IPCC Forth Assessment Report: Climate Change 2007. Retrieved 8 August 2017. https://www.ipcc.ch/publications_and_data/ar4/wg1/en/spmsspm-projections-of.html.

Islam, M.S., and Edson Kieu. 2020. Tackling Regional Climate Change Impacts and Food Security Issues: A Critical Analysis across ASEAN, PIF and SAARC. *Sustainability* 12 (883): 1–21.

Islam, M.S., and L. Si Hui. 2015. When 'Nature' Strikes: A Sociology of Climate Change and Disaster Vulnerabilities in Asia. *Nature and Culture* 10 (1): 57–80.

Islam, Md Saidul. 2014. *Confronting the Blue Revolution: Industrial Aquaculture and Sustainability in the Global South*. Toronto: University of Toronto Press.

Kaur, Simrit, and Harpreet Kaur. 2016. Climate Change, Food Security, and Water Management in South Asia: Implications for Regional Cooperation. *Emerging Economy Studies* 2 (1): 1–18.

Khadka, Narayan. 1990. Regional Cooperation for Food Security in South Asia. *Food Policy* 15 (6): 492–504.

Kher, P. 2012. Political Economy of Regional Integration in South Asia. Background Paper, UNCTAD. Retrieved 6 August 2017. http://unctad.org/en/PublicationsLibrary/ecidc2013misc1_bp5.pdf.

Lal, M. 2011. Implications of Climate Change in Sustained Agricultural Productivity in South Asia. *Regional Environmental Change* 11 (Suppl 1): S79–S94.

Ministry of Foreign Affairs of Finland. 2014. Development Cooperation between Finland and Nepal. Retrieved 10 August 2017. http://www.finland.org.np/public/download.aspx?ID=112594&GUID={D13F0081-6826-4B4F-AEAB-F2E771185004}.

Mirza, M.M.Q. 2011. Climate Change, Flooding in South Asia and Implications. *Regional Environmental Change* 11: 95–107.

Mittal, S. 2011. Regional and International Cooperation. In *Climate Change and Food Security in South Asia*, ed. Bipul Chatterjee and Manbar Khadka, 87–106. Jaipur, India: CUTS International.

Nelson, Gerald C., Mark W. Rosegrant, Jawoo Koo, Richard Robertson, Timothy Sulser, Tingju Zhu, Claudia Ringler, Siwa Msangi, Amanda Palazzo, Miroslav Batka, Marilia Magalhaes, Rowena Valmonte-Santos, Mandy Ewing, and David Lee. 2009. *Climate Change Impact on Agriculture and Costs of Adaptation*. Washington, DC: International Food Policy Research Institute.

Paroda, R.S., and P. Kumar. 2000. Food Production and Demand in South Asia. *Agricultural Economics Research Review* 13 (1): 1–24.

Rahman, Mustafizur, Estiaque Bari, and Sherajum Monira Farin. 2017. SAARC FOOD BANK (SFB): Institutional Architecture and Issues of Operationalisation.

Rahman, Mustafizur, Estiaque Bari, and Sherajum Monira Farin. 2018. Operationalizing the SAARC Food Bank: Issues and Solutions. ESCAP South and South-West Asia Office.

SAARC. 1987. Agreement on Establishing the SAARC Food Security Reserve. SAARC Agreements and Conventions, Asian Legal Information Institute. Retrieved 9 August 2017. http://www.asianlii.org/saarc/other/agrmt/aoetsfsr537/.

SAARC. 2007. Agreement on Establishing the SAARC Food Bank. Retrieved 10 August 2017. http://www.ifrc.org/Docs/idrl/N646EN.pdf.

SAARC. 2008. Workshop Climate Change and Disasters: Emerging Trends and Future Strategies. Retrieved 16 October 2015. http://saarc-sdmc.nic.in/pdf/publications/climate/chapter-2.pdf.

SAARC. 2009a. SAARC Charter. Retrieved 1 August 2017. http://saarc-sec.org/saarc-charter/5/.

SAARC. 2009b. Fifth Meeting of SAARC Technical Committee on Agriculture and Rural Development. SAARC Agenda Item Six of SAARC Agriculture Vision 2020.

SAARC. 2009c. Area of Cooperation (Environment). SAARC. Retrieved 9 August 2017. http://globalsummitryproject.com.s197331.gridserver.com/archive/saarc/saarc-sec.org/areaofcooperation/cat-detail1a12.html?cat_id=54.

SAARC. 2010. Thimphu Statement on Climate Change. Sixteenth SAARC Submit Thimphu, 28–29 April.

SAARC (South Asia Association for Regional Cooperation). 2015. SAARC Agriculture Vision 2020. Retrieved 7 August 2017. http://www.sac.org.bd/vision/saarc-agriculture-vision-2020/.

SAARC Group on Statistics. 2009. Key-Statistics; Real GDP Per Capita. Retrieved 3 August 2017. http://saarcstat.org/db/statistics/real_gdp/real_gdp_per_capita?year=2007&search=Submit.

Sharma, S. 2011. Existential Threat to Human Security in South Asia and Regional Response: A Case Study of Climate Change and SAARC Initiatives. WISC.

Sivasubramaniam, K. 2009. The Sustainable Contribution of Fisheries to Food Security in the South Asian Subregion. Food and Agriculture Organization. Retrieved 14 August 2017. http://www.fao.org/docrep/003/x6956e/x6956e08.htm.

South Asia Cooperative Environment Programme. 2015. What We Do. Retrieved 10 October 2015. http://www.sacep.org/.

Subasinghe, R. 1997. Review of the State of World Aquaculture. FAO Fisheries Circular No. 886 FIRI/C886 (Rev.1). Retrieved 14 August 2017. http://www.fao.org/docrep/003/w7499e/w7499e32.htm.

US Department of State. 2015. US-India Commercial, Trade and Economic Cooperation. Retrieved 10 August 2017. https://in.usembassy.gov/fact-sheet-u-s-india-commercial-trade-and-economic-cooperation/.

USAID (United States Agency for International Development). 2015a. Afghanistan Agriculture. Retrieved 12 August 2017. https://www.usaid.gov/afghanistan/agriculture.

USAID (United States Agency for International Development). 2015b. Pakistan Economic Growth and Agriculture. Retrieved 12 August 2017. https://www.usaid.gov/pakistan/economic-growth-agriculture.

World Bank. 2007. *South Asia: Growth and Regional Integration*. Washington, DC: World Bank.

World Bank. 2021. World Development Indicators. Retrieved March 14, 2021. https://databank.worldbank.org/source/world-development-indicators.

CHAPTER 5

Climate Change and Food Security in PIF

Founded in 1971, the Pacific Islands Forum (PIF) comprises of 18 members: Australia, Cook Islands, Federated States of Micronesia, Fiji, French Polynesia, Kiribati, Nauru, New Caledonia, New Zealand, Niue, Palau, Papua New Guinea, Republic of Marshall Islands, Samoa, Solomon Islands, Tonga, Tuvalu, and Vanuatu (Shibuya 2004). As the region's premier political and economic policy organization, the work of the Forum has been guided by the Framework for Pacific Regionalism since 2014. The pattern of cooperation developed among the countries in Oceania is well established and should provide many lessons for other regions. On the other hand, many critics view the Forum as an example of unrealized potential, where endless discussions have replaced action as the measure of effectiveness, while refusing to take the next step in its evolution, from regional organization to regional community. Through governments, intergovernmental organizations, or civil society organizations, the Pacific Islands were some of the most highly vocal proponents of a climate change mitigation agreement at COP21. However, even with these long-standing efforts to speak with one voice, the multiple climate change declarations that came out of the Pacific during the final months leading up to COP21 exhibited a series of differences and some tensions (Denton 2017; Islam and Kieu 2020).

M. S. Islam and E. Kieu, *Climate Change and Food Security in Asia Pacific*, International Political Economy Series,
https://doi.org/10.1007/978-3-030-70753-8_5

This chapter provides an understanding of PIF and its member states, highlights the impacts of climate change and food security on PIF, and provides an overview of regional initiatives undertaken and their efficacy in mitigating regional risks related to food security due to climate change impacts. PIF adaptive and mitigating measures on issues regarding food security and climate change will be assessed, thereby elucidating the current state of action within the region. Like earlier chapters, this PIF case study examines regional policies, although individual member states may develop their own national-level policies and programs to mitigate climate change impacts and food security risks. This chapter refers only to policies specific to both food security and climate change in tandem; policies considering climate change and food security as discrete matters are beyond the scope of this chapter.

Background and History of PIF

The Pacific Islands Forum (PIF) was established in 1971 as the South Pacific Forum; the name was later changed to the Pacific Islands Forum to reflect its new members and therefore encompassed both the north and south Pacific. The founding nations of the PIF were Australia, Cook Islands, Fiji, Nauru, New Zealand, Tonga, and Western Samoa (now Samoa). The Federated States of Micronesia, Kiribati, Niue, Palau, Papua New Guinea, Republic of Marshall Islands, Solomon Islands, Tuvalu, and Vanuatu were included later (PIF Secretariat 2015). The objectives and resolutions of the PIF inscribed as its mission and vision are as follows: "Our mission is to ensure the effective implementation of the Leaders' decisions for the benefit of the people of the Pacific. Our goals are to stimulate economic growth and enhance political governance and security for the region, through the provision of policy advice; and to strengthen regional cooperation and integration through coordinating, monitoring and evaluating implementation of Leaders' decisions" (PIF Secretariat 2015). In achieving these goals, the Primary Roles of the Forum Secretariat, as set out in the 2005 Agreement Establishing the Pacific Islands Forum, are to provide: (a) Policy advice and guidance in implementing the decisions of the Leaders; (b) Coordination and assistance in implementing the decisions of the Leaders; and (c) Support to the Leaders' meetings, ministerial meetings, and associated committees and working groups.

In addition to the above, the PIF adopts the following guiding principles and values: (a) Address the priority needs and rights of our most vulnerable members, communities, and people (Special and Differential Treatment); (b) Embrace the cultural diversity of the region with tolerance and respect (The Pacific Way); (c) Facilitate the debate on how to position the region to meet emerging challenges both now and in the future (Foresight); (d) Strive for recognition of the region's responsibility for guardianship of the world's largest ocean and its resources (Common Heritage); (e) Foster quality interaction with all our stakeholders, both internal and external (Communication); and (f) Embrace good governance and gender equality, and seek peak performance (Continuous Performance) (PIF Secretariat 2015).

The Pacific Island Countries and Territories (PICTs) are characterized by their relatively small physical size and geographical remoteness, delicate biodiversity, and limited natural resources. There are over 7000 inhabited Pacific Islands among 7500 islands in 30 million square kilometers of the tropical Pacific Ocean. The land area is divided into three main regions, Melanesia, Micronesia, and Polynesia. These are again divided into 14 independent countries and 6 American and French territories.

The majority of Pacific countries' exports are based on the extraction of natural resources: agricultural and marine products, forestry, and mining. Since many of these countries grow and export similar commodities, inter-island trade is limited (ADB 2011). Nevertheless, all PIF nations have experienced a steady trend of economic growth over the last few years. The gross domestic products per capita of the PIF nations can be seen in Table 5.1.

The total population for all PIF member nations is around 34.4 million, with Australia having the largest population, around 23 million, and Niue having the smallest, with only 1626 people, based on 2015 estimates (CIA 2017). The population growth rates in these nations remain small, ranging from +2% per year to a decline of −1% per year. Although these nations are not expecting tremendous changes and shifts in their economies and demographics relative to other regions, climate change and its impacts may nonetheless impact food stability for the region due to its fragile biodiversity and environment.

Table 5.1 Gross domestic product per capita in PIF at current prices (nominal) in US dollars (as of September 2017)

Country	*2010*	*2011*	*2012*	*2013*	*2014*	*2015*
Australia	51,874.1	62,245.1	67,677.6	67,792.3	62,214.6.	56,554.0
Cook Islands	12,578.7	–	–	–	15,002.5	–
Federated States of Micronesia	2838.5	2998.9	3148.1	3044.5	3057.9	3016.0
Fiji	3652.0	4353.1	4546.7	4763.1	5046.0	4921.9
Kiribati	1493.2	1692.6	1763.8	1724.4	1684.5	1424.5
Nauru	4912.6	7233.9	10,099.4	10,036.2	9872.6	8052.9
New Zealand	33,691.3	38,426.6	39,970.3	42,889.9	44,503.2	38,201.9
Niue	5800 (2003 estimates)					
Palau	8979.0	9704.4	10,318.9	10,932.1	11,894.4	13,500.6
Papua New Guinea	1366.9	1770.9	2071.3	2030.0	2182.7	–
Republic of Marshall Island	3142.6	3286.4	3514.0	3617.8	3461.6	3385.9
Samoa	3453.5	3942.0	4234.6	4219.1	4179.0	4149.4
Solomon Island	1272.4	1642.8	1858.7	1880.5	2009.7	1922.0
Tonga	3547.6	4045.0	4501.5	4266.6	4192.4	4093.8
Tuvalu	3021.9	3698.9	3718.0	3542.1	3415.8 lePara>	2970.0
Vanuatu	2965.8	3275.1	3158.6	3167.3	3148.4	2805.8

Source Adapted from World Bank (2015), United Nations Statistics Division (2015), and CIA (2017) [no copyright issue]

Climate Change Impact on Food Security in PIF Member States

The larger, higher islands among Pacific countries have more agricultural potential as fertile volcanic islands, while the low-lying countries generally are more reliant on coastal fisheries, with marine resources shaping local cultures, food, income, and livelihood. Amidst climate change, other threats to future food security in the Pacific region include global economic volatility and food price crises, rapid urban population growth, rural to urban migration, land degradation and declining land productivity, erosion of crop genetic diversity, coastal and coral degradation and declining productivity of fisheries, and breakdowns in traditional social safety nets. Food systems are changing from subsistence agriculture and fishing to commercial agriculture, with increasing dependence on imported food, overtaking local produces, especially rice and wheat flour. With an increasing high-calorie low-nutrition imports, the Pacific Island countries' rates of obesity, diabetes, and micronutrient deficiencies were among the world's highest (20% undernourished in 2003–2005), with considerable improvements and a downward trend over the years (ADB 2011; Islam and Kieu 2020).

Places at risk in the PIF include atolls, coastal communities, river floodplains, and deltas. Many parts of the region are exposed to drought events. Papua New Guinea Highlands and most atolls face a loss of potable water supply both in terms of quality and quantity. The combined impacts of climate change have serious tolls on habitat security and agricultural production threatening livelihood including food security. Changes in tropical cyclone frequency and magnitude are quite apparent (Campbell 2014). Increasing natural disasters and rising sea levels directly affect food security in the long term, particularly in smaller atoll countries, further reducing the declining agricultural output per capita. Crop yields will also be affected by wetter or drier conditions, in the El Niño and La Niña events due to climate change. Increased atmospheric carbon dioxide concentrations and warmer temperatures are less conducive for growing feed, reducing the nutritional value of animal production, particularly beef. Coastal and low-lying farms may also suffer from seawater inundation and intrusion of saltwater into the groundwater. Coastal fisheries will suffer from overfishing to meet demand, destroyed habitats and coral death due to acidification of seawater. Offshore fisheries (mainly of skipjack tuna in the tropical Pacific) may suffer a net loss by the end of the century. Forests, water resources, human health, and infrastructure will also be impacted by climate change and food insecurity (ADB 2011; Islam and Kieu 2020).

Impact on Land and Agricultural Productivity

Global warming and climate changes are expected by experts to cause significant disruptions to the PICTs' food production systems through direct and indirect impacts. The impacts of extreme weather events on agriculture are highly critical since this sector is the main source of food, livelihood, and income for many Pacific Island communities. Severe droughts, intense floods, salt water inundation and intrusion, and tropical cyclones reduce both crop yields and total production, increasing the risks of food insecurity in communities. Most rural people in the Pacific rely directly on staple crops and farming for food (Iese et al. 2018).

Direct impacts on agricultural production such as weakening easterly winds, increases in high-intensity rainfalls, rising mean temperatures, rising sea levels, and greater cyclone frequency (Lebot 2013) may lead to declining agricultural output. According to the FAO (2008), 70% of gross crop areas are strategically located to benefit from rain during the summer season during November to April, making local agriculture particularly dependent on seasonal rainfall. Although there may be gains in some crop yields as the overall mean temperature rises, these may be offset by drier or wetter conditions (ADB 2011). Crop losses and livestock production will be impacted by excess heat and drought in some locations and oversaturation of soil and land damage in other parts. These impacts and variations in weather will be further exacerbated by El Niño and La Niña frequency and intensity, making agricultural production more susceptible to fluctuations based on climatic extremes (ADB 2011). Coastal and low-lying farms will face seawater inundations, and saltwater intrusion of groundwater will impact agricultural productivity and discourage future investment in affected areas.

Impact on Marine Ecosystems, Fisheries, and Aquaculture

Many Pacific Island communities depend on their local, nearshore fisheries for food security, livelihoods, and cultural purposes; however, fisheries in the tropics are currently threatened by major changes in fish distribution, with a predicted net movement of fish stocks out of the tropics into higher latitudes. Coral reef degradation, resulted from changes in water temperature and chemistry, is among the major threat to essential fisheries habitat. Besides, there is an increase in intensity and variability in coastal storms which poses safety hazards to fishers and reduces access to fishing. Therefore, the livelihoods based on fishing, food security, culture, safety, health, and sovereignty are at stake (Finkbeiner et al. 2018). Ocean acidification, triggered by climate change, is another problem that affects fisheries in various ways. It can, for example, alter behavior of fishes as well as sensory perception, making them increasingly vulnerable to predation. Ocean acidification has significant negative effects on coral reef calcification which in turn decreases the amount of habitat available to reef-associated fishes. It can also potentially alter marine food webs through its effects on the calcification, growth, mortality rates, and reproductive success of a variety of marine organisms that serve as prey, predators, and competitors of fishes (Asch et al. 2018).

Marine ecosystems, fisheries, and aquaculture are vital to PICTs, as they play an intricate part in the lives and culture of its inhabitants. Per capita consumption in PICTs is very high, with an average of 70 kg of fish per person annually consumed in the early 1990s (FAO 2008). The exacerbating problem with fisheries and aquaculture in PICTs is that good nutrition must come from fish, because fish provides 50% of the total animal protein supply (SPC 2008). Subsistence and commercial farming have been threatened by environmental degradation and over-exploitation, and when these issues are compounded by climate change, the sustainability of the industry and food security could be in severe danger. The survival of fisheries is intricately linked to environmental variables: increases in water temperature and salinity can disrupt ecosystems and complex food chains (FAO 2008). Projected increases in temperatures and rising sea levels will affect plankton activity and ultimately cause a decline in fisheries' productivity (Lal 2004). Furthermore, widespread coral bleaching during ENSO episodes will cause additional ecosystem disruptions. Fish stocks may be impacted by the destruction of coral and coastal habitats, and in the longer term by acidification (ADB 2011).

Outside of ecosystems, more frequent and intense storms could also render fishing more hazardous, which will reduce fish supplies and affect the livelihoods of fisher folks and communities dependent on this industry. Coastal fisheries will face overfishing as the population and urban area grow faster than the fish population, resulting in an overall net loss by the end of the decade (ADB 2011). The global financial and food crisis since 2007 is a reminder how food security cannot be taken for granted anywhere in the world. The crisis highlights the importance of precautions for food security, due to the compounding risks exacerbated by climate change, larger world populations, and future economic volatility. Additional threats faced in the Pacific region highlighted by the ADB (2011) include rapid urban population expansion, land degradation coupled with declining land productivity, erosion of crop genetic diversity, and coastal and coral degradation, which will result in a decline in the productivity of fisheries and the breakdown of traditional social safety nets.

Future Policy Implications

Regional action by the PIF has been slow, but objectives for the region have centered on ensuring sustainable food security. Given current trajectories, PICTs could face worsening economic growth due to adverse climatic impacts, existing development problems, and worsening trade imbalances (ADB 2011). According to the ADB (2011), future collaboration and developments to address climate change and food security in the region will be pursued in various directions. The first is related to increasing economic growth and productivity, which is a vital point of departure for food security in the region. The changing demands of agriculture under rapid urbanization, the decline of agricultural interests, chronic land disputes, and the uncertainties of food production systems in a changing climate need to be managed effectively. Greater focus on fish as a food source is also touted as a method to meet protein deficiency and shortfalls as a short-term measure.

The second direction relates to institutional capacity development to address changing climate scenarios. However, there must be sufficient domestic capacity to support institutional needs, which may be difficult to maintain, especially for smaller and economically weaker countries. An alternative for countries that are unable to build the necessary institutional capacity to rely on coordination by the Council of Regional Organizations in the Pacific. Such coordination and efficient implementation may become fruitful by utilizing existing external resources, drawing upon knowledge, technology, and services from regional organizations. Because most Pacific countries are largely rural, community-level engagement in decision-making to partake in climate change adaptation initiatives is seen as a viable way to establish stronger food security in terms of nutrient-rich foods.

The third direction involves establishing climate resilience in multisectoral infrastructure development in hopes of improving growth, productivity, trade, and distribution of goods. These will be integral to strengthen food security in the region. Investment in climate-resilient infrastructure like proper management of land use and water supply, well-established roads, and shipping ports could increase regional connectivity and productivity, and thereby provide a more resilient food supply chain. Furthermore, the ADB (2011) highlights that the region's current free-trade regime tends to increase the importation of processed goods that are nutritionally poor, and may weaken food security.

The fourth direction relates to information, education, and communication between PICT nations. The dissemination of information, data, and knowledge is critical to raise public awareness and mutual understanding and to foster effective partnerships and cooperation to address climate change adaptation and mitigation. Disaster management and emergency response systems should be established to mitigate threats from natural or man-made disasters. This approach could address the threats of extreme weather caused by climate change and provide more efficient food assistance to those affected by disasters.

PIF as a Regional Forum for Climate Change and Food Security Initiatives

In 2009, during the Forum Leaders Communiqué, the Pacific Leaders issued a call to action on climate change. They claimed that the "very viability of some of our communities" and the "security of our communities and the health of populations are in great jeopardy. And some habitats and islands States face obliteration" (PIF Secretariat 2009). The call to action drew attention to the Niue Declaration on Climate Change during the Pacific Islands Forum's Smaller Island States (SIS) Leaders' Summit, held on August 19, 2008. The Niue declaration was a watershed, highlighting the seriousness of potential climate change impacts on the region and asking for the support of the international community. The Pacific Leaders' 2009 call to action similarly urged the international community to pursue effective global agreements.

The threat of climate change is generally accepted in the region, and the PIF Secretariat has fervently acknowledged that climate is an "immediate and serious threat to sustainable development and poverty eradication" (PIF Secretariat 2015). Many member countries of the PIF have to bear a large disproportion of climate change impacts relative to their contribution to global emissions. The leaders of member countries of the PIF have tasked the PIF Secretariat with exploring options to effectively manage climate change and to facilitate the management of resources at the national level. The PIF Secretariat engages in multi-tiered dialog with multiple stakeholders. Apart from engaging member nations, the PIF Secretariat also collaborates with Council of Regional Organizations in the Pacific (CROP) agencies like the SPREP and Secretariat of the Pacific Community (SPC), the United Nations Development Programme (UNDP), Australian Aid (AusAID), the European Union

(EU), the United States Agency for International Development (USAID), the Asian Development Bank (ADB), and the World Bank (WB).

PIF and PICTs' Regional Initiatives

Although the PICTs have multiple partnerships addressing climate change and food security, the main coordinating body, the Pacific Islands Framework for Action on Climate Change, was established in 2005. This framework aimed to ensure that Pacific Island communities can build resilient and risk-adverse capacities to mitigate the risks associated with climate change. The founding principles and key objectives according to the Secretariat of the Pacific Regional Environment Programme (SPREP) (2006) are as follows:

1. Implementing adaptation measures
2. Governance and decision-making
3. Improving our understanding of climate change
4. Education, training, and awareness
5. Contributing to global greenhouse gas reduction; and
6. Partnerships and cooperation.

These principles align with action plans intended to contribute to the implementation of the framework, which is primarily regional in nature. In support of this framework, the Pacific Climate Change Roundtable (PCCR) attempts to ensure the coordination of activities and to provide monitoring and evaluation mechanisms for activities under the framework (SPREP 2006). The SPREP, acting as the secretariat for the PCCR, was envisioned as cooperating with CROP to help in drafting agendas for the PCCR. These agendas were to be circulated to national climate change focal points that will involve relevant organizations; financing arrangements will be shared among PICTs. CROP and other agencies are expected to appoint focal points for the PCCR to ensure participation in the meetings PCCR has laid out. All PCCR meetings are open to all stakeholders and allow for "interactive, multi-disciplinary and inclusive dialogue" (SPREP 2006). Accordingly, the SPREP ensures that all relevant stakeholders are updated. Food security and climate change initiatives for the region routinely involve organizations external to the PIF nations, as either implementing agencies or development partners.

Some of the projects, as tabulated in the Pacific Climate Change Portal Database (2012), are outlined in Table 5.2.

Table 5.2 summarily shows collaborative efforts to coordinate regional organizations with international partners for development at the national level. The programs foster a multidisciplinary approach by consulting technical and scientific experts and disseminating best practices and strategies to boost national development sustainability related to food security and adaptive capacities for climate change. Programs for PICTs engage with climate change by gathering information and developing innovative adaptive mechanisms to mitigate the threats they face. Through improved knowledge about climate change, the region will be able to develop Action Plans to communicate between stakeholders, thereby budgeting for and implementing institutional capacity to address regional climate change variability and vulnerability (SPREP 2006; Islam and Kieu 2020). Notwithstanding, apart from such multilateral programs, individual nations have undertaken similar studies and programs, which will be discussed in the following section.

PIF Framework for Action on Food Security in the Pacific

The Framework for Action on Food Security is a call to action issued by Pacific Islands leaders during the 39th Pacific Islands Forum. The agenda set out by this framework was unanimously accepted by all PIF nations. This framework recognizes five themes that will be the foundation for cooperation among member states. These six themes are summarized in Table 5.3.

Potential initiatives have been drafted to address regional goals at the national level, so as to strengthen legislative frameworks and public sector monitoring, involve all stakeholders in legislation formulation, strengthen private sector compliance, and facilitate collaboration between private and public sectors for food quality and safety (SPC 2011). The desired outcomes are to strengthen policy, increase the productivity of agriculture and fisheries, increase the contribution of oceanic fisheries to domestic supplies, enhance food processing capacity while value-adding to agriculture and fish products, and increase the competitiveness of agriculture and fisheries in the domestic and international markets while actively promoting sustainable management of these land and marine resources. The conceptual model in Fig. 5.1 highlights the needs for food security and how all sectors and groups should ideally collaborate with one another.

Table 5.2 Pacific regional climate change and food security project listings

Title	*Implementing agencies/development partners*	*Objectives*	*Implementing Countries*
ADAPT Asia-Pacific	*USAID *USAID ADAPT Asia-Pacific	ADAPT Asia-Pacific aims to be a platform for knowledge sharing to disseminate adaptation-related subject matter with the Asia-Pacific Adaptation Network (APAN). It will also engage in capacity-building programs that will provide skills training for adaptation projects. Lastly, the project will identify and prepare for potential projects, fielded by highly skilled technical specialists	- Federated States of Micronesia - Palau - Marshall Islands - Cook Islands - Fiji - Kiribati - Samoa - Tonga - Solomon Islands - Tuvalu - Niue - Papua New Guinea - Vanuatu
Coping with Climate Change in the Pacific Island Region	*GIZ (*Gesellschaft für Internationale Zusammenarbeit*)	This project aims to enhance the capabilities of local populations, national governmental institutions, and regional organizations; specifically, helping SPC and SPREP to cope with and combat causes of climate change. The project involves the review of policies by considering the management of land and coastal resources and tourism. At the regional level, this project aligns with the Pacific Island Framework for Action on Climate Change (2006–2015)	- Federated States of Micronesia - Palau - Marshall Islands - Cook Islands - Fiji - Kiribati - Samoa - Tonga - Solomon Islands - Tuvalu - Niue - Papua New Guinea - Vanuatu

Title	*Implementing agencies/development partners*	*Objectives*	*Implementing Countries*
	^SPC ^SPREP		
Food Security in the Pacific and East Timor and Its Vulnerability to Climate Change	^AUSaid ^Australian Government Department of Climate Change and Energy Efficiency	This is a report that examines food security and climate change in 15 Pacific Island economies based on four main pillars: adequacy, availability, stability, and utilization	- Federated States of Micronesia - Palau - Marshall Islands - Cook Islands - Fiji - Kiribati - Samoa - Tonga - Solomon Islands - Tuvalu - Niue - Papua New Guinea - Vanuatu
Gap Analysis on Loss and Damage to Climate Change in Selected Pacific Island Countries	*SPREP	This is a commissioned study to examine damages and losses from climate change in the Kiribati, Samoa, and Vanuatu. The study focuses on key sectors such as the environment, fisheries, agriculture, tourism, and the social and private sectors. Based on the findings, the information will be utilized to align with negotiation processes and future designs to support regional attempts to deal with losses and damages	- Kiribati - Samoa - Vanuatu

(continued)

Table 5.2 (continued)

Title	*Implementing agencies/development partners*	*Objectives*	*Implementing Countries*
Implementation of Strategic Programme for Climate Resilience: Pacific Region-ADB Project	*SPREP *ADB ^ADB/WB CIF (Climate Investment Fund) ^PIF Secretariat ^SPC ^FFA (Forum Fisheries) ^SPTO (South Pacific Tourism Organization) ^GIZ	The strategic program for climate resilience addresses core concerns from climate change. These are; (1) climate change adaptation and disaster mitigation; (2) the ability to respond to climate change risks and strengthening adaptive capacities; and (3) enhancing regional capacity development. The program will integrate climate change adaptation with disaster risk reduction as part of development processes, utilizing partnerships with ADB, CROP, and WB	- American Samoa - Cook Islands - Federated States of Micronesia - Fiji - French Polynesia - Guam - Kiribati - Marshall Islands - Nauru - New Caledonia - Niue - Northern Mariana Islands - Palau - Papua New Guinea - Samoa - Solomon Islands - Tokelau - Tonga - Tuvalu - Vanuatu - Wallis and Futuna

Title	*Implementing agencies/development partners*	*Objectives*	*Implementing Countries*
Pacific Adaptation to Climate Change	*SPREP ^UNDP	This project aims to reduce climate change vulnerability while at the same time strengthening the adaptive capacities of all 14 participating nations in key development sectors, such as (1) coastal zone management; (2) food production and food security; and (3) water resource management	- Cook Islands - Federated States of Micronesia - Fiji - Marshall Islands - Nauru - Niue - Palau - Papua New Guinea - Samoa - Solomon Islands - Tokelau - Tonga - Tuvalu - Vanuatu
Pacific iCLM	*SPREP *Griffith University ^SPC ^PIF Secretariat ^USP (University) ^SPC-GIZ Pacific German Regional	Goals of this project center on enhancing resilience and adaptation planning in the Pacific by supporting regional information management	- Fiji - Tonga - Vanuatu

(continued)

Table 5.2 (continued)

Title	*Implementing agencies/development partners*	*Objectives*	*Implementing Countries*
Pilot Programme for Climate Resilience	* PIF Secretariat * FFA * SPC * SPREP * ADB/WB CIF	The pilot will demonstrate methods by which climate risk and resilience can be subsumed under core development planning, which will be consistent with the pursuit of development goals such as poverty reduction	- Papua New Guinea - Samoa - Tonga
Vegetation and Land Cover Mapping and Improving Food Security for Building Resilience to a Changing Climate in Pacific Island Communities	* SPC	This is a joint study that will evaluate and subsequently implement techniques to improve land-based food production systems by making them more resilient to climate change	- Samoa - Fiji - Kiribati - Solomon Islands - Tonga - Vanuatu
Vegetation and Land Cover Mapping and Improving Food Security for Building Resilience to a Changing Climate in Pacific Island Communities	* SPC	This is a regional endeavor that aims to evaluate and implement techniques to improve the resilience of food production systems for participating PICTs. The three main objectives are as follows: (1) to improve the understanding of present and future climate constraints and the adoption of adaptive responses; (2) to strengthen national and community capacity-building that can proactively respond to climate change; (3) to improve the integration of successful approaches as part of national and sectoral climate change adaptation strategies	- Fiji - Kiribati - Samoa - Solomon Islands - Tonga - Vanuatu

Title	*Implementing agencies/development partners*	*Objectives*	*Implementing Countries*
Freshwater Under Threat—Pacific Islands Publication	*SPC-SOPAC	This is a report that addresses the challenges of freshwater resources due to limited technical and governance capacity. Hence, this report will examine innovative approaches and tailoring solutions to address the socioeconomic constraints of freshwater resources of the various nations participating in this study	- Cook Islands - Fiji - Marshall Islands - Papua New Guinea - Nauru - Tuvalu - Samoa
Application of Latest IPCC Climate Models to Forecast Marine Ecosystem Changes in the North Pacific Over the Twenty-first Century	*NOAA (National Oceanic and Atmospheric Administration) PIFSC (Pacific Islands Fisheries Science Center)	The program will retrieve the output from the latest IPCC climate models to make estimations about high trophic level impacts, which will include three main approaches; (1) a biome approach; (2) driving ecosystem/fisheries models with phytoplankton output from the climate model; and (3) a size spectrum model	- Marshall Islands - Northern Mariana Islands - Guam - Palau - Federated States of Micronesia

Source Secretariat of the Pacific Regional Environment Programme (2012) [no copyright issue]
*Refers to implementing agencies
^Refers to development partners

Table 5.3 Six themes to improve food security: the PIF framework for action

Theme	*Recognition*	*Intention*
Theme 1	Leadership and Cooperation—Recognizes that sectors cannot operate alone. The government needs to rely on important partners such as civil society, healthcare, the food industries, and trade and donor partners that can cooperate and build a more resilient food system	Rectifies issues with coordination, communication, and resources as obstacles to food security
Theme 2	Regulatory frameworks, enforcement, compliance, and public–private sector collaboration—This theme recognizes the importance of partnerships and collaboration across the public and private spheres, which will be able to legislate food frameworks, based on formulation, implementation, and enforcement	Assures consumers of access to quality food
Theme 3	Enhanced and sustainable production, processing, and trading of safe and nutritious local food—This theme is based on the understanding that food security can be improved with better availability, access, stability, and sustainability of local food production	Ensures that consumers are able to obtain all vital aspects of food security
Theme 4	Protect infants and vulnerable groups—This theme stresses that food security issues should also pay attention to the needs of infants and vulnerable groups	Safeguards all social groups, including infants
Theme 5	Consumer empowerment and mobilizing partners—This theme recognizes that all sectors and agencies should provide consumers with information and enable them to make informed decisions about food	Enables the promotion of healthy options and better environmental changes
Theme 6	Food security information system—This theme recognizes the need for robust evidence-based information about food security	Develops a framework that can help monitor and evaluate progress while aiding the dissemination of new ideas and initiatives

Source Adapted from: Secretariat of the Pacific Community (2011), Islam and Kieu (2020) [no copyright issue]

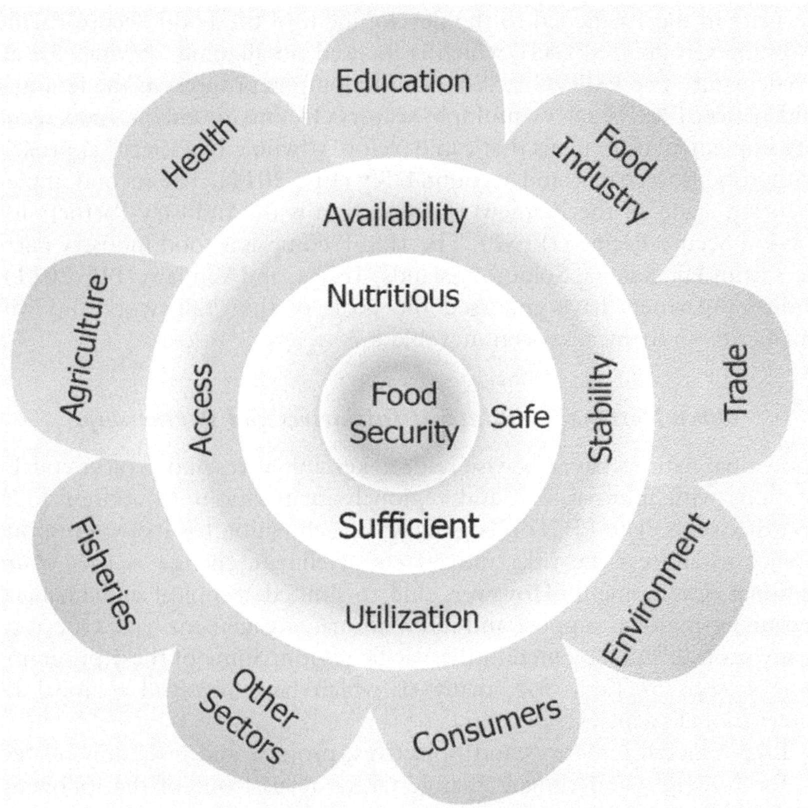

Fig. 5.1 Conceptual model of food security in the Pacific (*Source* Secretariat of the Pacific Community [2011] [public document; no copyright issue])

As in many other regions, food security in the Pacific is complex and multifaceted. To attain food security would be to encourage a coordinated multisector approach, engaging all stakeholders in capacity-building within food production and food distribution networks. As such, the Framework for Action aims to adopt close partnerships to build regulatory cost-effective and efficient frameworks that can operate at the regional level. This approach will promote investments, research and development, capacity-building, and adaptation that can mitigate climate change threats (SPC 2011). The implementation of the Framework for Action on Food

Security in the Pacific led to the development of the Food Secure Pacific Working Group (FSPWG), which is focused on aligning activities for all participants. The FSPWG facilitates and monitors progress at the regional and national levels across multiple sectors. It aims to enable food security implementation plans that can develop a "whole of society" approach with good governance and accountability (PIC 2011). The second implementing agent of the Framework for Action is the Industry Partners for a Food Secure Pacific (IPFSP). The IPSFP comprises food industry partners from Fiji, Samoa, Solomon Islands, Tonga, and Vanuatu (PIC 2011). Industry partners have endorsed the goals of the Framework and will pursue its six themes, as seen in Table 5.3.

Other National or Bilateral Initiatives and Partnerships

Individual nations have likewise undertaken initiatives and project collaborations with international and regional organizations to address food security issues. The PICTs recognize that each nation has its own responsibility to address the risks and effects of climate change as part of its national development. However, due to limited technical and financial resources, regional support and international engagement have crucial to many projects implemented in the Pacific region. Some of these programs can be seen in Table 5.4, many of which have involved regional or international agencies:

Like regional initiatives and objectives, projects and programs related to food security and climate change target at least one of the following goals:

1. To enhance institutional capacity for adaptation to climate change variabilities between stakeholders;
2. To develop policies that can provide sustainable development in conjunction with the pursuit of developmental agendas;
3. To provide support to local communities in mitigating climate change threats;
4. To improve knowledge and facilitate dissemination and communication between stakeholders and agencies.

By building these systems and projects, the associated ecological, economic, and social vulnerability coupled with its remoteness can help

Table 5.4 Summary of national and bilateral initiatives undertaken by PICTs

Country	*Program*	*Year beginning*
Cook Islands	Adaptive Capacity Study	2011
	Agrobiodiversity Case Study in Mauke.	2011
	Agrobiodiversity Case Study in Pukapuka	2011
	Distribute Climate Ready Crops from CEPACT for Climate Change Evaluation	2009
	Develop a Comprehensive Geospatial Framework to Inform Climate Change Adaptation in the Coastal Zone of Selected Areas in Mangaia Island	2011
	Establish Evaluation Sites in Cook Islands	2011
	Remote Sensing Mapping Using Geographic Information Systems to Map Forest Cover, Agriculture, Pasture, Mangroves, Plantations, Coral Reefs, Water bodies, and Biodiversity	2012
	Support for Agrobiodiversity and Climate Change Study	2011
	Support for Evaluating Crops and Varieties for Tolerance to Water-Logging	2011
	Support Taro Improvement Programmes to Breed Taro for Good Performance in Drought Conditions	2012
	University of the South Pacific—EU Global Climate Change Alliance Project	2013
Kiribati	Agricultural Good Crops Development	2012
	Papua New Guinea Disaster Risk Management and Climate Adaptation Programme	2011
Samoa	Climate Early Warning System Project	2012
	Integrating Climate Change Risks into the Agriculture and Health Sectors in Samoa	2009
	Integration of Climate Change Risk and Resilience into Forestry Management	2011
	Securing Community Water Resources Project	2012
Fiji	Duck and Poultry Project	2007
	Milk and Beef Project	2007
	Rice Revitalization	2007
Tuvalu	Enabling Activity for the Preparation of Tuvalu's Second National Communication to the UNFCCC	2005

(continued)

Table 5.4 (continued)

Country	*Program*	*Year beginning*
	Implementing a "Ridge to Reef" Approach to Protect Biodiversity and Ecosystem Functions in Tuvalu	2014
Papua New Guinea	PNG-Smallholder Agriculture Development	2007
	Seeds for Needs	2008
Solomon Islands	USAID Adaptation to Climate Change	2012

Source Authors' own investigation

strengthen their resilience. The engagement of multiple stakeholders and integrated sectoral development strategies will help improve long-term capacity-building.

Analysis of Initiatives and Programs

The previous sections examined various programs implicated in PIF's future food security, in light of the threats it faces from climate change. With the PIF nations' acknowledgment that food security and climate change are vital concerns in the future, PIF has undertaken numerous initiatives to address matters related to climate change and food security. Beyond providing an overview of current initiatives, we will examine their efficacy in this section.

Some of the factors utilized to evaluate PIF initiatives and programs are highlighted in Table 5.5.

Planning

PIF nations acknowledge the threats posed by climate change to food security in the region, and have taken numerous steps toward a coordinated regional effort. The themes adopted by the Framework for Action in both climate change and food security highlight support and commitment across multiple sectors, from the formulation of legislation to implementation of programs at the community level. The scope of programs is also comprehensive, including disaster mitigation, responses to climate change, and capacity development. Additionally, the notion of nutrition for vulnerable populations and infants has not been neglected.

Table 5.5 Summary table for PIF regional initiatives' efficacy

	Factor	*Justification*
1.	Planning	This criterion involves the overarching frame of the programs and initiatives. It is mainly concerned with their goals and objectives
2.	Implementation	This criterion concerns the nature of the programs and initiatives laid out, and the execution of the initiatives
3.	Cooperation	The criterion concerns the state of relations between PIF nations and relative commitment levels. It will highlight the level of commitment and cooperation PIF has fostered among its member states for its programs
4.	Legal obligation	This criterion concerns the enforcement and legality of various agreements, treaties, and initiatives. Legal obligation involves the enforcement rights of PIF as a regional organization to ensure its member nations comply with various initiatives
5.	International contribution	This criterion assesses how the region has contributed to or impacted global climate change and food security

Source Authors' own investigation

Hence, the PIF projects and discussions to date have been extensive, encompassing all crucial aspects of climate change and food security.

Implementation

Like many other regions, the PIF lacks firm knowledge of the implications of climate change and best practices. However, PIF has already begun to fill these knowledge gaps through numerous case studies and pilot projects, as shown in Table 5.3. Projects have targeted the region as a whole, across many sectors, and have covered agriculture, fisheries, and aquaculture; private and public sector food networks; and sustainable production. However, due to the varied partnerships of multiple projects undertaken within the region, arguably PIF as a regional forum plays only a facilitative role in drafting agendas for the region, and it is therefore overly reliant on uptake from partners in supporting its programs and agenda. Furthermore, PIF requires external funding arrangements for PICTs, which may be a hindrance in developing a regionally coordinated effort. The reliance on short-term projects and programs may be a major shortcoming, which could be detrimental in the long run due to the lack of resilient mechanisms.

Cooperation

PIF endorses partnerships with international organizations to manage not only regional but international climate change, as PIF nations are keenly aware that they bear a disproportionate risk from the threats of climate change compared to other regions. Hence, the PIF, through its regional mechanisms, has engaged with a multitiered system involving multiple stakeholders. Cooperation is not relegated to the regional level, but also involves bilateral initiatives by PICTs. Cooperation is vibrant in the region, with many ongoing projects undertaken not only by SPREP but also with USAID, AusAID, UNDP, and even the private food sector, which has pledged to work with the Framework for Action on Food Security. Such a level of commitment and cooperation is promising for the Pacific Islands region. However, this cooperation is based on short-term programs and goals, which may be redrawn at the discretion of its international partners.

Legal Obligation

While PIF nations have shown their support for PIF's goals and aims regarding food security and climate change, the legal obligations of these nations to abide by the principles laid out is uncertain. Based on the structure of the programs, initiatives related to food security and climate change are still subject to the political will and commitment of individual states to abide by PIF aims and goals, with little or no legal ramifications for failure to do so. The same is true for international and private sector partners, as they may have no legal obligation to cooperate with PIFS and its member states until new legislation has been drafted to ensure support and compliance. Hence, as of this moment, there is little evidence to suggest that states and partners in the public and private sectors are obliged to adhere to PIF programs.

International Contribution

While climate change will undeniably impact food security in the Pacific Islands, PIF's engagement with the international community remains unidirectional, as the PIF has been reliant on the international community for support and financial aid. External international agencies play a vital role in PIF's climate change and food security initiatives. Although PICTs face disproportionate impacts from climate change, their role in actively addressing these issues by internationally furthering climate change mitigation is minimal. Arguably, PICTs can provide vital information about climate change impacts and best practices for community adaptation; such a possibility has yet to come to fruition at this juncture. Nevertheless, PIF has vast potential for contributing to international discourse on climate change and food security in the future, as it is on the frontlines of this fight.

Conclusion

This chapter has closely examined PIF's regional initiatives for dealing with climate change and food security. It is undeniable that PIF has been progressive in its attempts to coordinate efforts between member states, international partners, and the private and public sectors for a collective regional response. Evidence shows that PIF's pilot programs have begun to expand knowledge on the impact of climate change and possible adaptation measures. However, PIF still relies on external aid agencies for financial and technical support, which may be a shortcoming in the future. Given the facilitative avenues already in place, the PIF's potential to address climate change and food security issues are boundless. As climate change becoming an increasing concern, the PIF should address its weaknesses by formulating long-term measures and legislation, building capacity and operational mechanisms, and utilizing its strength to further regional long-term interests. Table 5.6 summarizes the overall efficacy of PIF regional initiatives for climate change and food security.

Table 5.6 Summary table for PIF initiatives' efficacy

	Factor	*Summary conclusion*
1.	Planning	PIF has extensive individual programs that engage its member states in multitiered, multisector partnerships
2.	Implementation	PIF has been active in implementing both reactive and proactive mitigation measures, and many projects have been undertaken. However, these programs may be short-lived, as PIF has yet to implement a mechanism for regional self-sufficiency
3.	Cooperation	Support for programs has been cursory and lacks effectiveness
4.	Legal obligation	The legal obligations of individual states are still uncertain, but cooperation on issues of climate change and food security is based on the goodwill of member states and their partners; there is no evidence that failure to adhere to regional goals has ramifications
5.	International contribution	PIF's role within the international community is minimal and it is still dependent on international and external agencies. However, there is vast potential for PIF to contribute to the international community, as it is at the frontlines of impact from climate change

Source Authors' own investigation

References

ADB (Asian Development Bank). 2011. Food Security and Climate Change in the Pacific: Rethinking the Options. Pacific Studies Series. Mandaluyong, PH: ADB.

Asch, Rebecca G., William W.L. Cheung, and Gabriel Reygondeau. 2018. Future Marine Ecosystem Drivers, Biodiversity, and Fisheries Maximum Catch Potential in Pacific Island Countries and Territories Under Climate Change. *Marine Policy* 88: 285–294.

Campbell, John Richard. 2014. Development, Global Change and Traditional Food Security in Pacific Island Countries. *Regional Environmental Change* 15 (7): 1313–1324.

CIA (Central Intelligence Agency). 2017. The World Factbook. Retrieved 1 September 2017. https://www.cia.gov/library/publications/the-world-factbook/index.html.

Denton, Ashlie. 2017. Voices for Environmental Action? Analyzing Narrative in Environmental Governance Networks in the Pacific Islands. *Global Environmental Change* 43: 62–71.

FAO (Food and Agriculture Organization of the United Nations). 2008. Climate Change and Food Security in Pacific Island Countries. Retrieved 1 September 2017. http://www.fao.org/3/a-i0530e.pdf.

Finkbeiner, Elena M., Fiorenza Micheli, Nathan J. Bennett, Adam L. Ayers, Elodie Le Cornu, and Angee N. Doerr. 2018. Exploring Trade-Offs in Climate Change Response in the Context of Pacific Island Fisheries. *Marine Policy* 88: 359–364.

Iese, Viliamu, Elisabeth Holland, Morgan Wairiu, Robin Havea, Soane Patolo, Minoru Nishi, R. Taniela Hoponoa, Michael Bourke, Annika Dean, and Logotonu Waqainabete. 2018. Facing Food Security Risks: The Rise and Rise of the Sweet Potato in the Pacific Islands. *Global Food Security* 18: 48–56.

Islam, M.S., and Edson Kieu. 2020. Tackling Regional Climate Change Impacts and Food Security Issues: A Critical Analysis across ASEAN, PIF and SAARC. *Sustainability* 12 (883): 1–21.

Lal, M. 2004. Climate Change in Small Island Developing Countries of the South Pacific. *Fijian Studies* 2 (1): 15–31.

Lebot, Vincent. 2013. Coping with Insularity: The Need for Crop Genetic Improvement to Strengthen Adaptation to Climatic Change and Food Security in the Pacific. *Environment, Development and Sustainability* 15: 1405–1423.

PIC (Pacific Island Countries). 2011. Progress on Food Security in the Pacific. Ninth Meeting of Ministers of Health for the Pacific Island Countries. Retrieved 2 September 2017. http://www.wpro.who.int/southpacific/pic_meeting/2011/documents/PIC9_10_progress_on_food_security.pdf.

PIF Secretariat (Pacific Islands Forum Secretariat). 2009. Pacific Leaders' Call to Action on Climate Change. Annex A to the 2009 Forum Leaders' Communique. Retrieved 3 September 2017. http://www.forumsec.org/resources/uploads/attachments/documents/Pacific%20Leaders'%20Call%20to%20Action%20on%20Climate%20Change%202009.pdf.

PIF Secretariat (Pacific Islands Forum Secretariat). 2015. Climate Change. Retrieved 3 September 2017. http://www.forumsec.org/pages.cfm/strategic-partnerships-coordination/climate-change/.

Secretariat of the Pacific Community. 2011. Towards a Food Secure Pacific; Framework for Action on Food Security in the Pacific 2011–2015 (Draft). Retrieved 1 November 2015. www.spc.int.

Secretariat of the Pacific Regional Environment Programme. 2012. Pacific Climate Change Portal. Retrieved 3 September 2017. http://projects.pacificclimatechange.net/.

Shibuya, Eric. 2004. The Problems and Potential of the Pacific Islands Forum. In *The Asia-Pacific: A Region in Transition*, ed. Jim Rolfe, 102–115. Asia-Pacific Center for Security Studies.

SPC (Secretariat of the Pacific Community). 2008. Fish and Food Security. Policy Brief 1/2008, Secretariat of the Pacific Community: Noumea, New Caledonia.

SPC (Secretariat of the Pacific Community). 2011. Towards a Food Secure Pacific; Framework for Action on Food Security in the Pacific 2011–2015 (Draft). Retrieved 4 September 2017. www.spc.int.

SPREP (Secretariat of the Pacific Regional Environment Programme). 2006. Pacific Islands Framework for Action on Climate Change 2006–2015. Retrieved 4 September 2017. http://www.sprep.org/climate_change/pycc/documents/PIFACC.pdf.

United Nations Statistics Division. 2015. UNdata. Retrieved 5 September 2017. http://data.un.org/CountryProfile.aspx?crname=CookIslands.

World Bank. 2015. Data; GDP Per Capita (Current US$). Retrieved 5 September 2017. http://data.worldbank.org/indicator/NY.GDP.PCAP.CD/countries/S2?page=1&display=default.

CHAPTER 6

Climate Change and the Environment: The Chindia (China and India) Dilemma

"Chindia," a term coined by India's former environment minister Jairam Ramesh, highlights the importance of cooperation between both nations on global issues such as climate change (Ramesh 2005). In recent decades, China and India's economic development brought both countries to the forefront as the two largest emitters today. Reports by the Intergovernmental Panel on Climate Change and a plethora of other studies highlight that both countries face similar threats from ecological degradation and food and water scarcity due to agricultural shifts from the impacts of climate change. However, as emerging players in the international economy, China and India face other developmental challenges such as socioeconomic development and poverty. Climate change, environmental degradation, and food security will have to be balanced precariously with developmental goals. This chapter examines Chindia's (China and India) Dilemma by looking at the challenges both countries face. In this chapter, we will examine (1) Chindia's economic developments thus far, (2) the impacts of climate change on food security in Chindia, and (3) approaches Chindia undertake to address the associated problems.

M. S. Islam and E. Kieu, *Climate Change and Food Security in Asia Pacific*, International Political Economy Series,
https://doi.org/10.1007/978-3-030-70753-8_6

Chindia as the Epicenter of the New Global Economy

Chinese and Indian economies have a large influence on the global economy and both countries have been contended to take over the role of economic growth engines. The last three decades brought about phenomenal economic growth by China and India with global output rising from less than 10% to over 20% and from 6 to 10% in GDP annual rates, respectively. In terms of GDP per capita for China and India, there are stark increases. China rose from $194.80 in 1980 to $10261.68 by 2019 and India saw increases within the same timeframe from $266.58 to $2099.60 (World Bank 2021). Projections by the International Monetary Fund (IMF), World Bank and, World Economic Forum posit that current economic trends by China and India will continue in the coming years. By comparison, economic growth in the United States, Europe, and Japan was significantly lower (Hölscher et al. 2010).

Structural features of development and institutional changes in China and India have been posited to be the drivers behind high rates of economic growth. China's policy support, strengthening of external demands, and supply-side reforms have helped to maintain its strong growth. With tighter enforcement of capital flow management and the reduction of exchange rate pressures, China is projected to sustain strong growth (IMF 2017a). Similarly, India's economic growth have also been attributed to policy actions and key structural reforms, trade gains, supply-side measures, and tight monetary stance (IMF 2017b).

However, development comes at a cost. The extent of China and India's economic growth has brought with it exponential increases in global carbon emissions from fossil fuels. Since the 1980s till 2010, carbon emissions from fossil fuels doubled from 5 billion to 10 billion metric tons of carbon. In 2014, the top CO_2 emitters were China (30%), the United States (15%), the European Union (9%), India (7%), Russian Federation (5%), and Japan (4%), respectively (Boden et al. 2017). The fourth assessment report by Intergovernmental Panel on Climate Change (IPCC) reveals that effects from excessive carbon emissions will be most consequential for Asia if adequate measures are not implemented. While economic and national development in China and India lifted millions out of poverty, this has not been without trade-offs as the adverse effect from emissions and climate change may become consequential in the long run (Wang et al. 2018).

Socioeconomic Developments and Poverty in Chindia

Both China and India recognize the importance of macroeconomic stability to poverty reduction, seeing rapid growth; but with rising inequalities, that were far greater for China than India (Ravallion 2009). By 2005, poverty in China fell to 16% (from 84% in 1981), while India's fell to 42% (from 60% in 1981). In its market-oriented economic reform, China had favorable initial conditions for rapid poverty reduction through market-led economic growth, although inequality has since risen. India, on the other hand, concentrated opportunities in the hand of the wealthy, amplifying prior inequalities in various dimensions which handicapped poverty reduction. India hence needs to do more to assure that poor people are able to participate in both the country's growth process and its social policies.

Growth in the primary sector, mainly agriculture, accounted for most of China's success and poverty reduction (Ravallion and Chen 2007). From the 1980s, China started the Household Responsibility System (HRS) and other reforms to liberalize markets for farm outputs and inputs. The allocation of land within communes appears to have been relatively equitable as the allocation did not neglect individual farmers (Fan 1991; Lin 1992). As a result of these reforms, agricultural growth was pro-poor, and relatively low inequality in access to basic health and education also helped reduce poverty. Meanwhile in India, economic growth had disappointing outcomes for the poor. Some argued that the agricultural growth stimulated by the green revolution brought little gain to the rural poor, while others pointed farm-output growth as key to rural poverty reduction (Datt and Ravallion 1998a, b). From 1991, India's economic reforms to address the balance of payment crisis promoted a more open economy, supporting the private sector and restructuring the public sector. However, agriculture had been neglected in these policies.

Although economic growth have been reducing extreme poverty, the rise in rural and urban inequalities dampened its effects. India's large inequalities in dimensions like human development, including gender inequalities, literacy rates, and infant mortality rates, also handicapped the country's progress against poverty. Non-farm economic growth also reflect inequalities and impact poverty, as low farm productivity, low rural living standards relative to urban areas and poor basic education, inhibited the prospects of the poor participating in growth of the nonfarm sector (Ravallion 2009; Christiaensen et al. 2010; Datt and Ravallion 1992, 2002, 2009).

With a developing economy, the agricultural wage rate in India and China had also been rising sharply (Zhang et al. 2011). The introduction of machinery, with rapidly growing machine rental markets replaced rising labor costs, resulting in large farms in China and India becoming more productive (Otsuka et al. 2016). This however decreased the advantage of small farms, which relied on family labor. Even though small farms in China contracted with machine service providers to minimize the user cost of machine use, they were unable to save on labor costs as much as large farms.

Impact of Climate Change on Food Security in China and India

Impact on Land and Agricultural Productivity

As postulated in previous chapters, climate change affects agriculture and food production systems in numerous aspects. Agriculture, forestry, and other types of land use play a central role in enduring food security and sustainable development. Crop production such as growth periods and crop cycle are affected by rising temperatures, patterns of precipitation, and increased atmospheric CO_2 levels. Global food production may be required to increase by as much as 70% in 2050 for a world populated by over 9 billion people (Schmidhuber and Tubiello 2007). Noting current trajectories, attaining global food security under the looming threat of climate change will be an uphill task.

Agriculture, mainly food production, is heavily dependent on weather and climate. Yet, global climate change is happening at an exceedingly fast rate, interrupting crop growth and reducing yields. Seasonal water scarcity, rising temperatures, and extreme weather patterns have all negatively affected crop productivity. Rice and wheat yields in Asia had declined since the 1980s by approximately 8% for every temperature increase of 1 °C. Climate change-induced and numerous extreme weather events resulted in agricultural yield losses and have a significant negative impact on food production and prices, affecting food security in South Asia. For instance, erratic monsoon weather conditions in India during 2009 reduced production of the main crops and led to higher food prices as domestic demand remained high during the period of flood. Indian food price inflation also spread to its neighboring countries. Furthermore, nearly half the world's poor reside in this region, and over 70% live in rural areas and depend on agriculture, as a key source of GDP and employment to reduce poverty (Cervantes-Godoy and Dewbre 2010). Thus, apart from food security, the projected decline in agricultural output is expected to reduce the country's GDP as well, inhibiting its ability to eradicate poverty. Although current economic growth and policies contribute to a reduction in poverty and vulnerability in South Asia, the region is likely to face a high degree of vulnerability by 2030 as a result of predicted climate-induced changes in crop productivity (Bandara and Cai 2014).

The combined population of China and India (2.746 billion in 2018) is too large to rely on the world food market for its food supply. Furthermore, distribution of large quantities of imported food will be the major challenge and impediment for both countries. Self-sufficiency becomes a vital touchpoint for China and India. While there have been positive estimates for China's food production capacity, India is in a less favorable position. According to estimates for Chinese's food production, China is positioned to increase food production yields of around 497–646 million tons due to 30% production intensification in multi-cropping index values (see Ye et al. 2013). On the other hand, current estimates of projected crop yields for India are expected to decline in 2035 and continue to do so for the next few decades. Birthal et al. (2014) highlight these projections based on IPCC projections of temperature and precipitation that will affect crop yields like rice, maize, barley, and chickpeas, all of which are important dietary components for the Indian population.

Cropland loss resulting from climate change is seen to be one of the biggest concerns for China and India. Despite China's positive estimates for agricultural intensification, cropland losses remain a problem (Godfray et al. 2011; Tilman et al. 2002). India faces significant land constraints in two aspects: (1) agricultural land suffering from degradation and (2) difficulties in raising food supplies beyond current levels with net crop area stabilizing at 140 million hectares indicating limited areas for expansion (Birthal et al. 2014). Based on estimates, India will suffer a loss of 120 million hectares of land through various forms of degradation (Singh 2011). India's glacier Himalayan region as one of the main sources of freshwater at the Gangetic basin is melting and could have a devastating impact on that region. Half a million people depend on the Gangetic basin for their livelihood and hundreds of millions more who live in coastal India may see an increase in sea levels which could cripple their communities (Malone 2010). Consequentially, cropland and crop yield losses due to climate change can affect China and India's food security and agriculture-dependent economy.

Impact on Marine Ecosystems, Fisheries, and Aquaculture

China and India are traditionally considered as the world's major fishing nations (FAO 2018). Climate variables can impact fisheries through a wide range of direct and indirect ways, these include: changes in air and water temperatures, precipitation, salinity, oceanic circulation nutrient levels, glacial melt, storm, and flooding (Barange 2002; Stenseth et al. 2003; Lehodey et al. 2006; Brander 2007). Such changes can influence ecosystem productivities and aquatic habitat quantity and quality as well as the distribution of predators and preys (O'Reilly et al. 2003; Edwards and Richardson 2004; Hall-Spencer et al. 2008). Hence, the adaptation of fisheries must be adequately managed as climate change may result in a decrease in output due to stresses caused via reduced water quality.

Despite the threats of reduced output from the impact of climate change, the FAO reports great potential for the development of fisheries and aquaculture due to rapid development in China and India (FAO 2001, 2006). China's construction of fishery infrastructure and service systems has been expanding to develop efficiency in ecological aquaculture (FAO 2001). For India, inland fish production has been showing rapid growth via area expansion, diversification of farmed specifics, and augmenting productivity across existing farms (FAO 2006). Hence, food security and climate change at this juncture is not an imminent threat due to increased productive capacities.

Apart from impacting ecosystem properties, climate change repercussions on fisheries and aquaculture have wider socioeconomic implications. Fisheries serve as a means of livelihood for large segments of the population in China and India (Rosegrant and Cline 2003). Fishers, aquaculture farmers, and the relevant communities are particularly susceptible and vulnerable to climate changes as seasonal weather patterns change with more frequent extreme weather patterns such as drought, floods, and storms (Avnimelech 2009). Ripple effects are numerous: (1) impacts fish farming via coastal flooding and the incursion of saltwater, (2) species distributions and fish physiology, and (3) fish processing methods (FAO 2012). The total value of national fisheries for China reached \$30.52

billion in output (FAO 2001). Data from 1999 highlights that the work-force engaged in fisheries totalled 12.57 million people, with around 59% as full-time workers (FAO 2001). In India, the sector is worth $4.84 billion dollars in output during 1997–1998 (FAO 2006). Estimated population working in the sector totals 14.66 million people (FAO 2006). For both countries, this sector plays a crucial role in supporting a large section of the economy as well as livelihoods of millions, the potential devastation caused by climate change on economic, social, and food security is tremendous.

Chindia's Approaches to Climate Change

In both China and India, sulphur dioxide originating from coal-burning power stations has had a devastating effect on crop yields in many areas (Wahlqvist et al. 2012; Galli et al. 2012). To address the climate change issues, China established the National Committee on Climate Change (NCCC) in 1988. Later on, the National Leading Group to Address Climate Change headed by the Chinese Premier was set up in 2007 to come up with important measures to tackle climate change, and to coordinate for solving of major problems related to climate change. Various other measures include the formation of the National Development and Reform Commission (NDRC) and Experts Committee for Climate Change. The goals include improving scientific decision-making on climate change and supporting government decision-making and enhancing international cooperation and nongovernmental activities. The National Plan for Coping with Climate Change directed the provincial governments "to further improve industrial, financial, taxation, credit and investment policies, make full use of price leverage, form institutions and mechanisms conducive to reducing greenhouse gas emissions, increase financial input and improve corresponding rules conducive to decelerating and adapting to climate change, thus enhancing work on climate change" (Bazaz and Seksaria 2014). Although improvements are noted, there remains looming crisis and vulnerabilities related to climate change (Kedia 2016; Wang et al. 2018).

The consideration of climate change in national development planning for India has been acknowledged by the government but not explicitly mentioned in the plan document. However, the National Action Plan for Climate Change (Government of India 2008), unveiled by the Prime

Minister of India in 2008, does emphasize the need for such consideration. The plan has explicitly considered certain missions, aimed at specific sectoral interventions, which have both mitigative and adaptive possibilities vis-à-vis climate change. One of the eight National Missions is the National Mission for Sustainable Agriculture. It includes adaptation in agriculture through the development of climate-resilient crops, expansion of weather insurance mechanisms, and promotion of sustainable agricultural practices (Bazaz and Seksaria 2014; Prime Minister's Council on Climate Change 2007). While India is still hesitant with international voluntary commitments to reduce GHG emissions, political pressures are increasing over the years to reduce local environmental pollution.

As Chindia face imminent threats from ecological degradation, food and water scarcity, agricultural shifts due to climate change, they have begun to emerge as crucial players in the international climate change negotiations, seeking to attain equity and justice in the international arena. Climate diplomacy has been touted as a point of convergence between both countries. Chindia found semblance in climate diplomacy over the years, facilitated by having shared concerns and similar positions as developing countries. Both countries have determinedly championed the need for a fair and just climate change deal and stress the importance of taking all countries to take initiatives via a common principle but differentiated responsibilities (National Development and Reform Commission 2007; Ministry of Environment and Forests Government of India 2011). Cooperation has been argued to be the best option for China and India as they face similar pressures from economic development and the loom threats of climate change. With increasing emission rates and stringent global policies on emission trajectories, Chindia will be on the same page. Some of the common issues Chindia have regarding climate change is highlighted below (Mizo 2016):

- China holds the developed north historically responsible for climate change and its relevant problems.
- Despite becoming leading emitters of carbon in recent years, based on emission rate per capita, Chindia's emission rates are still much smaller than that of the developed North.
- Chindia as the two largest countries in the world face the task of tackling socioeconomic development for their people; hence the similar calls for common but differentiated responsibilities.

- The gravity of climate change is more severe for Chindia due to current states of underdevelopment.
- Chindia face enormous pressures from the international community to adopt quantifiable emission targets, the Stern report in 2007 highlights the need for Chindia to commit to binding emission targets.
- As emerging economic giants, Chindia's economic policies in the coming decades will have strong environmental consequences.

As seen, China and India responded to the issues related to climate changes within their own national capacities but found convergence on two main points: (1) the primary responsibility of cleaning carbon mess should lie with the developed countries' due to their historical culpability, (2) they stressed on the responsibilities of all to protect the planet according to one's ability. In 2007, China and India instituted national-level climate change initiatives and began to show greater commitment toward emission reduction. These climate change action plans such as India's National Action Plan for Climate Change and China's National Climate Change Programme are frameworks to determine actions to deal with the implications of climate change and serves as a major milestone for China and India (National Development and Reform Commission 2007; Ministry of Environment and Forests Government of India 2011). Prior to this period, both China and India found difficulties in rectifying international agreements such as the 1992 Rio Earth Summit and the 1997 Kyoto Protocol. Some selected key milestones are simplified in Table 6.1, highlighting shifts in China's stance before and after 2007.

Despite earlier tensions with the international community, the developments from 2009 Copenhagen and 2015 Paris Agreement bolstered both China and India's role and commitments in mitigating global climate change. Prior to these watershed agreements, China and India found contention and skepticism regarding international climate change negotiations and commitments to the proposed agreements. Nevertheless, ratified agreements by both countries have mechanisms of accountability embedded through the United Nations Framework Convention on Climate Change (UNFCCC) brought about by four main provisions. These are as follows (Dubash 2015; Mizo 2016):

1. A mandatory five-yearly update of all pledges;

Table 6.1 Selected milestones for China and India

Agreement	*China*	*India*
1992 Rio Earth Summit	Joined the group of 77, Non-Alignment Movement as a united south initiative to highlight historical responsibility of the developed north	Concerns raised about responsibilities and highlights for the need to have equitable development opportunities
1997 Kyoto Protocol	China was not interested in negotiating until all parties within Annex 1 implemented their commitments	As with other developing countries, India does not have any biding mitigation commitments through the application of the Principle of Commons
Chindia instituted national-level climate change initiatives		
2009 COP15 Copenhagen	Voluntarily agreed to reduce emissions of carbon dioxide per unit of economic growth by 40 to 45% by 2020 with respect to 2005 levels	To reduce domestic emissions intensity of 20 to 25% in comparison to 2005 levels
2015 COP21 Paris Agreement	Raised its emission reduction targets in terms of carbon intensity from 60 to 65%	Maintained the carbon intensity approach and increased its emission reduction pledge from 33 to 35% by 2030 compared with 2005 levels

Sources Adapted from UNFCCC (1998, 2009, 2015), Chmutina (2010), Ministry of Environment and Forests, Government of India (2011) [no copyright issue]

2. A review process of both climate actions and financial contributions;
3. Transparency provisions;
4. Global stocktaking of aggregate effects from the actions.

The four mechanisms not only ensure follow-up actions by China and India but also pushes for the enhancement of actions and goals intermittently (Mizo 2016). To date, Chindia remain very active in all international forums related to environmental protection with few exceptions and they continually play a major role in forming the position of developing countries in international agreements.

Food Security: A Historical Overview of Chindia's Woes

On China's Agriculture

Since 1949, the Chinese Communist Party (CCP) rule China as a party-state and adopted a planned economy that included agricultural growth policies and targets which instituted land reform and collectivization. As opposed to a market economy, the state sets prices via a centralized planning bureau and ministries to determine production targets expressed in five-year plans. During that time, 80% of the population was involved in agricultural pursuits. McBeath and Mcbeath (2010) highlight that China underwent four stages of agricultural organization. The first stage was land reform and collectivization which was concluded in 1952. Agricultural productivity did increase after the land reform but fell short of meeting the expectations of the leaders due to the growing urban and industrial population. The Great Leap Forward during 1958–1960 is identified as the second stage with the CCP realizing that grain production was not keeping up with population growth. Hence, to develop agriculture, the peasants were made to organize to increase land reclamation, improve irrigation systems, and improve fold control efforts (Fairbank and Goldman 2006).

However, peasants during this period were also required to contribute toward steel production under Mao Zedong's "walking on two legs" strategy which saw efforts shifting toward farm to steel labor that led to many crops rotting in the fields. This brought about man-made famine throughout China that saw 20–30 million lives lost to starvation and malnutrition (Fairbank and Goldman 2006). The third stage was identified as the Cultural Revolution between 1966 and 1976. This period was a tumultuous period for political China and its food security. Due to the first-generation governance that made several disastrous policy choices, China's ecological stability was shaken. Reclamation works had damaged wetlands and forests that brought about gradual desertification and adverse impacts on the environment. The last stage saw policy reforms from 1978 to 2009 that called for long-term industrial agricultural, military, and technological development. The reforms focused on increasing incentives for production particularly on agricultural development while increasing global trade, foreign investors, and improving infrastructures. All of these were vital aspects for food security. Since the Maoist era,

China has been pushing for self-sufficiency in grain production and by 2000, China progressed to become the world's ninth largest exporter of food products (worth $16.38 billion or 2.9% of global exports) and the eighth largest importer ($19.54 billion or 3.2% of global exports). While China has been increasing its exports and imports of agricultural products, these transactions only comprise less than 15% of the agricultural GDP, highlight that China has a relatively low dependence on the international market (McBeath and McBeath 2010).

While production of agricultural products has been increasing, access to food is not equal and it varies across geographic and economic variables. Peripheral areas such as Inner Mongolia, Xinjiang, Tibet, and Yunan have difficulties to access grains due to their distance from grain processing regions (McBeath and Mcbeath 2010). Hence, overall food costs are higher for these central and eastern areas while incomes are also lower. Furthermore, inequality between the rural and urban regions has greatly increased since economic reforms took place, and the income gap seen between both groups is 2.33:1 (Saich 2004). Changing food preferences due to increased wealth and significant reduction of poverty brings about demand-side pressures. A growing middle-class sees greater demand apart from grains and more on higher quality food such as meat and fresh produce (Jussaume 2001). Due to income and food preference changes, it is noted that as China's economic development continues, grain sufficiency alone cannot be considered as a worthy measure of food security.

To tackle insecurity in farmer's individual land rights, China has taken several measures to facilitate land rental transactions, land consolidation, and farm size expansion. In some provinces, like Chongqing, farmland rental arrangements are facilitated through the internet by county governments. Land banks for borrowing and lending farmland, and rural land banks registered in 2008, also facilitate farm size expansion (Huang and Ding 2015; Otsuka et al. 2016). Yet, the average farm size remained at 0.6 ha in 2010, increasing only by 0.05 ha per year since 2000, even though land rental markets have become increasingly active (Kimura et al. 2011; Huang et al. 2012; Otsuka et al. 2016). This may be because subsidies for farm size expansion are distortive and do not lead to immediate efficiency gains (Rada et al. 2015).

On China's Fisheries Sector

Since 1949, Chinese fisheries began to develop which saw production steady increases in production of marine, inland capture fisheries as well as aquaculture. Within the course of China's numerous five-year plans, fisheries production saw an average increase of 110,000 mt/year. By 1995 fisheries production reached 25.17 million mt, contributing to one-fifth of the world's total output. Specific types of economic reforms in fisheries that began in 1978 include: the introduction and implementation of production responsibility system; allowing private or individual fisheries and fish farming operations; shifting fisheries trade from government control to a free market system; and relaxation of price controls for all aquatic products (Song 2000). Further breakdown of the major policies identified to promote segments of China's fisheries is highlighted in Table 6.2.

As compared to agriculture and animal husbandry, the average yearly growth rate and value of fisheries were the highest. From a policy standpoint, changes in the production and management of China's fisheries were considered the most successful. These products are nutritious and are vital for dietary balance. Current estimates suggest that one-third of the animal food consumed comes from aquatic products. Yet, total protein intake for China is low, standing at only 10% which is below the world average of 17%. Hence, the CCP regards that the development of fisheries and supply of aquatic products as a vital measure for improved living standards and food security (Yu and Han 2020).

On India's Agriculture

India is primarily an agricultural nation with over 70% of the population engaging in this economic activity (FAO 2000). Since independence in 1947, agricultural policies have been targeted at the reduction of hunger, food insecurity, and malnourishment (Acharya 2009). India's food security champions that food should be sufficient and accessible to all individuals at sustainable levels by fulfilling every individual's dietary needs for a productive and healthy life. However, since independence till the period of 1983–2000, estimates of calorie deprivation in India highlight that much of the population across all states are still facing calorie intake deficits (Table 6.3). In principle, 2400 kcal figure repre-

Table 6.2 Major policies for China's fisheries

Marine fisheries	Controls over the intensity of fishing effort Restrictions on further entry to inshore waters and diversion of would-be fishermen to aquaculture, processing, transport, etc. Closed seasons for the East China Sea and Yellow Sea Prevention of illegal fishing methods Restriction of fishing boats to their designated areas; Protection of the inshore environment allied with large-scale stocking and enhancement programs; and Strengthened enforcement of fisheries laws
Freshwater capture fisheries	Improved use of water bodies and recognition of special needs of fisheries Conversion of reclaimed land into lakes Enforcement of licensing systems and other regulations Protection of ecological environments from pollution; and Stocking programs for large water bodies
Aquaculture	Further expansion of aquaculture water areas Promotion of high-yielding technologies Further integration of aquaculture with agriculture and animal husbandry Research to improve variety bases, feed and fry quality, etc. Improved utilization, processing, and marketing systems for aquacultural products; and Better control over fish diseases and aquaculture-derived pollution

Sources Adapted from Song (2000) and FAO (2000) [no copyright issue]

sents an average requirement by incorporating a margin of safety which is necessary for good health (Meenakshi and Vishwanathan 2003).

As seen in Table 6.3, figures highlight that there have been some incremental improvements for calorie intake in certain states but large percentages of populations across all states are still consuming lower than 2400 kcal. Hence, despite high economic development for India in the last few decades, ensuring food security remains a priority and need for India. The rise of food prices since the end of 2006 has aggravated the situation of hunger worldwide. Regional-level impacts led to greater

Table 6.3 Calorie deprivation by state 1983–1999/2000

States	*Average calorie intake per capita per day (kcal)*		*Percent (%) Consuming less than 2400 kcal per day*	
	1983	*1999/2000*	*1983*	*1999/2000*
Andhra Pradesh	2204	2021	68.5	80.7
Bihar	2189	2121	67.6	74.9
Gujarat	2133	1986	72.6	80.5
Haryana	2554	2455	54.1	55.1
Himachal Pradesh	2636	2454	44.5	56.5
Jammu and Kashmir	2569	2631	44.5	39.7
Karnataka	2260	2028	64.0	78.9
Kerala	1884	1982	81.5	81.2
Madhya Pradesh	2323	2062	62.5	78.4
Maharashtra	2144	2012	73.1	83.3
Orissa	2103	2119	70.9	74.6
Punjab	2677	2381	46.2	62.8
Rajasthan	2433	2425	54.2	56.7
Tamil Nadu	1861	1826	80.6	86.5
Uttar Pradesh	2399	2327	58.4	64.5
West Bengal	2027	2095	76.0	75.6

Sources Adapted from Meenakshi and Vishwanathan (2003) and Chakraborty (2005) [no copyright issue]

number of people suffering from hunger due to rising prices in Asia and Sub-Saharan Africa (FAO 2008). Driving forces behind food supply and prices are complex with both demand and supply-side factors playing a part. Cyclical and temporary factors interact with long-term structural trajectories which can impact overall food demand and supply tension. Rapid rise in the costs of petroleum saw upward pressures on food prices due to increased cays of fertilizers and transportation from 2006 to 2008. On the demand side, increased use of sugar, maize, cassava, oilseeds, and palm oil due to the emerging biofuels industry lead to price increase. Increases in demand by middle-class Indians as well as China have been pointed out as reasons for price increases. Additionally, Acharya (2009) highlights that the adoption of export restrictions by countries has led to speculative re- and pre-stocking by large importers leading to new types of investors. These investors have therefore brought about an increase in speculative activities on agricultural commodities. Based on these shifts in events and the threats from climate change, the attainment of food security is a precarious situation in India.

Acharya (2009) highlights three main strategies that India aims to achieve in terms of food security directed toward agricultural farmers: (1) the provision of improved technology packages, (2) the delivery of modern farm inputs, technical knowledge, and institutional credit, and (3) the assurance of remunerative marketing and pricing environments. To attain these objectives, policy instruments adopted by India are summarized in Table 6.4.

The instruments highlighted in Table 6.4 are vital steps toward ensuring food security from the supply-side perspective. Yet, chronic food

Table 6.4 Main policy instruments adopted by India

1.	Creation, strengthening, and expansion of the national agricultural research system (NARS) for developing and perfecting new production technologies for food grains and other agricultural commodities
2.	Establishment, strengthening, and expansion of agricultural education and training system for agricultural extension workers and farmers for transfer of new technologies at the farm level
3.	An arrangement for the production and/or import and distribution of high-yielding farm inputs like improved seeds, fertilizers, agrochemicals, and improved implements/farm machines to the farmers
4.	Planning and execution of major, medium, and micro-irrigation schemes for increasing the area under irrigation
5.	Nationalization of commercial banks, creation of cooperative credit institutions, and reorientation of monetary policy to increase institutional credit flow to the farmers
6.	Creation and expansion of physical and institutional infrastructure (primary market yards, roads, storage facilities, farmers' cooperatives, and public-sector organizations) for improvement of the marketing system to handle and distribute the emerging marketed surplus
7.	Regulation of traders' exploitative marketing practices through a series of legal and regulatory measures such as licensing, levies, stocking limits, and movement restrictions
8.	Fixation of minimum support prices (MSPs) and arrangements for price support purchases and procurement by public or cooperative agencies
9.	Building-up and maintenance of buffer stocks of cereals and distribution of cereals through public distribution system (PDS)
10.	Provision of food and input subsidies, explicit or implicit, for reconciling the conflicting objectives of cereal producers and consumers in terms of prices
11.	Canalization, licensing, minimum export prices (MEPs), and custom duties for maintaining price stability in the domestic market

Source Adapted from Acharya (2009) [no copyright issue]

insecurity may persist the next few decades if problems of low-calorie intake and high incidences of malnutrition follow on current trajectories with only incremental improvements. The persistence of low nutritional status is an important consideration specially when the impact is mostly felt by vulnerable populations such as women, children, and the elderly. Numerous reports suggest that several types of programs need to be targeted exclusively at vulnerable segments of the population. This can be done via (1) the elimination of inadequate access to food during crisis, (2) enhancing capabilities enabling participation in India's growth process to reduce chronic food insecurity, (3) reducing malnutrition of preschool children and women as well as, (4) improving basic services and infrastructure such as safe drinking water, healthcare to the poor (Chakraborty 2005; Dev and Sharma 2010; Radhakrishna and Reddy, n.d.; Pingali et al. 2017). India's latest agricultural strategy is not sufficiently focused on increasing smallholder productivity, while aiming to reduce the current unsustainable levels of groundwater overexploitation and build a resilient agriculture in the face of climate change, which is affecting India more severely than China (Lele and Goswami 2020).

The land-to-the-tiller programs implemented in India (like Nepal and the Philippines) facilitate the transfer of land from large landowners to landless or near landless tenants, enhancing both efficiency and equity, given the inverse relationship between farm size and productivity. However, the reduced incentives for a large number of small landowners to rent land to a few large farmers hinders land consolidation (Otsuka 2007). India also developed new varieties of crops, land use switching, changes to planting seasons, investment in irrigation infrastructure, and flood migration strategies (Bandara and Cai 2014).

In China, there is a potential for redistributive policies in reducing poverty, such as the "Minimum Livelihood Guarantee Scheme" also known as "Dibao," to guarantee a minimum income in urban areas. However, Dibao's coverage is imperfect as the poor living in poor areas fared worse in access to the program (Ravallion 2009). India's interventions, on the other hand, were through food subsidies, farm-input subsidies, subsidized credit schemes, and workfare schemes. The subsidies on food and fertilizers, in particular, have been costly in budgetary terms and economically inefficient. The "National Rural Employment Guarantee Scheme," influenced by the "Employment Guarantee Scheme" in Maharashtra, aims to assure income support in rural areas by providing unskilled manual labor at low wages, and appears promising to reduce poverty (Murgai and Ravallion 2005).

On India's Fisheries Sector

The fisheries sector in India is generally small in scale with the use of nonmotorized craft having a larger percentage than larger scale fishermen with motorized trawlers (Sivasubramaniam 2000). The industry is mostly made up of subsistence fishermen without much means to purchase more efficient means of fishing. Considering the size of India, there is an inherent lack of financial ability for the government to provide financial assistance to fishermen. As such, due to the lack of income derived from this economic activity, many fisherfolk work in other sectors during low-peak seasons (Sivasubramaniam 2000). Inland fish farming on the other hand is more common in countries like India and Bangladesh as compared to other countries of the subregion and it contributes significantly to fish production. Aquaculture for India contributes to 50% of the Indian Ocean's production with close to 100,000 mt annually. Estimated supply and demand analysis for India highlights demand–supply deficits for the years 2020 and 2030 (Salim et al. 2014).

The demand–supply deficits highlight the importance of improving fisheries productivity in India. Numerous problems related to marine capture fisheries are abound. Some of the problems include: debt trap and lack of institutional credit, nonmodernization of existing fleets, post-harvest losses due to improper handling and transportation (Salim et al. 2014). For sustainable development for this sector, there must be equitable development that is financially feasible to drive ecologically sound practice for food security. With growing demand and lack of development in this sector, there must be future policies to aid growth. Salim et al. (2014) further highlight that the inland sector for India will be the most important sector to bridge the demand and supply gap and the aquaculture field shows great promise.

The Chindia Dilemma

For Chindia, climate change is exacerbating environmental devastation and expanding mitigation efforts will pose as an additional hurdle to the continued high growth rates and economic development. Additionally, attaining food security for a bludgeoning population with greater demands for quality food produce will be an uphill battle for Chindia. Nevertheless, Chindia can play a big role in building a harmonious global system via climate change to deal with one of the most crucial problems of our time. However, as rapidly developing countries, they must deal with their domestic demands. Chindia face three challenges: (1) maintain high economic growth rates, (2), economic growth must be supported by sustainable practices, and (3) manage rising demand for food. The interplay of developmental ambitions to alleviate poverty, coupled with the emissions associated with higher development both directly and indirectly impacting the supply and demand of food supply poses a dilemma. To move ahead, Chindia must carefully navigate the problems via careful policies which is by no means an easy task.

Given the assumption ability and motivation of Chindia to address the problems faced, there are still obstacles due to key knowledge gaps in our current understanding of the full range of impacts that climate change may have on marine ecosystems and fisheries. There is much more to be done to improve our understanding about the biophysical impacts of climate change and how numerous interlocking factors can affect marine life and economic activities such as fishing costs, jobs, and income (Sumaila et al. 2011). Compounding this, policymakers face additional tasks of dealing with policy implications and national development trade-offs.

References

Acharya, S. 2009. Food Security and Indian Agriculture: Policies, Production, Performance and Marketing Environment. *Agricultural Economics Research Review* 22: 1–19.

Avnimelech, Y. 2009. *Biofloc Technology—A Practical Guide Book*. Baton Rouge, USA: World Aquaculture Society.

Bandara, Jayatilleke S., and Yiyong Cai. 2014. The Impact of Climate Change on Food Crop Productivity, Food Prices and Food Security in South Asia. *Economic Analysis & Policy* 44 (2014): 451–465.

Barange, M. 2002. Influence of Climate Variability and Change on the Structure, Dynamics and Exploitation of Marine Ecosystems. In *Global Environmental Change: Issues in Environmental Science and Technology*, ed. R.E. Hester and R.M. Harrison, 57–82. Cambridge: Royal Society of Chemistry.

Bazaz, Amir B., and Vrinda Seksaria. 2014. (De)Constructing India's and China's Energy and Climate Change Policy Choices: Interfaces of Co-Operation. *Procedia—Social and Behavioral Sciences* 157: 322–329.

Birthal, P., M.T. Khan, D. Negi, and S. Agarwal. 2014. Impact of Climate Change on Yields of Major Food Crops in India: Implications for Food Security. *Agricultural Economics Research Review* 27 (2): 145–155.

Boden, T.A., G. Marland, and R.J. Andres. 2017. Global, Regional and National Fossil-Fuel CO_2 emissions. Carbon Dioxide Information Analysis Center. Oak Ridge National Laboratory. Oak Ridge, TN, USA: US Department of Energy.

Brander, K. 2007. Global Fish Production and Climate Change. *Proceedings of the National Academy of Sciences* 104 (50): 19709–19714.

Cervantes-Godoy, D., and J. Dewbre. 2010. Economic Importance of Agriculture for Poverty Reduction. OECD Food, Agriculture and Fisheries Working Papers No. 23. OECD Publishing, OECD.

Chakraborty, D. 2005. Food Security in India: Policy Challenges and Responses. Asia Programme Briefing Paper ASP BP 05/-2. New Delhi: Chatham House. Retrieved 28 March 2018. https://www.chathamhouse.org/sites/files/chathamhouse/public/Research/Asia/india_food_security.pdf.

Chmutina, K. 2010. China's Participation in Global Climate Change Cooperation: From the 1980s to the Post Kyoto Era. Briefing Series—Issue 63. China Policy Institute: The University of Nottingham.

Christiaensen, Luc, Lionel Demery, and Jesper Kuhl. 2010. The (Evolving) Role of Agriculture in Poverty Reduction: An Empirical Perspective. WIDER Working Paper, No. 2010/36. ISBN 978-92-9230-273-3. Helsinki: The United Nations University World Institute for Development Economics Research (UNU-WIDER).

Datt, Gaurav, and Martin Ravallion. 1992. Growth and Redistribution Components of Changes in Poverty Measures: A Decomposition with Applications to Brazil and India in the 1980s. *Journal of Development Economics* 38: 275–295.

Datt, Gaurav, and Martin Ravallion. 1998a. Farm Productivity and Rural Poverty in India. *Journal of Development Studies* 34 (4): 62–85.

Datt, Gaurav, and Martin Ravallion. 1998b. Why Have Some Indian States Done Better Than Others at Reducing Rural Poverty? *Economica* 65: 17–38.

Datt, Gaurav, and Martin Ravallion. 2002. Has India's Reform Economic Growth Left the Poor Behind. *Journal of Economic Perspectives* 16 (3): 89–108.

Datt, Gaurav, and Martin Ravallion. 2009. Has India's Economic Growth Become Less Pro-Poor in the Wake of Economic Reforms? Policy Research Working Paper. Washington, DC: World Bank.

Dev, M.S., and A. Sharma. 2010. Food Security in India: Performance, Challenges and Policies. Oxfam India Working Papers Series: Oxfam India.

Dubash, N. 2015. Comment: A Climate More Congenial to India. *The Hindu*. Retrieved 31 March 2018. http://www.thehindu.com/opinion/op-ed/cop-21-and-paris-agreement-a-climate-more-congenial-to-india/article7992802.ece.

Edwards, M., and A.J. Richardson. 2004. Impact of Climate Change on Marine Pelagic Phenology and Trophic Mismatch. *Nature* 430 (7002): 881–884.

Fairbank, J.K., and M. Goldman. 2006. *China: A New History*, 2nd ed. Cambridge, MA: Harvard University Press.

Fan, Shenggen. 1991. Effects of Technological Change and Institutional Reform on Growth in Chinese Agriculture. *American Journal of Agricultural Economics* 7: 266–275.

FAO (Food and Agricultural Organization of the United Nations). 2001. Fishery Country Profile: The People's Republic of China. Fisheries and Aquaculture Department, FAO. Retrieved 29 March 2018. http://www.fao.org/fishery/facp/CHN/en.

FAO (Food and Agricultural Organization of the United Nations). 2006. Fishery Country Profile: The Republic of India. Fisheries and Aquaculture Department, FAO. Retrieved 29 March 2018. http://www.fao.org/fishery/facp/IND/en.

FAO (Food and Agricultural Organization of the United Nations). 2012. *The State of World Fisheries and Aquaculture 2012*. Rome, Italy: FAO Fisheries and Aquaculture Department.

FAO (Food and Agriculture Organization of the United Nations). 2000. Sustainable Contribution of Fisheries to Food Security. Asia-Pacific Fishery Commission Food and Agriculture Organization of the United Nations. Retrieved 23 March 2018. http://www.fao.org/3/a-x6956e.pdf.

FAO (Food and Agriculture Organization of the United Nations). 2008. Assessment of World Food Security and Nutrition. Agenda Notes for 34th Session of Committee on World Food Security.

FAO (Food and Agriculture Organization of the United Nations). 2018. The State of World Fisheries and Aquaculture 2018 - Meeting the sustainable development goals. Retrieved 14 March 2021. http://www.fao.org/3/i9540en/i9540en.pdf.

Galli, Alessandro, Justin Kitzes, Valentina Niccolucci, Mathis Wackernagel, Yoshihiko Wada, and Nadia Marchettini. 2012. Assessing the Global Environmental Consequences of Economic Growth Through the Ecological Footprint: A Focus on China and India. *Ecological Indicators* 17: 99–107.

Godfray, H., J. Pretty, S. Thomas, E. Warham, and J. Beddington. 2011. Linking Policy on Climate and Food. *Science* 331 (6020): 1013–1014.

Government of India. 2008. National Action Plan on Climate Change. Retrieved 14 March 2021. https://archivepmo.nic.in/drmanmohansingh/climate_change_english.pdf.

Hall-Spencer, J.M., R. Rodolfo-Metalpa, S. Martin, E. Ransome, M. Fine, S. Turner, S. Rowley, D. Tedesco, and M. Buia. 2008. Volcanic Carbon Dioxide Vents Show Ecosystem Effects of Ocean Acidification. *Nature* 454 (7200): 96–99.

Hölscher, J., E. Marelli, and M. Signorelli. 2010. China and India in the Global Economy. *Economic Systems* 34 (3): 212–217.

Huang, J., and J. Ding. 2015. Institutional Innovation and Policy Support to Facilitate Small-Scale Farming Transformation in China. In Proceedings of Paper presented at 29th International Conference of Agricultural Economists in Milan.

Huang, Jikun, Liangliang Gao and Scott Rozelle. 2012. The Effect of Off-Farm Employment on the Decisions of Households to Rent Out and Rent In Cultivated Land in China. *China Agricultural Economic Review* 4 (1): 5–17.

IMF (International Monetary Fund). 2017a. *People's Republic of China: Staff Report for the 2017 Article IV Consultation.* IMF Country Report No. 17/247.

IMF (International Monetary Fund). 2017b. *India: Staff Report for the 2017 Article IV Consultation.* IMF Country Report No. 17/54.

Jussaume Jr., R.A. 2001. Factors Associated with Modern Urban Chinese Food Consumption Patterns. *Journal of Contemporary China* 10 (27): 219–232.

Kedia, Shailly. 2016. Approaches to Low Carbon Development in China and India. *Advances in Climate Change Research* 7 (4): 213–221.

Kimura, S., K. Otsuka, T. Sonobe, and S. Rozelle. 2011. Efficiency of Land Allocation Through Tenancy Markets: Evidence from China. *Economic Development and Cultural Change* 59 (3): 485–510.

Lehodey, P., J. Alheit, M. Barange, T. Baumgartner, G. Beaugrand, K. Drinkwater, K. Fromentin, S. Hare, G. Ottersen, R. Perry, C. Roy, C. van der Lingen, and F. Werner. 2006. Climate Variability, Fish and Fisheries. *Journal of Climate* 19 (20): 5009–5030.

Lele, Uma, and Sambuddha Goswami. 2020. Agricultural Policy Reforms: Roles of Markets and States in China and India. *Global Food Security* 26: 100371.

Lin, Justin. 1992. Rural Reforms and Agricultural Growth in China. *American Economic Review* 82: 34–51.

Malone, E. 2010. *Changing Glaciers and Hydrology in Asia: Addressing Vulnerabilities to Glacier Melt Impacts.* Washington, DC: USAID.

McBeath, J.H., and J. McBeath. 2010. *Environmental Change and Food Security in China.* New York: Springer.

Meenakshi, J.V., and B. Vishwanathan. 2003. Calorie Deprivation in Rural India, 1983–1999/2000. *Economic and Political Weekly* 38 (4): 369–375.

Ministry of Environment and Forests Government of India. 2011. *Sustainable Development in India: Stocktaking in the Run Up to Rio + 20*. New Delhi: Ministry of Environment and Forests Government of India.

Mizo, R. 2016. India, China and Climate Cooperation. *India Quarterly* 72 (4): 375–394.

Murgai, Rinku, and Martin Ravallion. 2005. Employment Guarantee in Rural India: What Would It Cost and How Much Would It Reduce Poverty? *Economic and Political Weekly* 40 (31): 3450–3455.

National Development and Reform Commission. 2007. China's National Climate Change Programme. People's Republic of China. Retrieved 30 March 2018. http://en.ndrc.gov.cn/newsrelease/200706/P020070604561191006823.pdf.

O'Reilly, C.M., S.R. Alin, P.D. Plisnier, A.S. Cohen, and B.A. McKee. 2003. Climate change Decreases Aquatic Ecosystem Productivity of Lake Tanganyika, Africa. *Nature* 424 (6950): 766–768.

Otsuka, K. 2007. Efficiency and Equity Effects of Land Markets. In *Handbook of Agricultural Economics 3*, ed. P. Pingli and R.E. Evenson. Amsterdam: Elsevier.

Otsuka, Keijiro, Yanyan Liu, and Futoshi Yamauchi. 2016. Growing Advantage of Large Farms in Asia and Its Implications for Global Food Security. *Global Food Security* 11: 5–11. https://doi.org/10.1016/j.gfs.2016.03.001.

Pingali, Prabhu, Bhaskar Mittra, and Andaleeb Rahman. 2017. The Bumpy Road from Food to Nutrition Security-Slow Evolution of India's Food Policy. *Global Food Security* 15 (2017): 77–84.

Prime Minister's Council on Climate Change. 2007. National Action Plan on Climate Change. Government of India. Retrieved 30 March 2018. http://www.moef.nic.in/downloads/home/Pg01-52.pdf.

Rada, N., C. Wang, and L. Qin. 2015. Subsidy or market reform? Rethinking China's Farm Consolidation Strategy. *Food Policy* 57 (1): 93–103.

Radhakrishna, R., and Reddy, K.V. n.d. Food Security and Nutrition: Vision 2020. Planning Commission Government of India. Retrieved 20 March 2018. http://www.planningcommission.nic.in/reports/genrep/bkpap2020/16_bg2020.pdf.

Ramesh, J. 2005. *Making Sense of Chindia: Reflections on China and India*. New Delhi: India Research Press.

Ravallion, Martin. 2009. A Comparative Perspective on Poverty Reduction in Brazil, China and India. Policy Research Working Paper No. WPS 5080. Washington, DC: World Bank Group.

Ravallion, Martin, and Shaohua Chen. 2007. China's (Uneven) Progress Against Poverty. *Journal of Development Economics* 82 (1): 1–42.

Rosegrant, M.W., and S.A. Cline. 2003. Global Food Security: Challenges and Policies. *Science* 302 (5652): 1917–1919.

Saich, T. 2004. *Governance and Politics of China*, 2nd ed. New York: Palgrave.

Salim, S.S., R.B. Pramod Kiran, N. Joshua, and B. Biju Kumar. 2014. Challenges in Food Security: The Fisheries and Aquaculture Policy Perspectives in India. *Journal of Aquatic Biology and Fisheries* 2 (2): 24–32.

Schmidhuber Josef, and Francesco N. Tubiello. 2007. Global Food Security Under Climate Change. *Proceedings of the National Academy of Sciences* 104 (50): 19703–19708.

Singh, R. 2011. *Towards an Evergreen Revolution—The Road Map*. National Academy of Agricultural Sciences: New Delhi.

Sivasubramaniam, K. 2000. The Sustainable Contribution of Fisheries to Food Security in the South Asian Subregion. In *Sustainable Contribution of Fisheries to Food Security Asia-Pacific Fishery Commission Food and Agriculture Organization of the United Nations*, 159–221. Retrieved 23 March 2018. http://www.fao.org/3/a-x6956e.pdf.

Song, Z. 2000. The Sustainable Contribution of Fisheries to Food Security in China. In *Sustainable Contribution of Fisheries to Food Security Asia-Pacific Fishery Commission Food and Agriculture Organization of the United Nations*, 19–20. Retrieved 23 March 2018. http://www.fao.org/3/a-x6956e.pdf.

Stenseth, N.C., G. Ottersen, J.W. Hurrell, M. Atle, M. Lima, K. Chan, N. Yoccoz, and B. Dlandsvik. 2003. Studying Climate Effects on Ecology Through the Use of Climate Indices: The North Atlantic Oscillation, El Nino Southern Oscillation and Beyond. *Proceedings of the Royal Society of London Series B-Biological Sciences* 270 (1529): 2087–2096.

Stern, N. 2007. *Stern Review: The Economics of Climate Change*. Cambridge: Cambridge University Press.

Sumaila, U.R., W. Cheung, V. Lam, D. Pauly, and S. Herrick. 2011. Climate Change Impacts on the Biophysics and Economics of World Fisheries. *Nature Climate Change* 1: 449–456.

Tilman, D., K. Cassman, P. Matson, R. Naylor, and R. Polasky. 2002. Agricultural Sustainability and Intensive Production Practices. *Nature* 418 (6898): 671–677.

UNFCCC (United Nations Framework Convention on Climate Change). 1998. Kyoto Protocol to the United Nations Framework Convention to Climate Change. United Nations. Retrieved 30 March 2018. http://unfccc.int/resource/docs/convkp/kpeng.pdf.

UNFCCC (United Nations Framework Convention on Climate Change). 2009. Copenhagen Climate Change Conference—December 2009. United Nations. Retrieved 30 March 2018. http://unfccc.int/meetings/copenhagen_dec_2009/meeting/6295.php.

UNFCCC (United Nations Framework Convention on Climate Change). 2015. The Paris Agreement. United Nations. Retrieved 30 March 2018. http://unfccc.int/paris_agreement/items/9485.php.

Wahlqvist, Mark L., John McKay, Ya-Chen Chang, and Ya-Wen Chiu. 2012. Rethinking the Food Security Debate in Asia: Some Missing Ecological and Health Dimensions and Solutions. *Food Security* 4 (4): 657–670.

Wang, Qiang, Su Min, and Rongrong Li. 2018. Toward to Economic Growth Without Emission Growth: The Role of Urbanization and Industrialization in China and India. *Journal of Cleaner Production* 205: 499–511.

World Bank. 2021. World Development Indicators. Retrieved 14 March 2021. https://datacatalog.worldbank.org/dataset/world-development-indicators.

Ye, L., W. Xiong, W. Li, P. Yang, W. Wu, G. Yang, Y. Fu, J. Zou, Z. Chen, E. Van Ranst, and H. Tang. 2013. Climate Change Impact on China Food Security in 2050. *Agronomy for Sustainable Development* 33: 363–374.

Yu, Jinkai, and Qingchao Han. 2020. Food Security of Mariculture in China: Evolution, Future Potential and Policy. *Marine Policy* 115 (2020): 103892.

Zhang, X., J. Yang, and S. Wang. 2011. China Has Reached the Lewis Turning Point. *China Economic Review* 22 (4): 542–554.

CHAPTER 7

Urban Food Security and Sustainability in Asian Cities

With Daisy Tam

For the first time in history, more than 50% of the world's population now lives in cities. As the trend continues, this figure will rise to 70% in the next 30 years. As the UN World Urbanization Prospects estimates, over 2.5 billion urban residents will be added by 2050 and the majority of this growth will take place in Asia and Africa, accounting for 90% of growth in these two parts of the world (United Nations 2017). In the rapidly changing world with increasing global population, massive urbanization and climate change, feeding cities will certainly be a major challenge to sustainability in the coming decades. In this chapter, taking the cases of two Asian cities, Singapore and Hong Kong, we will elucidate the mounting challenges for and grappling responses to urban food security in the age of vulnerability complicated largely by climate change.

Cities are resource-intensive places, despite only taking up 2% of the earth's surface; they consume 75% of global natural resources and produce equal amounts in carbon emissions (UNEP 2013). However, cities are also regarded as crucial sites for sustainable solutions especially where urban food systems are concerned (Ilieva 2017; Sonnino 2018). Urban food systems improve food security, defined by the FAO as when "all people, at all times, have physical and economic access to sufficient, safe

M. S. Islam and E. Kieu, *Climate Change and Food Security in Asia Pacific*, International Political Economy Series,
https://doi.org/10.1007/978-3-030-70753-8_7

and nutritious food to meet their dietary needs and food preferences for an active and healthy life" (FAO 2018) and contribute to the Sustainable Development Goals by reducing hunger and poverty, improving health, addressing inequality as well as reducing greenhouse gases through cutting down waste (Lang and Barling 2012; Shaw 2007; Ericksen 2008; Sonnino 2009).

Emerging sustainable urban food systems strategies (UFSS) yielded many insights into how cities developed plans on both a policy and governance level as well as grassroots and community level to tackle the issue. A combination of top-down and bottom-up initiatives can be observed, the term governance captures the "non-hierarchical modes of coordination, steering and decision-making" (Cattacin and Zimmer 2016) to describe the mixture of urban actors from both private and public sectors in addition to formal government structures (Zvolska et al. 2019). However, the vast majority of these case studies are based in Europe, Australia, and the United States (Ilieva 2017; Haysom and Tawodzera 2018), and there is a gap in the literature documenting cases in metropolitan cities in Asia. Taking into account how the next spurt of growth will take place in Asia (and Africa), this chapter offers a timely contribution to the global debate on food security by offering case-specific discussion of Hong Kong and Singapore, two of the four tigers in Southeast Asia, to map out some of the similarities and differences and also to offer a comparative study of how these two cities have approached the question of food security in the twenty-first century.

Singapore and Hong Kong exemplify the vulnerabilities of metropolitan food systems: as wealthy global cities, both are fully urbanized, capital-rich but resource-poor. Heavily dependent on imports, its population nevertheless has an appetite for premium energy-intensive foods. Scarcity and excess go hand in hand, while there is still want in the population, waste is also an issue. Against this backdrop, the chapter seeks to address three critical research questions: (i) Despite economic prosperity, why are both Singapore and Hong Kong vulnerable to food security? In other words, what are the central challenges both cities facing in ensuring food security? (ii) What is the current state of food security in terms of demand and supply in both cities? (iii) What broader responses and policies do both cities have to battle food insecurity for its growing inhabitants and to what extent are they successful? This chapter is intended to offer an understanding of how vulnerable highly dependent food-importing countries or cities like Singapore and Hong Kong can survive in increasingly urbanized, capitalistic, and environmentally eroding world.

Challenges for Urban Food Security

A close examination of our complex inextricable global food system reveals a number of core factors contributing to urban food insecurity around the world (Ericksen 2008). As cities offer lucrative jobs and modern amenities, there is an increasing trend of rural–urban migration, especially in Asian agricultural nations. Hence, even as billions of additional people need to be fed, fewer people will be working as food producers and less land will be allocated for food production. FAO, on the question of the trends related to the future of food and agriculture, identified a number of challenges (Table 7.1).

The four pillars of food security, as identified by FAO, are food availability, access, utilization, and stability (FAO 2006). We can discern a number of challenges associated with these pillars (Table 7.2), grouping

Table 7.1 Trends related to future agriculture and food system

No.	*Challenges and trends*
1	A rapidly increasing world population marked by growth "hot spots," urbanization, and aging
2	Diverse trends in economic growth, family incomes, agricultural investment, and economic inequality
3	Greatly increased competition for natural resources
4	Climate change impacts from extreme weather effects, droughts, floods, crop diseases, etc.
5	Plateauing of agricultural productivity for many crops and animals
6	Transboundary pests and diseases
7	Increased conflicts, crises, and natural disasters
8	Persistent poverty, inequality, and food insecurity
9	Dietary transitions affecting nutrition and health
10	Structural changes in economic systems and employment implications
11	Increased migration
12	Advanced food production systems and resulting impacts on farmers' livelihoods
13	Persisting food losses and waste
14	New international governance mechanisms for responding to food and nutrition security issues
15	Changes in international financing for sustainable development

Sources Adapted from FAO (2017) and Calicioglu et al. (2019) [no copyright issue]

Table 7.2 Challenges for urban food security

1.	Availability and stability • Sustainably improve agricultural productivity to meet increasing demand • Ensure a sustainable natural resource base • Address climate change and intensification of natural hazards • Prevent transboundary pests and diseases
2.	Access and utilization • Eradicate extreme poverty and reduce inequality • End hunger and all forms of malnutrition • Improve income-earning opportunities in rural areas and address the root causes of migration • Build resilience to protracted crises, disasters, and conflicts
3.	Systemic challenge • Make food systems more efficient, inclusive, and resilient • Address the needs for coherent and effective national and international governance

Sources Adapted from FAO (2017) and Calicioglu et al. (2019) [no copyright issue]

into three main clusters: challenges related to food availability and stability, challenges related to food access and utilization, and systematic challenges (Calicioglu et al. 2019).

Cities like Singapore and Hong Kong, where efficient infrastructure including affordable transportation and grocery facilities and numerous home delivery services are readily available, the physical "access" component of food security is not a major concern. Also, due to global trade and geopolitical significance, these two cities are regarded as Asian tigers inhabited largely by wealthy people. The "utilization" component in these two cities is a minor issue. Although obesity epidemic is still a major issue in the developed urban centers, today the overall burden of this epidemic and other chronic diseases is greater in the developing countries (Malik et al. 2013; Szabo 2016; Wang 2019; Assem et al. 2019). The food "availability" in terms of consumption patterns, food production, and supply process as well as food "stability" in terms of disaster preparedness, resilience, supplies, and policies are far more critical for these two cities. Although access and utilization are crucial for food security, our study mainly focuses on food availability and stability that have broader implications for sustainable food systems in both Singapore and Hong Kong. Figure 7.1 shows the framework of our analysis.

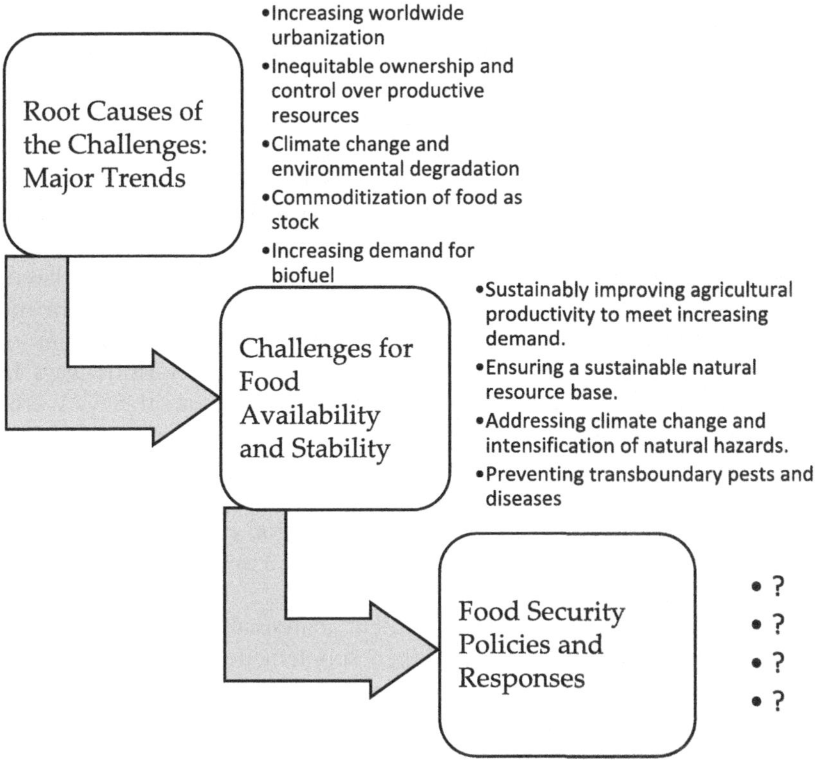

Fig. 7.1 Study framework [Authors' own; no copyright issue]

Materials and Methods

This chapter is based on a robust content analysis substantiated by a number of primary methods employed in both Singapore and Hong Kong in order to gain deeper insights into the food security dynamics. For the content analysis, we examined relevant materials in order to capture trends or patterns in food production systems and food security studies across the world. A number of approaches and variables suggested by academic journals to understand urban food security were identified and critically analyzed. Along with credible peer-reviewed sources, we also collected and examined other soft sources such as newspapers, government documents, and internet reports for our analysis.

For the Singapore case, the content analysis provided a bulk of data for our analysis, yet we employed focus group discussion, informal interviews, and ethnography to substantiate our findings. Three separate focus group discussions were held with three significant groups: the Agri-food and Veterinary Authority of Singapore (AVA) officials ($N = 9$), the NTU Food security expert group ($N = 10$), and regional experts on food security ($N = 15$). Informal qualitative interviews were conducted with 21 consumers, 5 food traders, and 3 government officials—a total of 29 respondents. We gained critical information regarding choice, habit, expectation on food security, and grocery and dining venues from the consumers; origin, management, demand, forecast, and regulations of various food commodities from the food traders; and various ways in which AVA is managing food security in Singapore from the AVA officials. For our ethnography, we visited wet markets in Jurong and Little India as well as a number of supermarkets such as Fairprice, Giant, and Prime Supermarket. We also visited a number of high-tech agrifarms in the Kranji areas. Taken as a whole, a combination of methods provided with us a comprehensive understanding of the complex issue of urban food security dynamics in Singapore.

For the Hong Kong case study, content analysis also provided the bulk of data for our analysis which was then supplemented by fieldwork and site visits, interviews, and participation observation. Over the course of research, the investigator visited 2 peri-urban farms and 2 rooftop farms, interviewed 6 local farmers, visited 10 local wet markets and 10 supermarkets in various districts, and interviewed members of staff from 2 food charities and interviewed 12 beneficiaries from food assistance programs. Taken as a whole, the research aims to get a holistic view of how food security is understood from different levels, from policy formulations to public reception. The 32 interviewees were stakeholders from a cross-section of the food system, farmers, retailers, consumers, charities, and their respective service users.

We employed almost similar methodologies in two cities: Content analysis substantiated by ethnography and qualitative interviews. Due to local dynamics, we used focus group discussions in Singapore as an additional method for consistency check, while participant observation as an additional method for Hong Kong. Singapore is robust in government policies and therefore the focus group discussion with the AVA, for example, was necessary; while Hong Kong has more civic activism and therefore the participant observation as an additional method was necessary. Taken as a whole, we tried our best to employ a robust triangulation of methods in both cities to capture the comprehensive dynamics for our analysis.

Foodscape in Singapore and Hong Kong

Singapore embraced remarkable transformation over the decades. Known widely as a "fishing village" in the precolonial era, Singapore was transformed as an Agricultural Hub in the 1960s producing 80% of its poultry demand, 60% of vegetable, 100% of eggs, and even exporting pork to neighboring regions before it became a trade hub for the world some fifty years later. It is now one of the wealthiest countries per capita in the world. Although small in size (721.5 km^2), Singapore has a GDP of around 486 billion dollars (Per capita GDP 57,714.30 USD in 2017). It is now widely known for its crystal skyscrapers and perfectly clean streets and not for its pork production (Eisenberg 2017).

With a population of 5.2 million people and a land area of 723 km^2, very little of Singapore's landmass has been allocated for the purposes of food production; the priority has been to build a modern urban city. In fact, the total farming area has declined by more than 9.5% since 2002 as the urbanized nation state has continued to develop. In 2011, only 729 ha or 1% of available land was allocated for food production. When the total food output from all the local farms is combined, it only accounts for 23% of eggs, 4% of fish, and 7% of leafy vegetables consumed (AVA 2010). As such, Singapore is highly dependent on food imports. It imported more than 90% of its food from 31 countries (AVA 2018). Figure 7.2 shows the major items imported by Singapore in 2017–2018.

Over the years, the household income for all income groups in Singapore increased, with households in the higher brackets registering higher income growth rates (AVA 2018). The increasing affluence of Singaporeans affects their food needs in two ways: quantity and quality. The average Singaporean's diet has seen an increase in chicken, pork, beef, vegetables, and hen eggs. There is a growing demand for high-end premium foods too. This trend is reflected in the increasing number of upscale supermarkets such as FairPrice Finest that "aimed at bringing the *fine* life closer to shoppers." The first FairPrice Finest outlet opened in 2007 and in only six years, FairPrice Finest expanded their operations to nine outlets. Examples of premium fare available at the store include live oysters from Australia, musk melons, Kyoho grapes and wagyu beef from

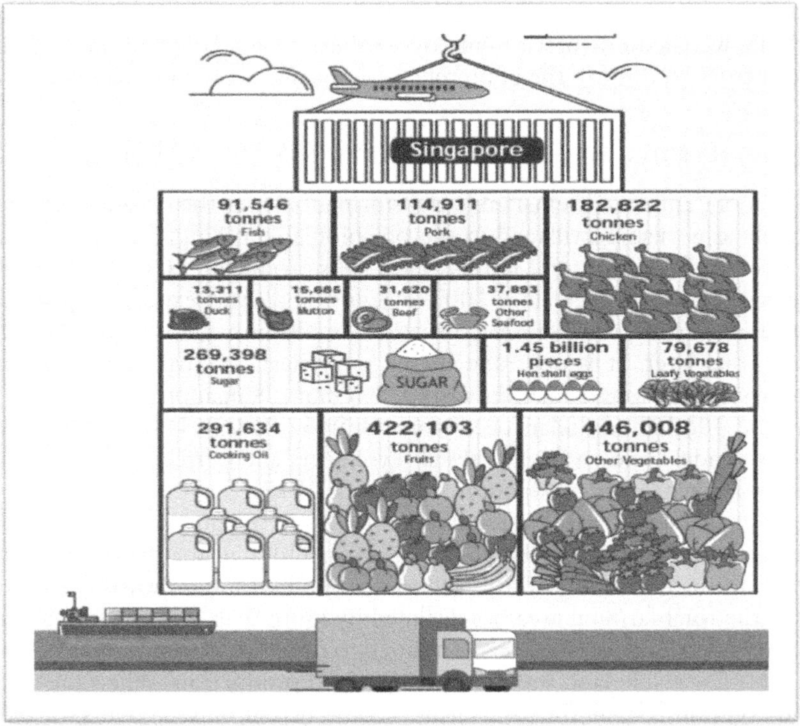

Fig. 7.2 Major food items imported by Singapore in 2017–2018 (AVA 2018) [public document; no copyright issue]

Japan, organic sugar from Brazil, organic eggs from New Zealand, Extra Virgin olive oil from France, and gourmet coffee from Italy (AVA 2018). Currently, FairPrice Finest supermarket chain has 25 locations in Singapore, including one at the Jewel Changi Airport (78 Airport Boulevard) (SHOPSinSG 2020).

Questions arise whether Singapore can continue to supply more and higher quality food as an increasing percentage of the population enters the upper and middle classes, and how these premium supermarkets can affect the economic access and nutritional welfare of citizens from the lower classes who cannot afford such luxury goods. Interestingly, in 2018 and 2019, Singapore topped the Global Food Security Index of 113 countries (GFSI 2019). Although Singapore scored high on food security measures such as affordability, availability, and safety, it is, as noted in the report, very vulnerable to climate and natural resource risks (EIU 2018; Koh 2018).

Hong Kong, alongside Singapore, is known as one of the four dragons of Southeast Asia because of its intense pace of modernization and urbanization. The city also had its humble beginnings as a fishing village and had a strong agricultural sector in the 1950s–80s, producing enough vegetables, livestock, poultry, fish, and seafood as well as rice and tea to support 30–40% of what the population consumed. Today Hong Kong has become a financial center, with a GDP of 340.1 billion USD (46,000 USD per capita) (PSR 2016), it is ranked 10th highest in the world. Like many urbanizing cities, agriculture was left behind as Hong Kong's economy took off. The lack of public investment in research and development coupled with continual decline of farming resources such as labor and land contributed to the fall in local production over the last five decades. In 2015, there are only around 4300 farmers left in Hong Kong, a far cry from 26,131 in 1986. Despite having nearly 4500 hectares of agricultural land, 84% is fallow and only 685 hectares are currently farmed producing a mere 1.7% of the population's consumption of vegetables (NGMR 2017; AFCD 2018).

With a population of 7.3 million and a landmass of 1106 km^2, Hong Kong relies mainly on imports, spending 5.26% of its GDP on buying food. The most important food source is Mainland China, which provides much of the city's fresh food needs: 94% of fresh pork, 100% of fresh beef, 92% vegetables, and 66% of its eggs (PSR 2018). The city also imports substantial amounts of chilled and frozen meat from Brazil, Australia, the United States, and New Zealand. Fresh fruit and vegetables, live and frozen seafood come from Thailand, Indonesia, the Philippines, and Norway (Figs. 7.3 and 7.4).

Hong Kong households spend on average 27% of their income on food (HKSAR 2016), and corresponding to global trends, increased affluence is also correlated to increased meat consumption. It is reported that Hong Kong consumes 664 g of meat/capita/day, equivalent to two pieces of 10 oz steak (Yau et al. 2018), one of the highest in the world. As consumer demands for resource-intensive and premium produce are high, supermarkets, which account for 56% of all retail food sales (USDA 2017) have shown continual expansion in premium and upscale outlets. Socioeconomic inequalities are a major challenge to food security in affluent

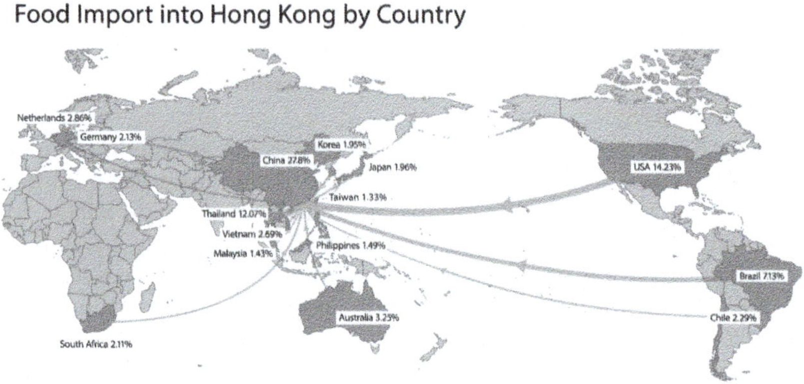

Fig. 7.3 Hong Kong food import map (*Credit* Jensen Choy) [no copyright issue]

Top 15 Countries of Food Import into Hong Kong by Quantity

Countries	Quantity	%
China	2,042,706,411	27.8%
USA	1,045,153,118	14.2%
Thailand	886,501,076	12.1%
Brazil	523,965,182	7.1%
Australia	238,744,246	3.3%
Netherlands	210,252,154	2.9%
Vietnam	197,429,763	2.7%
Chile	168,519,568	2.3%
Germany	156,711,703	2.1%
South Africa	155,076,952	2.1%
Japan	143,840,785	2.0%
Korea	143,502,292	2.0%
Philippines	109,156,742	1.5%
Malaysia	104,718,716	1.4%
Taiwan	98,020,583	1.3%
Other	1,122,366,845	15.3%

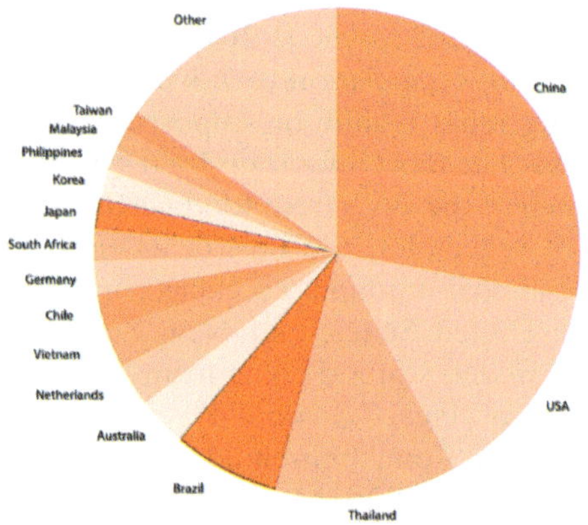

Fig. 7.4 Hong Kong food import figures (*Credit* Jensen Choy) [no copyright issue]

cities like Hong Kong and Singapore. From a macro-perspective, high-income countries are rated as more food secure due to their capacity to source food and lower average percentage of household income spent on food. While on the whole, wealthy cities fare better, this macro-perspective does not illuminate the polarized distribution of wealth, with an income disparity measured by the GINI index of 0.539 for Hong Kong and 0.458 for Singapore, the lowest 20% of Hong Kong's population spend 43% of their income provisioning for food (PSR 2016; NGMR 2017).

Responses to and Policies for Food Security

The Singapore Story

As Singapore imports more than 90% of its food from more than 31 countries worldwide, it is very difficult to solve Singapore's food insecurity without looking at the global picture. The issue, as expressed by the interview and focus group respondents, is thus whether supplying countries can continue to provide Singapore with food over the next 50–100 years. Without any increase in farm productivity from continued use of science and technology, an additional 1.6 billion hectares of land globally will be needed by 2050 to grow enough food (Syngenta Global 2012). This leaves Singapore with only two options: increasing the yield per unit of land or increasing the total area for agriculture. However, as stated earlier, due to greater urbanization and ecological devastation, increasing the total land area for agriculture might not even be possible. It is therefore vital to promote sustainable agriculture using modern techniques on a far greater scale, as the amount of arable land per person is in decline. Singapore responded to this crisis with the following strategies.

(i) *Singapore Food Fund*: As part of a larger push for ensuring a stable food supply, Singapore Food Fund was initiated in 2008 with the recommendation of the National Development Ministry and the Trade and Industry Ministry. In 2010, the AVA allocated $10 million to support local companies and farmers to enhance the production and import of leafy vegetables, eggs, and fish. The goal of this fund was to produce 30% of eggs, 15% of fish, and 10% of leafy vegetables Singapore consumes (Eco-Business 2011).

(ii) *Becoming a Food Research and Development Hub*: Due to land scarcity, Singapore may not be an agricultural hub, but it wishes to be an experimental hub and testing ground for different kinds of farming technologies and innovations. According to Feng (2012), a crop research laboratory in Singapore has developed a new type of rice that repels the brown plant hopper insect and is resistant to the viruses it spreads. The brown plant hopper is dangerous to rice crops in Asia because it feeds on them and spreads viruses which stunt their growth. By putting together knowledge and expertise from both the public and private sectors, Singapore sees itself in taking the lead in areas such as development of seed banks and improving seed varieties, farming systems, and post-harvest technologies for vegetables, breeding and farming systems for fish, and waste treatment and management systems. Such facilitation and technology transfer have a great potential in allowing Singapore to empower rural farmers in its supplying countries and improve their productive capacity (Teng et al. 2014). These were also echoed by the AVA officials during the focus group discussions.

(iii) *Increasing Fish Supply through Vertical Fish Farming*: Singapore is on track to reach its target for producing fish locally. Its 130 fish farms produced 10% of local consumption (5916 tons) in 2017 up from 4.5% in 2009 (AVA 2018). The AVA, targeting to raise this figure eventually to 15%, has been working closely with 120 coastal farms and 10 inland farms, providing different kinds of technical and research supports. The rise of vertical fish farming is another new initiative that promises to boost Singapore's fish production. Land-based fish farming is now moving toward multilayered fish farms on land, evading both the growing problem of land scarcity in Singapore and the vulnerability of sea farming, which can fall victim to pollution and plankton blooms (Lee 2012; AVA 2018).

(iv) *Jilin Food Zone*: In order to meet a substantial portion of its future food needs, Singapore supported a multi-billion-dollar proposal led by Temasek Holdings for a commercially driven enterprise that involves developing an "agricultural zone" twice the size of Singapore (1450 km^2, with a core area of 57 km^2) in the Chinese province of Jilin. This ambitious project, known as the Sino-Singapore Jilin Food Zone (SSJFZ), represents a "strategic step towards securing a safe, reliable, and sustainable supply of pork for Singapore in the long run," as opined by an AVA official. Investors have so far settled in the start-up area of SSJFZ and the first of the goods produced under the "Brilliance 430" brand, particularly the famed Jilin rice, has been launched for sale in Singapore. In December 2016, a batch of 60 tons of Japanese sticky rice from the Jilin Food Zone landed at FairPrice Xtra hypermarts and Finest supermarkets (Tan 2015).

(v) *Urban and Peri-Urban Agriculture (UPA)*: AVA has helped to develop six agrotechnology parks to promote agrotechnology-assisted food production methodologies in Singapore. The parks are well maintained and are equipped with modern infrastructure and facilities. The parks take up a combined land area of about 1465 hectares and are located at Lim Chu Kang, Murai, Sungei Tengah, Mandai, Nee Soon, and Loyang (AVA 2012a). Despite land scarcity in Singapore, a total of 700 hectares of land in the agrotechnology parks were allocated to 224 farms in 2012, while an additional 36 hectares of land outside the parks were allocated to 25 farms. The allocations include freshwater fish farms, layer farms for egg production, marine fish farms, goat and cattle farms, vegetable farms, orchid and floriculture farms, and ornamental fish farms. There were, in addition, 119 coastal fish farms (about 93 hectares of sea space) in the coastal waters of Singapore (AVA 2012b).

(vi) *Research and Development of Local Fisheries (R&D)*: To improve the quality of local produce while simultaneously achieving higher yields, as AVA officials reveal during the focus group discussions, AVA's research and development projects mainly focused on breeding, disease control, nutrition, aquaculture and vegetable production systems, and various post-harvest technology. AVA has two R&D centers for aquaculture. Research relating to marine aquaculture is carried out at the Marine Aquaculture Centre (MAC), while freshwater aquaculture research is done at the Sembawang Research Station (SRS). MAC was mainly established to oversee the development of tropical marine food fish aquaculture technology. It has succeeded in developing fish fry that are fast-growing and good-quality for intensive farming. AVA also conducts R&D projects with other private and public institutions. The knowledge, technology, and expertise exchange can add to synergies and deliver greater productivity and outcomes in research. For instance, AVA collaborated with Temasek Life Sciences Laboratory (TLL) on a "Selective Fish Breeding" project that aimed to develop cutting-edge genomics tools to find out, for example, Mozambique tilapia and Asian sea bass with good traits for breeding, fast growth, and disease resistance (AVA 2012b; 2018).

(vii) *Reducing Food Wastage*: Singapore is losing about 1 billion USD a year due to food waste. Although food waste is responsible for 10% of the total waste generated in Singapore, only about 17% of the food waste is recycled. National Environmental Agency in Singapore has recently taken a number of measures to reduce and manage food waste such as consumer education campaigns. According to Teng and Escaler (2011), "these campaigns must include messages that points to actions that consumers can adopt to reduce food wastage and draw attention to cost savings as a result of doing so." Looking at the retail, manufacturing, food service-sector level, strategies suggested by the interviewees include productive recycling of surplus food, improving demand-forecasting technologies, and developing sensor technologies to detect spoilage.

(viii) *Singapore Food Agency*: In order to consolidate all food-related functions—formerly carried out by the Agri-Food and Veterinary Authority of Singapore (AVA), National Environment Agency (NEA), and the Health Sciences Authority (HSA)—the Singapore government has introduced a new institution called Singapore Food Agency (SFA). SFA had set a target for 30% of homegrown food in Singapore by 2030, up from 10% now. Along with the "availability" component, SFA is working as a single umbrella to focus on access, utilization, and stability dimensions of food security (Wong 2018).

The Hong Kong Case

Compared to Singapore, Hong Kong does not have a clearly articulated urban food systems strategy as such; however, emerging initiatives on both a government and community level have begun to address different aspects of food security, creating a form of governance that is both formal and informal, bottom-up and top-down, involving private and public actors. In the following, we will adumbrate current responses and indicate opportunities and challenges for further development. Overall, the government's attitude toward food security is in line with its neoliberal values, so the response is largely market-driven in nature. In terms of local production, the Agricultural, Fisheries and Conservation Department (AFCD) pursues a high-value strategy. Going premium was identified as the way to help farmers sustain their livelihoods and a strategy to maintain competitiveness in a market-driven economy (AFCD 2018; EB 2014). Since the 2000s, the AFCD established a pilot conversion scheme for farmers to convert to organic farming as an extension of going premium. Hong Kong Organic Resource Center was established two years later and is currently the certification body for local organic production. To date, there are around 300 organic farms in Hong Kong (AFCD 2018; LCS 2019).

In order to reduce health risks and environmental pollution, the government aims to phase out animal husbandry, and has introduced a Buyout Scheme and a Volunteer Surrender Scheme for Poultry and Pig Farms in 2008, 2005, and 2006, respectively. The production has dropped despite annual figures showing a 94.6% increase in poultry supply, but that is due to a drastic cut to importing live chickens from mainland China due to the avian flu (LCS 2019). In addition to land-based production, new methods such as hydroponic and aquaponic cultivation were also included as part of the modernizing strategy for agriculture. In 2013, the Vegetable Market Organisation and AFCD established the Controlled Environment Hydroponic Research and Development Centre to explore and promote alternative methods of production, particularly models that are not dependent on land. The R&D center experiments with vertical cultivation, energy-saving technologies, and produces vegetables in shorter cycles in controlled indoor environments. Out of the 37 hydroponics farms, some have been set up privately in industrial buildings; however, without having changed the Town Planning Ordinance in parallel to support the use of industrial spaces for hydroponic farming, many farms face rezoning issues. Despite conservative policy initiatives, the public has responded with keen interest in urban agriculture. Driven by a combination of food scares and increased awareness for food and well-being, many urbanites have turned to growing their own food. Interviewees report concerns about unknown amounts of chemicals used in commercial produce and feel more confident about the health benefits if they produced their own. Subdivided agricultural plots of land provide allotments for families, while rooftop farming provides opportunities to grow in the heart of the city. In the last 10 years, over 60 rooftop farms have sprung up in the city (AFCD 2018; EB 2014).

The major challenge to producing food in the city is land, with real estate prices being one of the highest in the world, land is at a premium in Hong Kong. The scarcity, however, is man-made. There are 4400 hectares of agricultural land in Hong Kong of which 3686 hectares are left fallow. The government's rehabilitation initiative resulted in 22 hectares being successfully rented out to tenants in the last 5 years. This is not due to a lack of demand, as there are still 400 applicants waiting to be matched. The issue is to do with land ownership as 78% of the abandoned land is privately owned. This historical legacy has its roots in colonial times, where leasehold grants are sold by auctions or tenders (Dwyer et al. 1971). Selling land at a slow pace to the highest bidders was a very profitable model, accounting for 33% of government revenues between 1970 and 1996. Because of this controlled scarcity, developers are incentivized to hoard, buying up cheap agricultural land in the 1960s as land stock. Two major developers hold 56.8 million square feet of agricultural land, accounting to 1% of all non-built-up lands in Hong Kong (Poon 2011a, b).

The New Agricultural Policy launched in 2015 earmarked HKD$500 million for the Agricultural Development Fund aimed at modernizing and promoting sustainable agriculture. A key element is the setting up of Agri-Parks, which provides educational services to schools on the one hand and nurtures agrotech and agrobusiness on the other. Agriculture Priority Areas were also identified which will be supported for continued farming, and some 50 hectares of fallow farmland were promised to tenant farmers while the rest would be rezoned for development (FHB and AFCD 2014). Zoning is at the heart of contention between agriculture and development, both in the cases of industrial buildings for hydroponics, but also the rezoning of agricultural land. The policy has been criticized as a disguise to regain agricultural land for real estate development. Local farmers were also critical, saying that areas designated for farming are insufficient, lacking infrastructure and located even further out in the New Territories. Chuk, one of the farmers bitterly said "the only thing they know how to grow on our lands are buildings, not vegetables" referring to the policy.

Food waste is a major issue for cities, in Hong Kong, Municipal Solid Waste (MSW) is the single largest category of waste being thrown away at landfills, around 9000 tons everyday, of which 40% are putrescibles, organic matters that decompose and create greenhouse gases. Food waste constitutes the majority of putrescibles and the government has set the goal of reducing 40% by 2022, from 3600 tons a day to 2160 tons a day over the course of 8 years. This multipronged approach consists of 4 steps: the prevention and reduction of food waste at source through mobilizing the community, including the donation of surpluses; promoting separation and sorting of waste for better recycling; and an emphasis on food waste to energy where it is transformed into biogas or electricity as a form of renewable energy (Fig. 7.5). This aggressive target is largely due to the saturated landfill sites in Hong Kong, which are expected to be at capacity in 2020 (EB 2014).

Food waste management is another major policy area which touches food security. This is run by the Environmental Protection Department overseen by the Environment Bureau, responsible for environmental protection, energy conservation, and sustainable development. In 2014,

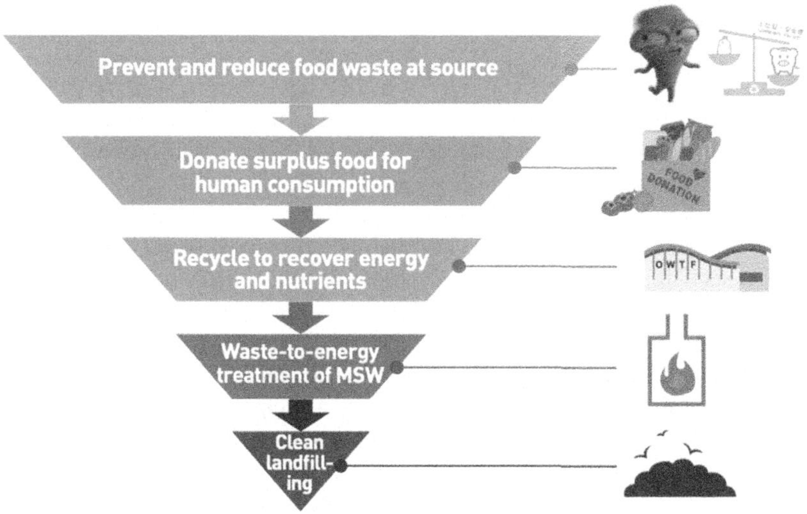

Fig. 7.5 Food waste and yard waste plan for Hong Kong 2014–2022 HKSAR Environment Bureau 2014 (EB 2014) [no copyright issue]

the Environment Bureau published a *Food Waste and Yard Waste Plan for Hong Kong 2014–2022* proposing a strategy that could be largely grouped into three areas—policy, social mobilization, and infrastructure. The two largest categories of the hierarchy: of prevention and reduction of waste at source and donating surplus for human consumption have been undertaken mainly as a social campaign, with sharing of best practices being promoted in the C&I sector and awareness-raising campaigns held in schools with $150 million HKD earmarked to retrofit schools to portion smaller meals on site. The Food Wise Campaign established in 2012 was expected to reduce 5–10% of the city's food waste by 2017/18 but figures continued to be on the rise. In terms of policy and legislation, this takes the form of MSW charging scheme, where quantity-based charging will be introduced to industries as well as private consumers (EB 2014). In terms of infrastructure, the Organic Waste Treatment Plant has been envisaged to employ anaerobic digestion technology to break down organic matter while producing biogas that can be converted to energy. The newly established OWTF in Siu Ho Wan is currently in operation and has a capacity of 200 tons a day and is currently in operation. If proven successful, the government plans a total of five to six for the city (Trading Economics 2020; EB 2014).

Conclusion

Like many other urban centers, both Singapore and Hong Kong face similar challenges with regard to their food security; however, they demonstrate different ways of response. On the whole, it could be observed that Singapore's development is driven by strong state policies, while Hong Kong's efforts are mainly led by civil society, advantages can be seen in both top-down and bottom-up approaches and insights from the comparison could help both cities move toward food security. The major vulnerability of Hong Kong and Singapore's food system is its heavy reliance on imports; and while self-sufficiency is not the goal, there is nevertheless a need to build resilience by anticipating the consequences brought about by volatilities in the global food supply chain. The immediate price hikes exhibited in the Hong Kong case study demonstrates how brittle the current systems are. Diversifying importing countries could alleviate some of the risks, and Singapore's partnership in the Jilin Food Zone offers an interesting model to consider for land-constrained cities; however, interruptions to transport and border logistics could still pose a risk as the most recent Corona virus outbreak demonstrates. In this regard, urban agriculture has been embraced by both cities as one of the ways to improve food availability. The Singapore Food Agency places its focus on increasing productivity, setting a goal of providing 30% of its nutritional needs by 2030 (Mahmud 2019). The strategy to increase yield is mainly through technology, using vertical farming for vegetables and protein sources such as fish. Despite similar farmed land area of 700 hectares, Singapore produces 38,000 tons—7% of their own consumption, 2.5 times more than Hong Kong's 14,900 tons, and 1.7% of its consumption (Szabo 2016). Clearly, a centralized drive from the Singapore government is much more effective in terms of increasing yield with little land resource input.

Urban agriculture in Hong Kong's governmental strategy took to quality over quantity, encouraging farmers to go premium and organic in the 2000s. This did answer the public's desire for more local produce in response to food scares and health concerns. Seasonal local produce has shorter, more transparent supply chains which alleviated the publics' distrust of goods from China. The increase in public demand saw an increase in land being farmed and production of market crops—the first time in forty years. The amount of land used for market crops went up from 408 to 419 hectares, and from 265 to 270 hectares for orchards. However, the increased availability of local produce does not necessarily answer to the needs of the food insecure as local, especially organic and premium produce are above market price, which does not answer to the requirements of food security. Personal allotments or other forms of informal urban farming on the other hand answer more directly to the needs of the food insecure as the distribution pathways are more direct (Opitz et al. 2016). While demographic groups in urban agriculture are context specific—it could be a lower income as well as middle-class neighborhood. But across class divide, it has been observed that the produce from the allotments go more directly to the growers and their immediate social network answering more to household needs.

Despite the low average household income spent on food, both Singapore and Hong Kong have a large income disparity and a significant number of its population live below means. While food insecurity does not appear as chronic hunger, malnutrition and undernutrition do affect low-income groups. In the case of Hong Kong, charities and community organizations actively fill the gap, using a combination of donation and surplus food rescue to provide for those in need, however this is not a sustainable solution in the framework of food security. It has been observed that there is an increased trend of premium supermarkets in both Hong Kong and Singapore, as supermarkets constitute a significant proportion of the food retail market, a presence of affordable food outlets should be maintained to avoid imbalance.

The chapter shows that Hong Kong and Singapore face similar challenges with regard to their food security despite their economic prowess. Heavy reliance on imports remains the number one vulnerability. Singapore's state-driven policies and investment in agritech have shown to be effective in terms of boosting yield and increasing self-sufficiency. The Singapore government's initiative to launch the Singapore Food Association (SFA) combining food-related activities, entrepreneurship and trade under one umbrella is a timely effort to boost its availability, access, utilization, and stability dimensions of food security. Hong Kong could benefit from a stronger governmental directive and a clearer goal to put food security on the agenda. On the other hand, Hong Kong's civic society is active, demonstrating a desire to have access to healthy, safe, and nutritious food. Small-scale urban agriculture has become popular which has the potential to fulfill both the availability and access requirements of food security needs of households. Social ventures and community partnerships offer an alternative model to market-driven solutions. Charities bridge the gap for those who are in need, often working within communities to provide food, but also other forms of support to the socially vulnerable. A combination of top-down and bottom-up initiatives would be most effective in terms of facing the challenges of food security. A stronger partnership between government, private small and medium enterprises and grassroots organizations could ensure the delivery of policy initiatives. A strong educational program could also alter attitudes toward food consumption in the long run, creating less pressure on our ecosystem.

Despite similar challenges yet diverse responses, there are multiple avenues in which both Singapore and Hong Kong can learn from each other's experience with regard to food security. While strong state policies for food security need to be accompanied with a vibrant grassroots food movement in Singapore, what Hong Kong needs is just the other way round.

Note: Md Saidul Islam and Daisy Tam claim equal authorship for this chapter.

References

AFCD (Agriculture, Fisheries, and Conservation Department). 2018. *Hong Kong Agriculture, Fisheries and Conservation Department: Departmental Annual Report 2017–2018*. Available online: https://www.afcd.gov.hk/misc/download/annualreport2018/eng/index.html. Accessed 12 January 2019.

Assem, A.H., M.E.R. Cavinato, A. Lindermer, and C.J. Lagerkvist. 2019. Urban Sprawl, Food Security and Agricultural Systems in Developing Countries: A Systemic Review of the Literature. *Cities* 94: 129–142.

AVA (Agri-Food and Veterinary Authority of Singapore). 2018. *Annual Report 2017/18*. Available online: https://www.sfa.gov.sg/files/annualreport/AR2017-18/. Accessed 30 November 2019.

AVA (Agri-Food and Veterinary Authority of Singapore). 2010. *AVA Vision, May 2010*. Singapore: Agri-Food and Veterinary Authority of Singapore.

AVA. 2012a. *Agrotechnology Parks*. Singapore: Agri-Food and Veterinary Authority of Singapore.

AVA. 2012b. *AVA Annual Report FY2011/12*. Singapore: Agri-Food and Veterinary Authority of Singapore.

Calicioglu, O., A. Flammini, S. Bracco, L. Bellù, and R. Sims. 2019. The Future Challenges of Food and Agriculture: An Integrated Analysis of Trends and Solutions. *Sustainability* 11: 222.

Cattacin, S., and A. Zimmer. 2016. Urban Governance and Social Innovations. In *Social Innovations in the Urban Context*, ed. T. Brandsen, S. Cattacin, A. Evers, and A. Zimmer, 21–44. Heidelberg: Springer.

Dwyer, D.J., P. Bishop, D.W. Drakakis-Smith, D.M.E. Evans, C.K. Leung, J.A. Prescott, E.G. Pryor, J.M. Wigglesworth, and L.S.K Wong. 1971. Introduction to Asian Urbanization. In *Asian Urbanization: A Hong Kong Casebook*, ed. D.J. Dwyer, 1st ed., 1–10. Hong Kong: Hong Kong University Press.

EB (Hong Kong SAR Environnent Bureau). 2014. *A Food Waste & Yard Waste Plan for Hong Kong 2014–2022*. Available online: https://www.enb.gov.hk/en/files/FoodWastePolicyEng.pdf. Accessed 16 March 2019.

Eco-Business. 2011. Singapore: Local Farming Promoted for Food Security. Available online at: https://www.eco-business.com/news/singapore-local-farming-promoted-for-food-security/. Accessed 10 April 2020.

Eisenberg, J. 2017. Islands of Agricultural Innovation—Singapore. *Medium*, November 27. Available online: https://medium.com/agri-futures/islands-of-agricultural-innovation-singapore-e9b68b7b31f0. Accessed 6 March 2019.

EIU (The Economist Intelligence Unit). 2018. *Global Food Security Index—2018 Overview*. Available online: https://foodsecurityindex.eiu.com/Index/Overview. Accessed 6 March 2018.

Ericksen, P.J. 2008. What Is the Vulnerability of a Food System to Global Environmental Change? *Ecology and Society* 13 (2): 14.

FAO. 2006. Food Security. *Policy Brief*, June 2006, Issue 2.

FAO. 2017. *The Future of Food and Agriculture: Trends and Challenges*. FAO: Rome, Italy.
FAO. 2018. *The State of Food Security and Nutrition in the World*. United Nations Food and Agriculture Organization.
Feng, Z. 2012. S'pore Lab Creates New Insect Resistant Rice. *The Straits Times* (Singapore). Available online: https://advance.lexis.com/document/?pdmfid=1516831&crid=61a911e7-3d2a-4260-8d3a-2549a89c4a40&pddocfullpath=%2Fshared%2Fdocument%2Fnews%2Furn%3AcontentItem%3A5734-RSV1-DYX4-02BB-00000-00&pddocid=urn%3AcontentItem%3A5734-RSV1-DYX4-02BB-00000-00&pdcontentcom. Accessed 16 February 2012.
FHB (Food and Health Bureau), and AFCD (Agriculture Fisheries and Conservation Department). 2014. *The New Agricultural Policy: Sustainable Agricultural Development in Hong Kong*, December.
GFSI (Global Food Security Index). 2019. Ranking and Trends. Economist Intelligence Unit. Available online at: https://foodsecurityindex.eiu.com/Index. Accessed 11 September 2020.
Haysom, G., and G. Tawodzera. 2018. Measurement Drives Diagnosis and Response: Gaps in Transferring Food Security Assessment to the Urban Scale. *Food Policy* 74 (2018): 117–125.
HKSAR (Hong Kong Special Administrative Region). 2016. *Census and Statistics Department Economic Analysis Division Household Expenditure Survey and the Rebasing of the Consumer Price Indices*. Hong Kong.
Ilieva, R.T., 2017. Urban Food Systems Strategies: A Promising Tool for Implementing the SDGs in Practice. *Sustainability* 9 (10): 1707. https://doi.org/10.3390/su9101707.
Koh, F. 2018. Singapore Tops Global Index for Food Security. *The Straits Times* (Singapore), October 18. Available online at: https://www.straitstimes.com/singapore/singapore-tops-global-index-for-food-security. Accessed 6 March 2019.
Lang, T., and D. Barling. 2012. Food Security and Food Sustainability: Reformulating the Debate. *The Geographical Journal* 178 (2012): 313–326.
LCS (Legislative Council Secretariat). 2019. *Agricultural Sector in Hong Kong*. Hong Kong.
Lee, A. 2012. Coming Soon—Vertical Fish Farming. *The Business Times Singapore*, March 6.
Mahmud, A.H. 2019. Singapore Aims to Produce 30% of Its Nutritional Needs by 2030, Up from Less Than 10%. *Channel News Asia (CNA)*, March 7. Available online: https://www.channelnewsasia.com/news/singapore/singapore-produce-30-own-food-up-from-10-nutritional-needs-11320426. Accessed 2 May 2019.
Malik, V.S., W.C. Willett, and F.B. Hu. 2013. Global Obesity: Trends, Risk Factors and Policy Implications. *Nature Reviews Endocrinology* 9: 13–27.

NGMR (Nomura Global Markets Research). 2017. *Asia Special Report*.

Opitz, I., R. Berges, A. Piorr, and T. Krikser. 2016. Contributing to Food Security in Urban Areas: Differences Between Urban Agriculture and Peri-Urban Agriculture in the Global North. *Agriculture and Human Values* 33: 341–358.

Poon, A. 2011a. *Hong Kong's Land Policy: A Recipe for Social Trouble*. Available online: https://carnegieendowment.org/hkjournal/PDF/2011_spring/3.pdf. Accessed 18 May 2018.

Poon, A. 2011b. *Land and the Ruling Class in Hong Kong*, 2nd ed. Singapore: Enrich Professional Publishing.

PSR (Poverty Situation Report). 2016. Hong Kong: Hong Kong SAR Census and Statistics Department. Available online: https://www.povertyrelief.gov.hk/eng/pdf/Hong_Kong_Poverty_Situation_Report_2016(2017.11.17).pdf. Accessed 9 May 2018.

PSR (Poverty Situation Report). 2018. Hong Kong Poverty Situation Report. Government of the Hong Kong Special Administrative Region. Available online: https://www.statistics.gov.hk/pub/B9XX0005E2018AN18E0100.pdf. Accessed 15 March 2021.

Shaw, J. (ed.). 2007. *World Food Security: A History Since 1945*, 1st ed. London, England: Palgrave Macmillan.

SHOPSinSG. 2020. FairPrice Finest Supermarkets in Singapore. Available online at: https://shopsinsg.com/fairprice-finest-supermarkets-in-singapore.html. Accessed 13 April 2020.

Sonnino, R. 2009. Feeding the City: Towards a New Research and Planning Agenda. *International Planning Studies* 14 (4): 425–435.

Sonnino, R. 2018. Feeding Urban Areas: Challenges and Opportunities. *Reference Module in Food Science* 1: 110–113. https://doi.org/10.1016/B978-0-08-100596-5.21986-0.

Syngenta Global. 2012. Available online: http://www.syngenta.com/global/corporate/SiteCollectionDocuments/pdf/publications/Our_industry_2012_EN_low_res_mail.pdf. Accessed 6 March 2013.

Szabo, S. 2016. Urbanisation and Food Insecurity Risks: Assessing the Role of Human Development. *Oxford Development Studies* 44 (1): 28–48.

Tan, A. 2015. Sino-Singapore Jilin Food Zone Harvests First Rice Crop for Sale in Singapore. *The Business Times*, October 29. https://www.businesstimes.com.sg/government-economy/sino-singapore-jilin-food-zone-harvests-first-rice-crop-for-sale-in-singapore. Accessed 13 April 2020.

Teng, P., and M. Escaler. 2011. Mind the Gap: Reducing Waste and Losses in the Food Supply Chain. Centre for Non-Traditional Security Studies, Singapore. Available online: https://www3.ntu.edu.sg/rsis/nts/HTML-Newsletter/Insight/pdf/NTS_Insight_jun_1101.pdf. Accessed 16 December 2017.

Teng, P., M. Caballero-Anthony, M. Escaler, and P. K. H. Khan. 2014. Ensuring Urban Food Security in ASEAN: Food Security Expert Group Meeting, Policy Brief. The RSIS Centre for Non-Traditional Security (NTS) Studies, 2014. Available online: https://www.rsis.edu.sg/wp-content/uploads/2014/07/PB100801_NTS_PB02.pdf. Accessed 30 November 2019.

Trading Economics. 2020. *Hong Kong - Food Imports (% of merchandise imports)*. Available online: https://tradingeconomics.com/hong-kong/food-imports-percent-of-merchandise-imports-wb-data.html Accessed 10 March 2021.

UNEP. 2013. *City-Level Decoupling: Urban Resource Flows and the Governance of Infrastructure Transitions*. http://www.resourcepanel.org/sites/default/files/documents/document/media/city-level_decoupling_summary_english.pdf. Accessed 20 January 2020.

United Nations. 2017. *United Nations Department of Economic and Social Affairs Population Division. World Population Prospects: The 2017 Revision*. Available online: https://population.un.org/wpp/Publications/Files/WPP2017_DataBooklet.pdf. Accessed 12 October 2018.

USDA. 2017. *Foreign Agricultural Services USDA GAIN Report*. No. SN7011, October 10.

Wang, Y.S. 2019. The Challenges and Strategies of Food Security Under Rapid Urbanization in China. *Sustainability* 11: 542.

Yau, Y.Y., B. Thibodeau, and C. Not. 2018. Impact of Cutting Meat Intake on Hidden Greenhouse Gas Emissions in an Import-Reliant City. *Environmental Research Letters* 13 (6): 1–11.

Zvolska, L., M. Lehner, Y.V. Palgan, O. Mont, and A. Plepys. 2019. Urban Sharing in Smart Cities: The Cases of Berlin and London. *Local Environment* 24 (7): 628–645.

Wong, Derek. 2018. New Stat Board Singapore Food Agency to Be Formed in April 2019; AVA Will Cease to Exist. *The Strait Times*, July 26. Available online at: https://www.straitstimes.com/singapore/environment/new-stat-board-singapore-food-agency-to-be-formed-in-april-2019-ava-will-cease. Accessed 13 April 2020.

CHAPTER 8

China and India's Involvement in Land and Water Grabs

With Teng Kuan Yung and Yuvaranjini D/O Mathiazakan.

Introduction

The attention toward land and water grabbing resurfaced on the international stage largely because of the spike in global food prices from 2007 to 2008. Initially, the global land and water grabs discourse highlighted new investments in farmland abroad by food-importing countries that were rich in capital but had limited land and water resources, such as the Gulf States, and by countries with large populations, like China, India, and South Korea. These investments were targeted at developing countries with abundant resources and lower production costs in countries like Madagascar and Ethiopia. These international investments in land and water resources were commonly framed as a solution to food security (IFFRI 2009).

Yet, over the years, it has become apparent that the framing of land and water grabs can also be understood differently when viewed in the lens of political economy (The Transnational Institute 2013). Through this lens, land and water grabs can be thought of as a form of "control grabbing," where influential actors, such as powerful states and organizations, wield power to control and benefit from these resources (Borras et al. 2012;

M. S. Islam and E. Kieu, *Climate Change and Food Security in Asia Pacific*, International Political Economy Series,
https://doi.org/10.1007/978-3-030-70753-8_8

Theesfeld 2018; Cotula et al. 2009). This framing of land and water grabbing, however, goes beyond the narrow definition of "control grabbing" as being "illegal appropriation," as the means by which contemporary actors secure these resources often involve legal, but illegitimate dynamics (Franco et al. 2014).

As there are varying perspectives on land and water grabbing, it is important to unpack and comprehensively examine its implications in today's context. In this chapter, we will explore global trends in land and water grabs, and the positive as well as negative effects of this phenomenon. As China and India are two major players of land and water grabbing around the world (Rulli et al. 2013), this chapter seeks to explore the involvement and consequences of both countries' involvement in foreign lands.

Land and Water Grabbing

Water Grabbing

Water grabbing is the distribution of water resources that is disproportionately allocated among the different groups or players. Often, influential state and organizational actors gain and maintain access over a bigger portion of valuable water resources for their own benefits. Such actions come at the expense of the livelihood of local communities that may depend on these resources and ecosystems. These influential actors also have the power to decide how, why, and where these resources should be used, now and in the future (Franco et al. 2014). While water resources have always been contested in water conflicts and water wars, contemporary water grabbing is differentiated by its advanced and globalized processes for appropriating resources. This process of appropriation undergoes a process of commodification, privatization, and large-scale capital accumulation. Grabbed water has been used for various activities globally, across domains of food, energy, mineral, and climate, including large-scale agriculture, biofuel projects, hydropower schemes, and even the privatization of water for drinking and sanitation (Mehta et al. 2012; Franco et al. 2013).

In addition to the various uses of grabbed water, there are also hydrological complexities in global water grabs that potential acquirers will take advantage of. The legal complexities enables acquirers the means to delegitimize claims and successfully grab resources. Some of these technicalities involves the ability to distinguish groundwater from surface water, and "blue" water (irrigation water) from "green" water (rainwater). There are also ecological complexities involved in determining the scale of water grabs due to the vast array and span of water systems. Furthermore, legal complexities are present due to ambiguous administrative boundaries and jurisdictions, encompassing a lack of clarity and in global property regimes including commons, customary, informal, and private tenure systems (The Transnational Institute 2014).

While some engage in delegitimization through claims, others engage in water grabs either through violent appropriation that dispossess its previous users, or through market mechanisms of privatization and monetization. While this may be enabling for grabbers, it mostly makes it difficult for local users to defend their claims over these resources. For instance, in Ghana, due to poor governance systems, investors took over water resources for biofuel plantations, dispossessing and disregarding its previous local users (Schoneveld et al. 2011). On a whole, water grabbing occurs globally across various contexts and forms, and frequently entails dispossession and ecological destruction.

Land Grabbing

Land grabbing involves the acquisition and appropriation of large plots of land. The process of land grabbing is done through the purchasing or leasing of land by individuals, governments, and businesses. This comprises "virtual" land grabs, where land remains dormant, and is acquired mainly to appropriate subsidies and get bank loans, using land permits as collateral, or increasing land value speculations; and "real" land grabs, where the land is physically exploited for agriculture, biofuel projects, and other industrial purposes (World Bank 2010; McCarthy et al. 2012). The phenomenon of land grabbing has been a long-term strategy by governments and corporations for food and energy security by acquiring inexpensive and productive agricultural land in a foreign country, often as a result of enhanced pressure on natural resources, due to rising food demands, population expansion, economic growth, increased biofuel production, contamination, and climate change (Chen et al. 2018). This is especially prominent in the regions of Latin America, Asia, and Africa where land is generally affordable, abundant, and arable too (Perrone 2017).

Land grabs are ultimately driven by capital accumulation, where the desire for profit affects the change of meanings, uses, and systems of management of land and its associated resources. Land grabs have produced a global shift in land use, from small-scale subsistence agriculture to large-scale, capital-intensive, resource depleting industrial monocultures, material extraction, and hydropower generation (White et al. 2012). Globally, land grabbing has caused a dramatic increase in transnational land deals since 2005, peaking in 2009, with Africa as the main target of the land rush accounting for 62% of 1217 project deals (Anseeuw et al. 2012). Today, land grabbing occurs across diverse agroecological contexts, including peri-urban corridors, forested uplands, floodplains, and rural outposts, and across diverse land rights regimes, such as private, public, and community domains and its legitimacy. Land grabbing also involves relocation, that may even involve intimidation and violence, depending on the varying political conditions in which it takes place.

The Nexus of Land and Water Grabs

Global land and water grabs are an aspect of broader changing patterns of control over land, labor, and markets (Huggins 2014). Agricultural land and freshwater flows tend to flow from resource-rich and less developed economies, such as India and Madagascar, to resource-poor and more developed economies, like the United Kingdom, EU, and so on (Chen et al. 2018). Regardless of resource endowment, all economies partake in global supply networks as exporters and importers of essential goods. The nature of land and water trade agreements is typically based on the nations' social-economic and environmental profiles. Failure to fulfil contracts and negotiate deals was found to occur more frequently to countries with larger territories and populations. For instance, Petrescu et al. (2020) found that China and India had higher numbers of intended and failed contracts with a higher proportion of contracts involving smaller land sizes.

The appropriation of land resources and water grabbing are deeply intertwined. As of 2010, about 40% of global food production was supported by 19% of irrigated agricultural areas (Molden and Fraiture 2010). Approximately 60% of total grabbed water was appropriated through land grabbing, demonstrating the close association between both land and water grabbing (Rulli et al. 2013). For example, the hydropower development along the Mekong River involved massive expulsion of people (Provost 2011). Likewise, in Mali and Sudan, investors have been granted unrestricted access to water that enables investors the ability to seek agricultural land that also has access to water for production (The Transnational Institute 2014).

Land and water grabs are largely driven by the emergence of new agroindustrial complexes and global commodity value chains (The Transnational Institute 2014). This was demonstrated with the rise of "flex crops" like soya, corn, and oil palm, which serve several purposes including feed, food, fuel, and industrial needs (Borras et al. 2012). Land and water grabs have been triggered by changing global food markets and agricultural production of crop monocultures that use up to ten times more water than biodiverse agricultural systems. Furthermore, recent developments with the rise in agrofuels and the need for renewable energy sources requires huge amounts of water that increases the constraints faced by competing demands. Compounding the situation, the increasing demands for consumer goods and technologies have spurred a growing need for raw materials. To meet such demands, industries have developed new technologies like hydraulic fracturing that may increase the incidences of land and water grabs by large corporations. The market-based management of water through privatization of water systems and services inhibits the access for marginalized groups in developing countries, leading to contestation over these resources. This is amplified with the financialization of water, including utilities and infrastructure, jeopardizing community rights, and access to water resources.

The Impact of Land and Water Grabbing

Typically, foreign-based land and water investments in developing countries were expected to promote rural development through modernization, diversification of agriculture, and the creation of job opportunities (Schoneveld et al. 2011). Hence, developing countries willingly participate in land and water grabs as these new jobs and investments also boost technological advances (Franco and Borras 2019). Furthermore, the logistical and legal benefits of greater land availability, permissive legislation, and lower land prices for land grabbing in Africa. Due to the host of benefits provided, acquiring land in certain countries were more attractive than acquiring land within one's home country. Other economic benefits of land grabbing included carbon trade opportunities, lower water cost of crop production, and enhanced resilience of food production by diversifying regions to rely on for food imports (Ahmed 2014; Lyons and Westoby 2014). Grabbed water, consisting of both green and blue water, was also found to be sufficient to improve food security and abate malnourishment (Rulli et al. 2013).

However, under the guise of enhancing these positive spillover effects of land grabs in developing countries and in the name of global food security, global institutions like the World Bank and Food and Agriculture Organization have been exploiting climate change politics to trigger transnational land and water grabs (World Bank 2010; Franco and Borras 2019). It has been posited that such deals lack transparency and took place without the consultation of locals, adequate compensation, and consideration for jobs and the environment. Some experts even categorized land grabbing as a new type of colonialism (Perrone 2017).

Other unintended effects of irrigating grabbed land include water stress, poor water quality, deforestation, land degradation, and smallholder agriculture losing access to land and water (Rulli et al. 2013; Lyons and Westoby 2014). Water grabbing can have harmful environmental effects as drainage basins are made unsustainable by the overuse of limited water. Land and water grabs especially causes social unrest as locals are dispossessed and displaced, where they become increasingly dependent on food aid and international subsidies due to a loss of livelihood (Rulli et al. 2013; Lyons and Westoby 2014). Existing investment contracts and urban agendas do not offer the tools to deal with rural elements, which is essential to address the effects of displacement and livelihood changes in new types of rural–urban landscapes (Zoomers et al. 2017).

World's Top Grabbers: China and India

China

As of 2013, China grabbed 34.116×10^5 hectares of agricultural land which accounts for 7.272% of total global grabbed land but effectively increasing China's cultivated land by 32.192%. This was associated with a gross irrigation of $5.4176\ 10^9\ m^3$, consisting predominantly of grabbed green water (Rulli et al. 2013). Despite its well-developed irrigation systems, China needed to grab land because in-country transfers of water from water-rich south to northern China costs more than investing in land grabbing in Africa, Mongolia, and other developing countries (Ananthaswamy 2011). As such, China remains the largest importer of agricultural land resource, and one of the top importers of freshwater resource at 73 billion m^3, highlighting the significance of its position in global resources flows (Chen et al. 2018).

China's food security is being threatened as China possesses only a third of the global average arable land per capita and is facing shrinking arable lands and the need to support one of the largest populations alongside increasing land urbanization (World Bank 2009). To ensure improved levels of food security, China implemented a "red line" on arable land area to be at least 120 million hectares in the 1990s (The Ministry of Land and Resources of the People's Republic of China 2016). China exported 27.18 million hectares of embodied arable land to Japan, the United States, and some parts of EU, who were consumption-oriented. As a production-oriented importer, China also imported 48.35 million hectares of land from Myanmar, Australia, Russia, and some African economies, emphasizing its status as the world's largest producer. Overall, large amounts of arable land are transferred with low utilization efficiencies, as transfers to economically developed countries (Germany, France, the United Kingdom, Sweden, Austria, New Zealand) increased land use pressure (Han and Chen 2018). Apart from large-scale land grabs in Africa, China also participates in small-scale land acquisitions. These smaller land grabs are done internationally, such as Northern Laos, and in local regions like the Guangxi province, where local villagers engage in "intimate land grabbing" (Friis and Nielsen 2016; Xu 2018).

India

As of 2013, India had grabbed 12.117×10^5 hectares of agricultural land, accounting for 2.583% of total global grabbed land, but resulting in the increase in their cultivated land by only 0.714%. This was associated with a gross irrigation of $22.1695\ 10^9\ m^3$, consisting of blue water and slightly less green water (Rulli et al. 2013). India also remains one of the top exporters, with an outflow of 94 billion m^3 of freshwater resources (Chen et al. 2018). India's growth in demands is expected to put pressure on their agricultural land and increase world biomass extraction by 3% (Singh 2010). Hence, to meet growing food and energy demands, India has largely targeted land grabbing from Ethiopia, which has optimal climate conditions, fertile land, and necessary water resources (Hules and Singh 2017; Teklemariam et al. 2017). Land grabbing within India is also prevalent, creating new layers of rural poor, as evident with Setipool slum in east Sikkim, despite it being a resource-poor state (Chettri 2020). These corporate land grabs, masked under state-led development policies, create different forms of exclusions to the locals and new socio-spatial changes in addition to environmental degradation too.

Selected Cases of Land Grab

India's Land Grab in Ethiopia

Since the 2007–2008 global financial and food crisis, instances of land grabbing have increased as governments and corporations sought to outsource their production of food and fuels. Back then, as an emerging economy, India invested heavily in farmlands in order to sustain their burgeoning population and rapidly increasing energy demands. One country that India looked toward was Ethiopia, a landlocked country in East Africa.

In Ethiopia, the government implemented an Agricultural Development-Led Industrialization (ADLI) strategy in order to attract foreign investors into agriculture as the agricultural sector plays a crucial role in Ethiopia's economy—with the industry accounting for 50% of the nation's GDP and 60% of its exports. Overall, the government tried to utilize foreign direct investments into agriculture to solve their food shortage issues while modernizing their agricultural sector as a whole. To attract investors, they offered low cost land acquisition opportunities and labor with tax exemptions. These lands boasted key benefits such as strategic locations, ease of export opportunities, and favorable climate conditions. With long-established trade and diplomatic relations with India, the Ethiopian Ministry of Agriculture as of 2015 revealed that India is the biggest foreign investor in Ethiopian farmland with a total acquisition of 300,715 hectares of land. To put the figure into context, only 553,503 hectares of farmland had been given by Ethiopia to foreign investors at that point in time. India accounted for 13 of 39 deals, with their largest land acquisitions conducted by Karuturi Agro Products PLC (111,700 ha), in Oromia (11,700 ha) and Gambella (100,000 ha). Other firms' land acquisitions averaged about 17,000 hectares of land (Hules and Singh 2017).

About 89% of all Indian agricultural projects are reported to be for food production, with Indian companies growing oilseeds, pulses, cotton, and rice, with 30–40% of these produce exported back to India or regional markets (Cotula et al. 2009; Rowden 2011; Shepard and Anuradha 2009; Yassin 2010). Other products include cereals, maize, wheat, sugar, soybeans, tea, floriculture, and a minority of other "flex crops" that have multiple uses including industrial production. Yet, it is unlikely that these land acquisitions and food production capabilities will address India's food security problems. For instance, Indian companies like Karuturi Agro Products PLC only cultivates 15% of their acquired land in Ethiopia thereby producing low yields and productivity. Furthermore, Ethiopia face greater dangers with foreign land grabs because it is a country with scarce food resources, and foreign investors are more likley to be incentivized to export their crops for more profits as opposed to selling the produce locally. This creates a harsh cycle of food insecurity in Ethiopia and intensifies the country's dependence on international groups for food aid. Observers note that Ethiopia benefits the least from India's land investments as the latter does not contribute in terms of infrastructural development, employment opportunities for locals nor do they engage in the transfer of technology and expertise (Hules and Singh 2017).

State-Mediated Land Grabs in India

Apart from transnational land grabs, India engages in land grabs within the country. These grabs are typically state-mediated and enacted through private corporations. One of the more prominent land grabs involves local dispossession in Rajasthan, due to one of the largest Special Economic Zone (SEZ), the Mahindra World City (MWC) which is primarily focused on IT services (Levien 2018; Singh 2019). This SEZ alone required 3000 acres (approximately 1214.06 ha) of both private and public land to be grabbed, which was predominantly sought from the village of Rajpura (Singh 2019).

To understand contemporary situations of dispossessions, David Harvey's concept of accumulation highlights that neoliberal capitalism centralizes wealth and power in the hands of a few by dispossessing public and private entities that result asymmetrical distribution of resources related to over-accumulation vis-à-vis land alienation (Harvey 2003). However, Levien (2018) argues against this concept of "new imperialism," and instead posits a concept of "regimes of dispossession". The concept of regimes of dispossession suggests that the influence of state forces under different regimes serve different phases of capitalist development that creates systematic changes in economic and social relations (Levien 2018; Singh 2019).

As exemplified with the case of Rajpura, the government used a market-based compensation system that involved giving 25% of the original dispossessed land near the SEZ (Levien 2018). However, due to "differentiation by speculation" some families with lower socioeconomic status were forced to sell their land, while others were able to wait to speculate on the added land value and profit from land commodification. Furthermore, as the SEZ did not generate a productive link with Rajpura, local villagers were excluded from the IT economy and new jobs created were filled by migrant workers instead. This shows that only their land was needed, and their labor was not (Li 2011). Instead, the villagers from Rajpura were contained into a "disinvested urbanizing village on the margins of a 'world city', a potential 'slum' in the making" (Levien 2018: 162).

Hence, apart from the destruction of agricultural livelihood and marginalization of rural labor, Levien (2018) also delineates the unevenness of infrastructure provision and the consequences of land value speculation on social inequality and village conflicts in Rajpura. While the Rajpura situation clearly demonstrates the effects of a state-mediated land grabs in India, this is also replicated in other regions. The Setipool slum in east Sikkim, is another example where a resource-poor state had lands systematically acquired by corporations under the influence of state-led development policies (Chettri 2020). Hence, apart from environmental degradation, these cases show how the rural poor are marginalized by the state's position in land grabbing locally.

China's Land Grab in Africa

In Africa, agriculture is touted as one of the key industries as the majority of the continent's population and poor depend on it. With an excessive amount of uncultivated and affordable land at their disposal, Africa is an attractive location for many international businesses looking for investment opportunities in agriculture. Furthermore, the continent is home to about 60% of the globe's arable land. It has been estimated that since 2008, between 20 and 100 million hectares of land have been leased by foreign investors. Among them is China, who have been accused of engaging in land grabs in Africa and exploiting the continent's agricultural industry (Sy 2015; Woodhouse 2012).

Since the 2007–2008 financial crisis, China's land acquisition in Africa increased exponentially. Such investments were expected to bring with them many positives for Africa—such as the creation of jobs for locals and transferring of technology and skills. In particular, rural areas will benefit from the improved infrastructure brought about by foreign investments to support newly established businesses. However, serious concerns have been raised over issues such as corruption, displacement of local communities, and even the negative connotations of colonialization. Foreign involvement in sovereign lands may experience pertinent dangers where foreign investors prioritized short-term profits at the expense of long-term environmental and economic sustainability. In some instances, local rights were neglected, as affluent investors wield considerable power over the small farmers (Sy 2015). Despite this, academics with an in-depth knowledge of China–Africa policies argued that China has a long-term interest in the development of Africa's infrastructure, primarily rooted on the premise that Africa's development will continue to increase China's yields in the future (Saunders 2010).

However, a research study published by Meine Pieter van Dijk (2016) contradicted claims that China is a major land acquisition player in Africa. The data revealed that as of 2013, China was ranked 19th in terms of land acquisition in Africa at 0.16 million hectares. Countries that were heavily involved in land grabbing in Africa included the UAE (1.9 million hectares), the United Kingdom (1.5 million hectares), and the United States (1.4 million hectares). As a whole, the differing sentiments is due to the fact that it is difficult to get an accurate evaluation of Chinese investments and land grab in Africa because of a lack of official data. Critics also warn that the facts and figures that are published might not be entirely reliable due to the lack of transparency through the use of different terminologies and classifications in the data (Conti 2017). Despite the inconclusive efficacy of data, it is still commonly accepted that China holds a significant position in the global flow of resources, as one of largest importer of agricultural land and accounts for 7.272% of total global grabbed land across many regions (Rulli et al. 2013; Chen et al. 2018).

China's Small-Scale Land Acquisitions in Northern Laos: Chinese Banana Investments

Laos has a reputation for being a resource-rich country with an abundance of fertile and free land. However, Laos have been earmarked by foreign investors for massive land grabs because of the government's keen interest in seeking foreign direct investments coupled with relatively weak land regulations. The Government of Laos's national strategy of "Turning land into capital" led to them yielding huge areas of land to local and foreign investors over the past few decades. This particular case highlights how seemingly small-scale and short-term contractual land grabs can still lead to hugely detrimental consequences—such as the alienation of land from local communities. This is in part due to the aggressive acquisition strategies implemented by investors as well as the swift land use conversion and corresponding cultivation practices.

Commercial banana plantations first gained traction in 2008 at the Muang Long district, when small-scale Chinese businesses rented land to grow bananas for mainland China. As compared to Laos which boasted cheap and high-quality lands that enjoyed decent climate, China was not an ideal location to grow bananas due to the "Panama disease" and typhoon risk among other reasons. As of 2014, a total of 820.75 hectares of land were used as banana plantations at the Muang Long district, with each plantation differing in size from as small as 1 hectare to around 62 hectares. However, one problem faced by the Muang Long District Agricultural and Forestry Office (DAFO) was that 3 out of the 13 legally registered companies acted as the middlemen for other investors, and were unregistered. As a result of this practice, many of these investors remain unknown, with some even using the land for their plantations without prior approval from the relevant authorities (Friis and Nielsen 2016).

One of these companies was the LFA company, a joint venture owned by 5 Chinese shareholders of mixed ethnicity. Utilizing their ethnic composition and personal relations, they engaged middlemen to help them convince local households within the Muang Long and Muang Sing districts to lease their land to the LFA. In total, the LFA managed to secure a total of 35 hectares of land, and this was later sold in 2015 to another group of Chinese investors. However, this sale was negotiated directly between the two Chinese companies, with the villagers and local authorities kept out of the loop. This was the same case for

XG company, who took advantage of their local connections to coerce local villagers to grant their land for banana plantation purposes. After a year of cultivation, XG company sold their plantation without consulting any of the district authorities and local community. In the aftermath of these cases, the villagers described the rapid land use change (from paddy rice fields to banana plantations) and the associated land degradation in the form of chemical population as two of the most negative impacts the plantations have had on their community. However, there were a host of other concerns related to the decline in rice production, destruction of traditional plot borders, and land restoration concerns (Friis and Nielsen 2016). In a nutshell, this case exemplifies how land grabbing on a small scale by foreign businesses can involve lasting ramifications on local communities.

Intimate Land Grabbing in the Industrial Tree Plantation Sector in Guangxi, China

As mentioned, prior literature mostly focuses on large-scale land grabbing by foreign and corporate organizations. However, the impacts of small-scale land acquisitions are equally significant as land grabs on a macroscale. In certain cases, land grabs by local actors have devastating consequences on local communities. In his paper, Xu (2018) argues that the crux of any land grab should not focus on its scale or the identity of the grabbers. Instead, land grabs should be evaluated based on its benefits, consequences, and distribution of cost among the stakeholders involved. Xu (2018) provide insights to the industrial tree plantation (ITP) sector in Guangxi, China and introduces the concept of "intimate land grabbing." In the Guangxi province of China, ITP has expanded rapidly and has become one of the most prolific sectors as it meets the demand for both food and biofuel. Guangxi is the top area for eucalyptus in China, producing commodities destined for Chinese domestic consumption, with domestic (timber, board, or furniture products from state-owned farms) and overseas (paper products by Finland's Stora Enso and Indonesia's Asia Pulp & Paper) investments. The prominence of ITP is stimulated by the crop boom, a phenomenon whereby rapid and extensive expansion of a sector is stimulated by increased demand for a crop through market incentives or favorable government policies (Hall et al. 2011). Thus, with the emergence of ITP as a booming sector in Southern China, more villagers in Guangxi have gained control over land areas from local or neighboring village collectives. As a result, these villagers benefit by becoming owners of eucalyptus tree plantations themselves through the acquisition of land which was originally owned and used by other villages. The term "intimate land grabbing" is used as these new landowners are deriving individual financial benefits at the expense of their own neighbors and kin.

When it comes to land grabbing, the "external vs internal" dichotomy is often raised. Outside actors such as foreign countries and corporations are often criticized for land grabbing as they are deemed to have no interest in local development nor care about the potential social and environmental repercussions their actions may cause. More often than not, they are also the sole stakeholders to benefit from the whole process (De Schutter 2011). However, Oya (2013) contends that there is a lack of evidence to suggest that the actions of local grabbers are less harmful or provide certain benefits for local development. We highlight that rather than focusing on discourse surrounding identity, the more pertinent concern is the power asymmetry between the land acquirer and targeted landowners. In fact, local actors may possess greater power than their foreign counterparts. This is because local investors are able to utilize their social bonds to both seek and maintain legitimacy over their land control activities. For example, when taking intimate relations into account, it can be difficult for villagers to evict or impose rental at market prices on their land when it comes to their own community. Furthermore, external actors often face high costs associated with the maintenance of land and production processes—issues that local actors are spared due to the lack of resistance from affected villagers, even though they have proven to be just as harmful to local communities and the environment. This demonstrates that villagers are not always the "victims" and "resistors," but sometimes grabbers themselves, using loans and land leases to grab land within China itself.

When evaluating the consequences of land grabs, it is vital to examine the plethora of social, economic and environmental impacts on various stakeholders. Although intimate land grabs occur on a relatively smaller scale, the changes in land control and land use affects local communities with their impacts not any less significant as bigger foreign corporations (Xu 2018). Firstly, when land ownership is transferred from village collectives to individual villagers, the former loses a portion of their original income source while also foregoing the possibility of expanding their livelihoods through the use of the plot of land for themselves. This issue is further exacerbated when these villagers are unable to find employment elsewhere. Furthermore, unlike in the case of external actors who solely depend on wage labor, local actors are guilty of exploiting family and kin for their labor. Secondly, there are environmental consequences as these plots of land are mainly used to grow eucalyptus trees. This affects adjacent lands as the ecological environment changes with factors such hydrologics, nutrition, and sunshine all playing a role in adversely influencing other villagers' farming yield. Moreover, local actors are also prone to using chemicals to grow their crops more densely and effectively. While their overall yield may be higher, the resulting repercussions may bring about to greater environmental destruction. However, these intimate land grabbers are able to get away with it as unlike external actors, they do not have to abide by environmental assessments from international non-governmental organizations (NGOs) (Oya 2013; Xu 2018).

Overall, the paper by Xu (2018) highlights the significance of the complex dynamics of social relations when it comes to land acquisitions. It also contributes to the discourse of global land grabbing, and provides a more comprehensive picture of the topic through the analysis of small-scale land acquisitions in a localized context. This also highlights the importance of understanding land grabs by its de facto consequences rather than scale or ownership.

China and India's Water Grab in the Himalayas

While water grabs typically occur as a part of land grabs, in 2013, India and China were involved in a massive "water grab" war that threatened the ecology of the Himalayas. Countries such as Pakistan, Bhutan, and Nepal were also engaged in this regional war as each of them sought new avenues to power their respective economies. By and large, it was estimated that over 400 hydroelectric schemes were planned across the Himalayas mountain region, causing the anticipation of colossal damage to the environment. China had intentions to build 100 dams along major rivers in Tibet, with another 60 planned along the Mekong river. Experts projected that with the construction of all these dams, China was on course to emerge as a water resource powerhouse as they would have control of water for almost 40% of the entire world population (Vidal 2013; Dell'Angelo et al. 2017).

Besides the implications brought about from dam constructions, it is estimated that about 150,000–200,000 mountain glaciers located in the vast Tibetan plateau had been shrinking at a speed of approximately 10 meters per year due to a new threat and consumer demand of "glacier water" (Xingmin 2014). China, especially, saw an emergence of Glacier mineral water companies, with 28 new companies licensed to produce bottle water from Tibet in 2014 (Liu 2015). These companies have extracted water from the glacier tongue itself, and even started building plants at higher altitudes, with one company, Qomolangma Glacier Water company, bottling water from a national reserve 80 km from Everest base camp (Liu 2015). Apart from disturbing these fragile environments, depleting resources, and influencing microclimate of the glacier ecosystem, ecological issues emerged, due to transportation, energy consumption, discharge, and treatment of wastewater arising from these plantations.

Furthermore, in light of the melting glaciers across the globe due to global warming, China's rampant dam construction plans in Tibet threatens the livelihood of hundreds of million people who rely on the Yangtze, Ganges, and Yellow rivers. This demonstrates that the extraction of glacier waters jeopardizes the quality of land and water use patterns in downstream areas, negatively impacting industries, agriculture, and urban life (Xingmin 2014). With over 90% of the water runoff from the aforementioned rivers flowing downstream into countries like India, Nepal, Thailand, and Bhutan, China's burgeoning political control of the Tibetan land and waterscapes were even predicted to escalate into deepening water wars within the region (Coca 2017). Notwithstanding, China is also investing and constructing huge dams in countries such as Burma, Pakistan, and Laos (Vidal 2013).

The "water grab" war between these two major players had resulted in a host of negative consequences. First and foremost, the overbuilding of dams have led to environmentalists becoming fearful about the increased instances of flooding and vulnerability to earthquakes. Secondly, tens of millions of people have been displaced from their communities due to the aggressive land acquisitions and dam-building efforts at Narmada and Three Gorges. Regional political tensions have also been on the rise as a result of the building of dams, with protest movements occurring in Tibet and certain India states such as Himachal, Sikkim, and Assam (Vidal 2013).

Reactions to Grabbing Involving India and China

As land grabs generally take on a top-down approach, with influential state or corporate actors acquiring land and dispossessing its previous users, such approaches inevitably has receives political reactions (Hall et al. 2015). These responses go beyond everyday resistance to include organized reactions which demand better terms incorporated into land deals. These demands range from the improvement of compensation for expulsion, inclusion in land deals as workers or contract farmers, and counter-mobilizations against land deal resisters. Some of these organized initiatives involving local and transnational alliances, have been successful, while others have not.

Often, pushback from land and water grabs come in the form of confrontation between affected stakeholders and the state through organized national mobilizations. To illustrate, agrarian movements in the Philippines in 2006–2007 resulted in the cancelation of investment agreements regarding the allocation of 1.4 million hectares of land to China (Hall et al. 2015). Such stakeholder–state conflict may also be demonstrated through individual protests directed at the state bureaucracy, which can also be referred to as "everyday forms of peasant politics," and is the most conventional form of land conflict in contemporary China itself. Chinese land conflicts also display "rightful resistance" where protests are individual, unorganized but noisy and overt (O'Brien and Li 2006). These may be gaining traction in places outside China, such as Vietnam which are moving beyond covert resistance, that is practiced in other countries like Ethiopia, Russia, and Ukraine (Visser et al. 2012; Kerkvliet 2014; Mamonova 2015; Moreda 2015).

Besides confrontation, in efforts to manage the effects of land grabs, there have been instances of mutual collaboration of relevant stakeholders as well as indirect resistance. In Laos for instance, the Khmu community was able to stall the planned plantation of rubber trees on half their territory by a Chinese company by working with state structures. Some of these acts of resistance include a variety of tools such as "anonymous acts of sabotage, refusal to work for the company, identification of powerful allies in the government and civil society, and recourse to law and state institutions" (McAllister 2015: 817). Meanwhile in India, land grabs were reverted and canceled due to the changes in the State's orientation. In the Indian state of Goa, a cross-class, cross-society coalition brought about the cancelation of 15 SEZs, some of which were in the midst of developing the land (Sampat 2015). Hence, states are also contested sites where land grabs may not always be successful for land acquirers.

Yet, a coalition may not always form due to divisions within farming communities based on classes and castes. These divisions impact their hostility toward dispossession as they stand to gain differently from expectations regarding land valuations (Levien 2018). Furthermore, the Indian government's market-based compensation plot system also worsens solidarities within the same castes and families, indirectly shaping resistance into a personal and individual fight, rather than villager–state conflict. Hence, land transfers are not as peaceful as current literature portrays it to be, with the various forms of resistance from locals and international allies affecting the success of land grabs.

Contract Farming—An Alternative to Land Grabbing?

With the proliferation of land grabs happening around the globe, contract farming (CF) was identified as an important form of land control and an inclusive alternative for smallholders to outright land acquisition by agribusiness capital. CF is a practice that has been around for decades and can be described as a way of organizing agricultural production. According to Shepherd (2013) from the Technical Centre for Agricultural and Rural Cooperation (ACP-EU), it is defined as such: "Contract farming is agricultural production carried out according to an agreement between farmers and a buyer, which places conditions on the production and marketing of the commodity" (p. 1). When it comes to CF, the buyer has a stake in how, where, and when crops are produced and harvested. The buyer is able to specify anything from the quantity needed, quality required, price offered, and expectations regarding delivery. Crucially, CF also allows farmers (and smallholders in general) to retain the ownership of their land while striving to meet the needs of corporate agribusinesses.

Potato Farming in Maharashtra, India

In the state of Maharashtra, several factors such as the restrictions implemented on foreign land ownership, land ownership ceilings and political aversion toward large-scale corporate farming have resulted in CF playing a key role in the land control discourse. The restriction in possession of agricultural land (both through sale and lease) by the 1961 Agricultural Lands Act led to the emergence of CF as an attractive alternative for corporate businesses to maintain some form of control over their productive land base. Although little research has been done to understand how CF influences patterns of agrarian change in India, Vicol (2017) argues that despite some individual households showing improvements in their livelihoods in part due to the CF schemes, others are not as fortunate. In particular, he suggested that CF agreements further exacerbate issues of inequality, with the unequal power relations between corporations and individual farmers playing a huge role. While much of the financial benefits are gained by businesses, farmers are left vulnerable as they suffer the loss of autonomy over the land use and rely on corporations for income and to sustain their livelihoods. As with all practices, CF has its own fair share of advantages and disadvantages.

Advantages of Contract Farming

CF can be an attractive alternative for several reasons. Firstly, while companies may prefer to have control over large plantations, finding one that is suitable and available is not a straightforward task. It may also be politically sensitive and reputation-damaging for foreign companies to simply grab huge chunks of land from another country. Secondly, when businesses diversify their production across several smaller plots of land, they spread the risks of pests, diseases, and natural phenomena such as drought or flooring that may be detrimental to crop yield. Certain types of crops such as tobacco and horticultural produce also thrive on smaller plots of land and are ideal for smallholder production. Moreover, businesses are able to provide smallholders with the relevant materials, extension advice, and scheduling to ensure they obtain their supplies at the appropriate times, and in the right amount and quality. One of the most important reasons for engaging in CF is that businesses are able to ensure all "organic" and "fairtrade" products are in compliance with their specific certification requirements (Shepherd 2013). CF can also be beneficial for farmers as they are guaranteed that the company who negotiated the contract with them will buy the crops and products that are produced on their land.

Disadvantages of Contract Farming

While CF has its advantages, it also has its shortfalls. One major disadvantage of this arrangement is that businesses have to trust that the farmers contracted would honor their side of the bargain. Unfortunately, more discreditable farmers have been known to use their inputs for other crops, as well as to sell their produce to different companies. The costs incurred for businesses can also be extremely hefty if contract farming agreements were to break down. For example, if farmers are unable to meet the production demand of companies, these companies in turn will not be able to meet the contracts they have with their own buyers. Bear in mind that businesses may also have to spend a lump sum of money on facilities, inputs, and services for farmers to utilize (Shepherd 2013).

Vicol (2017) also argues that contract farming can be problematic for small shareholders and landowners. He suggests that CF can be a method for businesses to maintain control over small plots of land while exploiting cheap labor. Farmers may also become overly dependent on corporations for income, market access opportunities and inputs. Evidence also suggests that CF agreements have resulted in detrimental consequences on smallholder communities that are equivalent to large-scale land acquisitions. Some examples include the loss of control and decision-making with regard to the plot of land, eventual outright loss of land, and growing inequality between the local elites and farmers.

Conclusion

The global financial crisis between 2007 and 2008 resulted in the sharp rise of land acquisitions as countries prioritized the production of food and fuel in times of shortages. China and India are recognized as the two of the biggest players in the global land grabbing scene, with both countries accounting for approximately 10% of the total land grabbed across the entire globe combined. Table 8.1 provides a brief comparative analysis of land and water grabbing by India and China.

Table 8.1 Comparative analysis of land & water grabbing by India and China

	China	*India*
Scope & Scale	China and India have higher numbers of intended and failed contracts for land grabs, and smaller sizes of contracts. This is due to them having larger territories and a greater population, resulting in territories being owned by smaller local communities (Petrescu et al. 2020)	
Large-Scale Land Grabs	Mainly in Africa Driven by: Production of food	Mainly in Africa (Ethiopia) Driven by: Production of food and fuels to sustain India's burgeoning population and rapidly increasing energy demands
Small-Scale Land Grabs	International: Northern Laos: Chinese Banana Investments: Land grabbing on a small scale by Chinese foreign businesses at Laos' Muang Long district Local: Guangxi, China: Intimate Land Grabbing: The emergence of the industrial tree plantation (ITP) as a lucrative sector resulted in instances of "intimate land grabbing" within the province of Guangxi	Local: State-mediated land grabs: Land in rural villages like Rajpura and Sikkim are grabbed by corporations under the influence of state-led development policies, such as to pave the way for new SEZs
Small-Scale Land Grabs: Impact	Small-scale land grabs have just as much environmental destruction and ramifications on local communities as large-scale land grabs but tend to get away with it	Poor rural villagers are dispossessed and ultimately marginalized and excluded from economic development, due to state-mediated land grabs
Water Grab in the Himalayas	On a whole, over 400 hydroelectric dams were planned across the entire Himalayas mountain region. This was expected to cause huge damage to the environment and would affect millions of people within the area. China alone had plans to build over 160 dams, with experts projecting the country to have control over 40% of the world's entire water resource in due course Negative Impacts of the Water Grab War in the Himalayas: 1. Increased risk of flooding and vulnerability to earthquakes 2. Tens of millions of people displaced from their communities 3. Regional political tensions have been on the rise	

Source Authors' own analysis

In general, developing countries are more open to land and water grabs agreements as they can obtain benefits such as the creation of job opportunities for their people, development of infrastructure, diversification of agriculture, and being introduced to and educated on new technologies (Schoneveld et al. 2011). Meanwhile, developed countries engage in land grabs in order to secure food and financial security for themselves. However, developed countries and foreign corporations that land grab in developing countries are often much more influential and powerful, and utilize their positions of power to gain a bigger portion of the pie. This comes at the expense of the poorer, developing communities that depend on the land for survival, as seen in Table 8.1.

When conducted on a large scale, land and water grabbing can be a politically sensitive and reputation-damaging activity. One suggestion as an alternative to land acquisition is contract farming, which involves the agreement between buyer and farmer for agricultural production. Such an agreement can be beneficial for both farmers and businesses. For farmers, they are guaranteed sales as their produce will be bought by the corporations involved. As for the businesses, they are able to spread out their risks over multiple plots of land and have free reign over exactly how, what, and when their crops should be produced and ready for pick up. However, as with all arrangements, contract farming has its shortfalls as well. Any breach of agreement may result in the corporation involved suffering hefty losses. Meanwhile, farmers may become over-reliant on these agribusinesses for income and to sustain their livelihood. In some cases, farmers may also lose decision-making and control over the plot of land they own. On the whole, land and water grabbing is increasingly seen as a problem around the world for a multitude of reasons. Unfortunately, it is difficult to accurately determine the exact extent to which a country engages in land acquisition and the negative consequences that arise due to issues surrounding transparency of the stakeholders involved and bureaucratic red tape.

References

Ahmed, Nafeez. 2014, December 1. Carbon Colonialism: How the Fight Against Climate Change Is Displacing Africans. Vice. Retrieved September 15, 2020. https://www.vice.com/en_us/article/kbzn9w/carbon-colonialism-the-new-scramble-for-africa.

Ananthaswamy, Anil. 2011, May 25. African Land Grab Could Lead to Future Water Conflicts. New Scientist. Retrieved September 15, 2020. https://www.newscientist.com/article/mg21028144-100-african-land-grab-could-lead-to-future-water-conflicts/.

Anseeuw, Ward, Mathieu Boche, Thomas Breu, Markus Giger, Jann Lay, Peter Messerli, and Kerstin Nolte. 2012. Transnational Land Deals for Agriculture in the Global South: Analytical Report Based on the Land Matrix Database. The Land Matrix Partnership 2012. CDE/CIRAD/GIGA, Bern/Montpellier/Hamburg. Retrieved September 15, 2020. https://landmatrix.org/stay-informed/transnational-land-deals-agriculture-global-south-analytical-report-based-land-matrix-database/.

Borras, S., J. Franco, S. Gomez, C. Kay, and M. Spoor. 2012. Land Grabbing in Latin America and the Caribbean. *Journal of Peasant Studies* 39 (3–4): 845–872.

Chen, B., M.Y. Han, K. Peng, S.L. Zhou, L. Shao, X.F. Wu, W.D. Wei, S.Y. Liu, Z. Li, J.S. Li, and G.Q. Chen. 2018. Global Land-Water Nexus: Agricultural Land and Freshwater Use Embodied in Worldwide Supply Chains. *The Science of the Total Environment* 613–614: 931–943. https://doi.org/10.1016/j.scitotenv.2017.09.138.

Chettri, Mona. 2020. From Shangri-La to de-facto SEZ: Land Grabs from 'Below' in Sikkim, India. *Geoforum* 109 (2020): 57–66.

Coca, Nithin. 2017. China's Water Grab in Tibet Risks Regional Devastation and Conflict. *Equal Times*. Retrieved December 10, 2020. https://www.equaltimes.org/china-s-water-grab-in-tibet-risks?lang=en#.X9jzgy0Rq3U.

Conti, Lucrezia. 2017. The Chinese Penetration in the African Continent: The Issue of Land-Grabbing. *Blog RISE*, November 27. Retrieved September 15, 2020. http://blogrise.altervista.org/the-chinese-penetration-the-african-continent-the-issue-of-land-grabbing/.

Cotula, L. 2012. The International Political Economy of the Global Land Rush: A Critical Appraisal of Trends, Scale, Geography and Drivers. *Journal of Peasant Studies* 39 (3–4): 649–680.

Cotula, L., S. Vermeulen, R. Leonard, and J. Keeley. 2009. Land Grab or Development Opportunity? Agricultural Investment and International Land Deals in Africa. IIED, FAO and IFAD, London.

De Schutter, Olivier. 2011. How Not to Think of Land-Grabbing: Three Critiques of Large-Scale Investments in Farmland. *Taylor Francis Online*. Retrieved December 11, 2020. https://www.tandfonline.com/doi/full/10.1080/03066150.2011.559008.

Dell'Angelo, J., M.C. Rulli, and P. D'Odorico. 2017. The Global Water Grabbing Syndrome. *ScienceDirect*. Retrieved August 23, 2020. https://www.sciencedirect.com/science/article/pii/S0921800916307121.

Franco, Jennifer C., and Saturnino M. Borras Jr. 2019. Grey Areas in Green Grabbing: Subtle and Indirect Interconnections Between Climate Change Politics and Land Grabs and Their Implications for Research. *Land Use Policy* 84 (2019): 192–199.

Franco, J., L. Mehta, and G.J. Veldwisch. 2013. The Global Politics of Water Grabbing. *Third World Quarterly* 34 (9): 1651–1675.

Franco, J., S. Kishimoto, S. Kay, T. Feodoroff, and G. Pracucci. 2014. *The Global Water Grab: A Primer*. Transnational Institute for Hands off the Land Alliance. Retrieved October 24, 2020. https://www.tni.org/en/publication/the-global-water-grab-a-primer.

Friis, C., and J.O. Nielsen. 2016. Small-Scale Land Acquisitions, Large-Scale Implications: Exploring the Case of Chinese Banana Investments in Northern Laos. *ScienceDirect*. Retrieved September 24, 2020. https://www.sciencedirect.com/science/article/pii/S0264837716301454.

Hall, D., P. Hirsch, and T. Li. 2011. Powers of Exclusion: Land Dilemmas in Southeast Asia. *Taylor Francis Online*. Retrieved December 11, 2020. https://www.tandfonline.com/doi/abs/10.1080/1747423X.2018.1499830?journalCode=tlus20.

Hall, Ruth, Marc Edelman, Saturnino M. Borras Jr, Ian Scoones, Ben White, and Wendy Wolford. 2015. Resistance, Acquiescence or Incorporation? An Introduction to Land Grabbing and Political Reactions 'from Below'. *The Journal of Peasant Studies* 42 (3–4): 467–488. https://doi.org/10.1080/03066150.2015.1036746.

Han, Mengyao, and Guiqian Chen. 2018. Global Arable Land Transfers Embodied in Mainland China's Foreign Trade. *Land Use Policy* 70 (2018): 521–534.

Harvey, David. 2003. *The New Imperialism*. New York, NY: Oxford University Press.

Huggins, Christopher. 2014. "Control Grabbing" and Small-Scale Agricultural Intensification: Emerging Patterns of State-Facilitated "Agricultural Investment" in Rwanda. *The Journal of Peasant Studies*, 41. https://doi.org/10.1080/03066150.2014.910765.

Hules, Magdalena, and Simron Jit Singh. 2017. India's Land Grab Deals in Ethiopia: Food Security or Global Politics? *Land Use Policy* 60 (2017): 343–351.

IFFRI (International Food Policy Research Institute). 2009. *IFPRI Policy Brief 13, April 2009.*

Kerkvliet, B. 2014. Protests Over Land in Vietnam: Rightful Resistance and More. *Journal of Vietnamese Studies* 9 (3): 19–54.

Levien, Michael. 2018. *Dispossession Without Development: Land Grabs in Neoliberal India*. Oxford: Oxford University Press.

Li, T.M. 2011. Centering Labor in the Land Grab Debate. *Journal of Peasant Studies* 38 (2): 281–298.

Liu, Hongqiao. 2015. China's Bottled Water Industry Eyes Up the Tibetan Plateau. Retrieved December 10, 2020, from https://www.theguardian.com/sustainable-business/2015/nov/16/chinas-bottled-water-industry-eyes-up-the-tibetan-plateau.

Lyons, Kristen, and Peter Westoby. 2014. Carbon Colonialism and the New Land Grab: Plantation Forestry in Uganda and Its Livelihood Impacts. *Journal of Rural Studies* 36: 13–21. https://doi.org/10.1016/j.jrurstud.2014.06.002.

Mamonova, N. 2015. Resistance or Adaptation? Ukrainian Peasants' Responses to Large-Scale Land Acquisitions. *The Journal of Peasant Studies* 42 (3–4): 607–634. https://doi.org/10.1080/03066150.2014.993320.

McAllister, K. 2015. Rubber, Rights and Resistance: The Evolution of Local Struggles Against a Chinese Rubber Concession in Northern Laos. *The Journal of Peasant Studies* 42: 3–4.

McCarthy, J.F., J.A.C. Vel, and S. Afiff. 2012. Trajectories of Land Acquisition and Enclosure: Development Schemes, Virtual Land Grabs, and Green Acquisitions in Indonesia's Outer Islands. *Journal of Peasant Studies* 39 (2): 523.

Mehta, L., G.J. Veldwisch, and J. Franco, eds. 2012. Water Grabbing? Focus on the (Re)Appropriation of Finite Water Resources. *Water Alternatives* 5 (2): 193–542.

Molden, David, and Charlotte de Fraiture. 2010. Comprehensive Assessment of Water Management in Agriculture. *Agriculture Water Management* 97 (4): 493–578.

Moreda, T.S. 2015. Listening to Their Silence? The Political Reaction of Affected Communities to Large-Scale Land Acquisitions: Insights from Ethiopia. *The Journal of Peasant Studies* 42: 3–4.

O'Brien, K.J., and L.J. Li. 2006. *Rightful Resistance in Rural China*. Cambridge: Cambridge University Press.

Oya, Carlos. 2013. Methodological Reflections on 'Land Grab' Databases and the 'Land Grab' Literature 'Rush'. *Taylor Francis Online*. Retrieved December 11, 2020. https://www.tandfonline.com/doi/full/10.1080/03066150.2013.799465.

Perrone, Tommaso. 2017. *What Is Land Grabbing and Why Land Acquisitions are Destroying the Planet*. LifeGate. Retrieved October 15, 2020. https://www.lifegate.com/land-grabbing.

Petrescu, D.C., T. Hartel, and R.M. Petrescu-Mag. 2020. Global Land Grab: Toward a Country for Future Land Negotiations. *ScienceDirect*. Retrieved August 31, 2020.

Petrescu, Dacinia Crina, Tibor Hartel, and Ruxandra Malina Petrescu-Mag. 2020. Global Land Grab: Toward a Country Typology for Future Land Negotiations. *Land Use Policy* 99 (2020): 1–10. https://doi.org/10.1016/j.landusepol.2020.104960.

Provost, C. 2011. Africa's Great "Water Grab." *The Guardian*. Retrieved from Retrieved December 10, 2020. http://www.guardian.co.uk/global-development/poverty-matters/2011/nov/24/africa-wategrab-land-rights.

Rowden, R. 2011. India's Role in the New Global Farmland Grab. An Examination of the Role of the Indian Government and Indian Companies Engaged in Overseas Agricultural Land Acquisitions in Developing Countries. Produced in Collaboration with GRAIN and the Economics Research Foundation.

Rulli, Maria Cristina, Antonio Saviori, and Paolo D'Odorico. 2013. Global Land and Water Grabbing. *PNAS* 110 (3): 892–897. Retrieved from https://www.pnas.org/content/110/3/892.

Sampat, P. 2015. The 'Goan Impasse': Land Rights and Resistance to SEZs in Goa, India.

Saunders, Doug. 2010. China's 'African Land Grab.' *farmlandgrab.org, April 4*. Retrieved October 15, 2020. https://www.farmlandgrab.org/post/view/12075-chinas-african-land-grab.

Schoneveld, G., L. German, and E. Nutakor. 2011. Land-Based Investments for Rural Development? A Grounded Analysis of the Local Impacts of Biofuel Feedstock Plantations in Ghana. *Ecology and Society* 16 (4): 10.

Shepard, D., and M. Anuradha. 2009. The Great Land Grab. Rush for Worldı´s Farmland Threatens Food Security for the Poor. The Oakland Institute.

Shepherd, A.W. 2013. An Introduction to Contract Farming. *Technical Centre for Agricultural and Rural Cooperation (ACP-EU)*. Retrieved December 14, 2020. http://www.fao.org/uploads/media/Contract-Farming-Introduction.pdf.

Singh, David. 2019. *Michael Levien, Dispossession Without Development: Land Grabs in Neoliberal India*, 2018. Oxford: Oxford University Press.

Singh, S. 2010. India's Biophysical Economy, 1961–2008: Sustainability in a National and Global Context. *Ecological Economics* 76: 60–69.

Sy, Amadou. 2015. What Do We Know About the Chinese Land Grab in Africa? *The Brookings Institution*. Retrieved October 11, 2020. https://www.brookings.edu/blog/africa-in-focus/2015/11/05/what-do-we-know-about-the-chinese-land-grab-in-africa/.

Teklemariam, D., J. Nyssen, H. Azadi, M. Haile, S. Lanckriet, F. Taheri, and F. Witlox. 2017. Commercial Land Deals and the Interactions Between Investors and Local People: Evidence from Western Ethiopia. *Land Use Policy* 63: 312–323.

The Ministry of Land and Resources of the People's Republic of China. 2016. Retrieved December 10, 2020. http://www.mlr.gov.cn/wszb/2016/zbph/jiabin/index_2842.htm (in Chinese).

The Transnational Institute (TNI). 2013. *The Global Land Grab: A Primer*. Amsterdam: TNI.

The Transnational Institute. 2014. *State of Power 2014*. https://www.tni.org/en/briefing/state-power-2014. Accessed 14 December 2020.

Theesfeld, Insa. 2018. From Land to Water Grabbing: A Property Rights Perspective on Linked Natural Resources. *Ecological Economics* 154 (2018): 62–70.

van Dijk, Meine Pieter. 2016. Is China Grabbing Land in Africa? A Literature Overview Study. Conference: Landac conference Utrecht.

Vicol, M. 2017. Is Contract Farming an Inclusive Alternative to Land Grabbing? The Case of Potato Contract Farming in Maharashtra, India. *ScienceDirect*. Retrieved December 14, 2020. https://www.sciencedirect.com/science/article/pii/S0016718517302117.

Vidal, John. 2013. China and India 'Water Grab' Dams Put Ecology of Himalayas in Danger. *The Guardian*, August 10. Retrieved October 15, 2020. https://www.theguardian.com/global-development/2013/aug/10/china-india-water-grab-dams-himalayas-danger.

Visser, O., N. Mamonova, and M. Spoor. 2012. Oligarchs, Megafarms and Land Reserves: Understanding Land Grabbing in Russia. *Journal of Peasant Studies* 39 (3–4): 899–931.

White, B., S. Borras, R. Hall, I. Scoones, and W. Wolford. 2012. The New Enclosures: Critical Perspectives on Corporate Land Deals. *Journal of Peasant Studies* 39 (3–4): 629.

Woodhouse, P. 2012. New Investment, Old Challenges: Land Deals and the Water Constraint in African Agriculture. *Journal of Peasant Studies* 39 (3–4): 777–794.

World Bank. 2009. *World Development Report 2009*. Washington, DC: The World Bank Group.

World Bank. 2010. *Rising Global Interest: Farmland: Can It Yield Sustainable and Equitable Benefits?* Washington, DC: World Bank.

Xingmin, Z. 2014. Bottled Mineral Water: The Industry That Consumes Glaciers. *Snow Alliance and TNI*.

Xu, Yunan. 2018. Land Grabbing by Villagers? Insights from Intimate Land Grabbing in the Rise of Industrial Tree Plantation Sector in Guangxi, China. *Geoforum* 96: 141–149.

Yassin, A. 2010. Large Scale Transnational Land Acquisition in Ethiopia? Is It an Acceleration for Development? The Case of Bako and Gambella Region in Ethiopia. Master thesis, Institute of Social Studies, The Hague.

Zoomers, Annelies, Femke Van Noorloos, Kei Otsuki, Griet Steel, and Guus Van Westen. 2017. The Rush for Land in an Urbanizing World: From Land Grabbing Toward Developing Safe, Resilient, and Sustainable Cities and Landscapes. *World Development* 92: 242–252. https://doi.org/10.1016/j.worlddev.2016.11.016.

CHAPTER 9

Green Movements, Food Justice, and Sovereignty in Asia

Integral Aspects of Environmental Politics

Environmental politics are closely intertwined with justice as the impact from environmental problems often disproportionately disadvantages poor sections of the populations or minority groups. The poorer sections of society are minuscule contributors to environmental damages but are disproportionately impacted by the severe repercussions of environmental problems. Unfortunately, the poorer sections of society both within and between nations are least capable to adapt to these impacts. Compounding the problems faced by the disadvantaged and marginalized, most nations situate environmental issues second to economic growth and development. Such macroeconomic choices made by governments and policymakers involves trade-offs and consequences for food security. Implications related to national pursuit of economic growth on food production are twofold: (1) as affluence in a population increases, consumption and likewise demand for food production will place strains on food production capacities and (2) environmental degradation exacerbated by emissions of greenhouse gases and the depletion of nonrenewable resources such as arable or fertile soil are a symptom as well as a result of unsustainable agricultural practices adopted to meet food production demands. Such stressors bring about a cascade of intensive agricultural practices to satisfy growing demands that intensify environmental damage.

M. S. Islam and E. Kieu, *Climate Change and Food Security in Asia Pacific*, International Political Economy Series,
https://doi.org/10.1007/978-3-030-70753-8_9

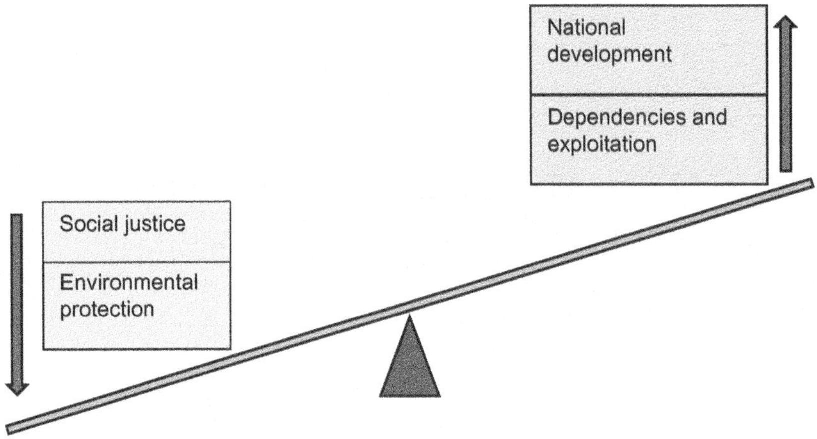

Fig. 9.1 Tensions of justice, dependencies, the environment, and development (*Source* Authors' own)

Social injustices partially contribute to environmental degradation due to the dependencies of developing countries on the developed world for investments (Garner 2011).

This dependency permits the acceptance of exploitative relations that indirectly lead developing countries to relax environmental standards on the premise of attracting investments from multinational companies from the developed world (Garner 2011). With the intensification of agricultural efforts, employment of unsustainable practices implicates the health and lives of many organisms which could bring about a cascade of unforeseen negative impact on biodiversity in the long run. Figure 9.1 summarizes the tensions and trade-offs of justice and the environment.

Food Sovereignty and Food Justice

Food sovereignty and food justice primarily seeks to establish institutional equity over food systems and advocate greater control over the ways in which food is produced and subsequently consumed (Cadieux and Slocum 2015). The notion of "sovereignty" is mostly used in the Global South whereas "justice" stemmed from the United States and is a more commonly used term (Romer and Farthing 2016). Food sovereignty, introduced in 1996, was the "right of each nation to maintain and develop its own capacity to produce its basic foods respecting cultural and productive diversity"; and it was later refined as the right of peoples and governments to choose the way food is produced and consumed in order to respect their livelihoods, as well as the policies that support this choice (La Via Campesina 2009: 57). It emphasizes the right of individuals and communities to define the processes that regulate their own food systems, from production to consumption. Hence, it is rooted in a "politics of local self-determination" rather than principles leading to a plan of action (Murphy 2014). Food sovereignty is thus a transformative process that aims to recreate the democratic realm and regenerate a diversity of local autonomous food systems in both rural and urban areas, based on equity, social justice, and ecological sustainability (Pimbert 2019). Food justice on the other hand refers to "a transformation of the current food system, including but not limited to eliminating disparities and inequities" (Gottlieb and Joshi 2010: ix). While some may use both focal terms interchangeably, Cadieux and Slocum (2015) outlined extensively the characteristics of food justice and food sovereignty based on its histories. Cadieux and Slocum (2015) posit that food sovereignty is akin to the notion of lacking in food as discourses in this arena revolves around food production while food justice is analogous to food consumption and access. Food justice, as an approach, was more aligned with the sociohistorical contexts of cities, due to its origins in broader class and race struggles, compared to food sovereignty.

Food sovereignty is a political campaign that has been active in the past decades that gained larger traction after the 2007 Nyéléni Declaration. Since its inception, the political movement stretches across multiple social domains and institutional space, as an expanding and inspiring social movement. Food sovereignty is the right of people and nations to determine their own system of agriculture and food, prioritizing local and national economies and markets and stimulating agriculture and food systems shaped by, for example, small farmers and family farms, artisanal fisheries, extensive animal husbandry, and sustainable food production, distribution. and consumption (Pimbert 2019; Donkers 2014). Drawing on the Forum for Food Sovereignty, Donkers (2014) discerned at least six principles of food sovereignty: (1) to ensure a food supply; (2) to appreciate producers of food; (3) to integrate agriculture and food systems into the local environment; (4) to keep local control; (5) to build upon local knowledge and experience; and (6) to cooperate with nature.

Edelman et al. (2014) see the food sovereignty movement as the "rights of farmers and consumers" as they are usually seen as occupying the two ends of the food chain. Food sovereignty comes through developing networks of aggregation, processing, commercialization, and distribution that are themselves linked to other sectors of the economy. One important source of political momentum in food sovereignty advocacy, according to Edelman et al. (2014), is the urban and peri-urban-based food initiatives. This advocacy is largely motivated by an idea of solidarity with farmers in the distant countryside as well as by immediate concerns around public health, access to healthy and affordable foods, dismantling racialized food systems, and the culture and lifestyle of food producers, food sellers, restaurant owners, and consumers. Food sovereignty, according to Alonso-Fradejas et al. (2015) is therefore a political project. The *how* questions in the political construction of food sovereignty involves questions about engaging with social forces external to the collective movement that may facilitate or hinder the attainment of food sovereignty. Food sovereignty spans across a wide range of domains that include, but are not limited to, food politics, agroecology, land reform, pastoralism, fisheries, biofuels, Genetically modified organisms (GMO), urban gardening, patenting of life forms, labor migration, feeding of volatile cities, community initiatives, state policies, public health, climate change, ecological sustainability, and subsistence rights. Food sovereignty today, according to Alonso-Fradejas et al. (2015), stretches across a manifold of sociopolitical and economic scaffolding: rural/agricultural, rural/nonagricultural, urban/agricultural, urban/nonagricultural, spheres of production, circulation/trade and consumption, the North–South hemispheric divide, state–society institutional spaces, as well as class and other social attributes and identities. Such is a key indication of the relevance—and power—of food sovereignty as an idea, a social movement, a campaign, and an analytical framework. It also provides us with a glimpse of why food sovereignty can be a complicated issue to negotiate within and between social classes and groups across societies.

The onset of the food sovereignty movement indicates the increasing recognition that agrarian sectors are critical in global patterns of production and consumption. Food sovereignty at present is a political struggle for sustainable food systems and a nexus of contestations between

North–South and rural–urban forces. Issues of contestations are further compounded by aspects of vulnerabilities that stretch from a variety of social attributes such as gender, race, castes, nationalities, religion (Alonso-Fradejas et al. 2015). Summarily, both food sovereignty and food justice revolve around four areas: (1) acknowledging and confronting historical, collective social trauma and persistent race, gender, and class inequalities; (2) designing exchange mechanisms that build communal reliance and control; (3) creating innovative ways to control, use, share, own, manage, and conceive of land, and ecologies in general, that place them outside the speculative market and the rationale of extraction; and (4) pursuing labor relations that guarantee a minimum income and are neither alienating nor dependent on (unpaid) social reproduction by women (Cadieux and Slocum 2015).

While there has been uptake on related subjects, Cadieux and Slocum (2015) point out the uncertainty that surrounds actors who champion such causes and questions if they are doing enough to elicit changes. They articulate that justice should stand for something that is practiced and without clarity in what justice means in practice runs the risks of standing for nothing. They highlight that the process of practice should involve the following: (1) an understanding of the distribution of power and incorporating this as part of the discourse, (2) a progressive sense of place and grapple with dynamic social relations, (3) analyzing and evaluating policies for capacities to enforce systematic changes, (4) identifying barriers and enabling elements, (5) considering the efficacy in engaging actors such as the state or markets, and (6) institutionalization of equity in a democratic and participatory process (Cadieux and Slocum 2015).

Food sovereignty and food justice echo the need to take steps toward a more sustainable production of food while playing a primary role in social justice and individual autonomy. It is seen as a political vehicle to which different people across the globe and communities understand about the relationships they share while working toward building networks that sustain and support one another (Chavez 2017; Schanbacher 2017). Food sovereignty and food justice both advocate greater control over food production and consumption by people who have been marginalized by mainstream agrifood regimes. These tend to be associated with less dependency on capital-intensive inputs, greater attention to social and environmental contexts, and systemic well-being, by demanding equity in the decision-making process and distribution of resources (Cadieux and Slocum 2015). However, because of the different histories, geographic contexts, and relations to state and capital, food justice and food sovereignty differ as strategies and approaches. Issues of food sovereignty are also tied to issues of racialized oppression and colonization, which has dismantled indigenous foodways through agricultural modernization and urbanization (Jarosz 2014; Clapp 2014). Yet, both are similarly limited by neoliberal structural contexts (Clendenning et al. 2016).

Green Movements in Asia

Green movements are anchored on political, economic, and environmental histories that seek to enact social transformation and development. Green movements are varied from bottom-up grassroots organizations to top-down international organizational reforms. Environmental movements are also markedly different across the developed and developing world. Gadgil and Guha (1994) highlight that environmentalism emerged in Western societies only after concerns with the quality of resources based on scarcity and resource management. On the other hand, developing countries' environmentalism has been characterized by issues related to land and resource depletion, pollution, and problems of biodiversity and resource degradation (Gadgil and Guha 1994). Asian NGO Coalition (ANGOC) establishes the approaches utilized by Asian NGOs in addressing the relationships between the environment and poverty in five main aspects: (1) information sharing across sectors of communities, governments, and businesses, (2) training and education of staff and community leaders on environmental protection, rehabilitation, processes and technologies, (3) field projects related to environmental protection, conservation, and rehabilitation, (4) creating linkages with local and international NGOs, and (5) projects related to community forestry, agricultural practices, alternative sources of energy, sanitation, and health facilities (ANGOC 1995).

According to Balsinger's (1998) report for the FAO, international organizations in Asia have a relatively greater influence compared to the local ones. Local organizations specifically concerned with environmental issues are relatively new, although communal self-help groups have been a long tradition. Examples of these are Indonesia's *gotong royong* and *bayanihan* in the Philippines which are distinct from Western variants of trade unions and NGOs. In recent decades, environmentalism in this region began to establish Western-type organizations in the newly industrialized countries such as South Korea, Taiwan, Singapore, Hong Kong, Malaysia, and Thailand. It is observed that many parts of the population have not benefitted from the rapid industrialization which may contribute to the expansion of environmental movements by these communities that are systematically disadvantaged.

The specific number of organizations that are active in Asia varies across countries and is hard to establish these actual figures but are estimated to be large and growing rapidly (Balsinger 1998; Serrano 1994). According to some sources, India is likely to have autonomous citizens' organizations numbering 100,000 even by the early 1990s and Bangladesh with numbers of up to 12,000 organizations (ANGOC 1995). The Philippines is similar to India and Bangladesh with a vibrant and active civil society. In the Philippines, there are 26,000 organizations listed by the country's Securities and Exchange Commission, 14,000 registered in Thailand and roughly 75% of 1000 NGOs in Indonesia involved in environmental protection, and 12,000 NGOs in Nepal even as early as the 1990s (ANGOC 1995; Serrano 1994). Japan estimates lie around 3000 grassroots organizations (Holliman 1990). While there are some indicators to show environmental civil movements, much of these organizations are not required to register formally and a great number of civil groups are established informally (Balsinger 1998). Based on information from UN Environment Programme (2018), we list some of the selected and accredited civil society organizations (CSOs) for Asia and the Pacific regions (Table 9.1).

In general, Asian CSOs generally stem from poverty reduction as the primary concern and therefore emplaces human concerns as central. In contrast, international environmental CSOs are more concerned with the conservation of nature and natural resources. However, both local and international CSOs collaborate across projects channeling international funds and establishing working partnerships to engage the local communities.

Table 9.1 National, regional, and International CSOs

National (Asia and the Pacific)	
The Philippines • Adec Foundation Inc. • Center for Environmental Concerns-Philippines INC. (CEC) • Global Alliance for Incinerator Alternatives (GAIA) • IBON International Foundation • Tebtebba Foundation Indigenous Peoples International Policy Research and Education (TEBTEBBA)	Bangladesh • Environmental and Social Development Organization (ESDO) • Environmental and Societal Development Foundation (ESDF) • The Environmental and Social Development Organization
China • All-China Environment Federation (ACEF) • Earth Council China/Oriental Environmental Institute • Ecumenical Coalition on Tourism (ECOT)/Ecumenical Coalition on Third World Tourism (ECTET)(ECOT/ECTWT • Global Energy Interconnection Development and Co-operation Organization (GEIDCO) • Ocean Recovery Alliance Limited • Society of Entrepreneurs & Ecology (SEE)	Japan • International Association of Ports and Harbours (IAPH) • International Lake Environment Committee Foundation (ILEC) • Japan Association for the United Nations Environment Programme
Thailand • Asia Indigenous Peoples' Pact (AIPP) • Thailand Environment Institute (TEI) • Women Organizing for Change in Agriculture and Natural Resource Management (WOCAN)	Nepal • Association of Protection of Environment and Culture (APEC) • Dalit Welfare Association (DWA) • NGO Federation of Nepal (NFN) • Rural Area Development Programme (RADP)

National (Asia and the Pacific)	
India • Asian Environmental Society • Center for Environment and Sustainable Development (CESDI) • Center for Science and Environment • Center for Science and Technology of the Non-Aligned and Other Developing Countries • Consumer Unity and Trust Society (CUTS) • Development Alternatives • Empower • Empower India • Govardhan Ecovillage • Gram Bharati Samiti (GBS) • India Water Foundation • Indian National Trust for Art and Cultural Heritage (INTACH) • Indo OIC Islamic chamber of commerce and industry (IICI) • International Movement for Advancement of Education Culture Social and Economic Development (IMAECSED) • International Society for Environmental Education • Nehru Foundation for Development - Centre for Environment Education • Sadayanodai Ilaignar Narpani Mandran (SINAM) • South Asian Forum for Environment (SAFE) • Terre Policy Centre • UDYAMA • Universal Versatile Society • Women & Child Welfare Society • Youth for Action	Pakistan • Community Initiatives for Development in Pakistan (CIDP) • Huqooq-ul-Ebad Development Foundation • International Human Rights Commission (IHRC) • LEAD Pakistan • New World Hope Organisation (NWHO) • Nippon Marks • Rural Educational Development and Welfare Organization (REDWO) • Sindhica Reforms Society • Society for Conservation and Protection of Environment (SCOPE) • Society for Roots for Equity • The National Forum for Environment and Health • World Muslim Congress (WMC)

(continued)

Table 9.1 (continued)

National (Asia and the Pacific)	
Democratic People's Republic of Korea • Future Forest Australia • Clean Up the World • Global Voices (GV) • Institute for Sustainable Futures	Kyrgyzstan • Independent Ecological Expertise The Lebanese Republic • Innovation and Development Association-INNODEV • Arab Forum for Environment and Development (AFED) • Green Globe • Green Hand Organization • Human Environmental Association for Development (HEAD) • IndyAct: The Leagues of Independent Activists • Society for the Protection of Nature in Lebanon (SPNL)
Malaysia • Global Environment Centre • Third World Network • World Youth Foundation	Singapore • Food Industry Asia • National Youth Achievement Award (NYAA) • Singapore Environment Council • World Toilet Organization
Mongolia • Development Horizon Foundation (DHF) Iran • Shakhes Pajooh International Engineering Research Institute of Natural Hazards	Cook Islands • Island Sustainability Alliance CI Fiji • The Pacific Islands Forum Secretariat (PIFS)
The Hashemite Kingdom of Jordan • Arab Group for the Protection of Nature (APN) • East Amman Society for Environment Protection (EASEP) • Jordan Environment Society (JES)	Bahrain • Bahrain Women Association for Human Development • Environment Friends Society (EFS)
The United Arab Emirates • Emirates Diving Association (EDA) • Emirates Environmental Group (EEG)	The Sultanate of Oman • Environmental Society of Oman (ESO)

National (Asia and the Pacific)	
The State of Qatar • Friends of the Environment Center - Qatar Israel • International Christian Embassy Jerusalem (ICEJ) The State of Kuwait • Kuwait Environment Protection Society • Kuwait Water Association	The Kingdom of Saudi Arabia • Gulf Research Center Yemen • International Youth Council-Yemen The Republic of Iraq • Nature-Iraq

Adapted from UN Environment Programme (2018) [no copyright issue]

Green Movements on Food Security

Both community food security and environmental justice shape discourse of sustainable agriculture, environmentalism, and social welfare advocacy. Yet, these remain relatively separate movements indicating an incomplete process in reshaping agendas and discourse (Gottlieb and Fisher 1996). The Green Revolution in the late 1960s boosted food crop production for domestic consumption, reducing calorie deficit for lowest income groups. However, it still required access to irrigation and fertilizers and had environmental challenges. Aquaculture and oil crops systems also offer improvements to environmental outcomes from intensive food production, attracting attention from development specialists, the environmental community, consumer groups, and the multinational agribusiness sector. Yet, these systems also have land rights environmental challenges, and freshwater and marine environmental challenges (Naylor 2016). Also, some responses to food security like large-scale commercialized farming, and even technological innovations in agriculture have received criticism on their environmental sustainability (Teng and Oliveros 2015). Influenced by the green movement and other food security factors, IRRI's (International Rice Research Institute) strategic plan for 2007–2015 showed a significant change from previous priorities, with more emphasis on marginal rainfed environments, diversification of rice systems, the sustainability and environmental consequences of intensive rice production, and genetic discovery research instead (Asia Society 2010). This shows their efforts directed at ensuring sustainability, particularly through scientific innovation, to address pushback and criticism from environmentalists.

Civil green movements and the global nature of environmental policies continue to influence policymaking across levels. By and large, governments are still one of the critical actors that make decisions and drive policies into effect. However, debates often revolve around *what* and *how* environmental policies and actions should be undertaken. Holt-Giménez and Shattuck (2011) identify distinctions between these varied forms of movements via the food regime–food movement matrix to trace the trends in food systems based on numerous key facets. The neoliberal food movement, for example, relies upon the discourse of food enterprise, reformist movement on food security, progressive movement on food justice, and radical food movement on the discourse of food sovereignty. Each of these strands of the food regime–food movement is entrenched with its own history and political proclivity. The focus and inclinations for food movement challenges the hegemony of the corporate food regime. Holt-Giménez and Shattuck (2011) in their paper "Food crises, food regimes and food movements: rumblings of reform or tides of transformation?" discusses the tensions within food movements. They highlight that for substantive changes to occur, collaborative alliances between progressive and radical trends of food movements are crucial to maintain pressures for reforms and food justice.

Singapore is an example where government initiatives for food security are accompanied by a host of activisms by NGOs, social enterprises, and community groups. With the recent announcement of the Ministry of Environment and Water Resource's (MEWR) goal of "30 by 30," where they intend to meet 30% of Singapore's nutritional needs locally by 2030, there has been a greater push to develop urban and smart farming capabilities in Singapore, particularly in aquaculture. With this, there has been the development and creation of more research institutes and training programs in universities and polytechnics to foster Singapore's capabilities in smart farming, as well as to train the next generation of farmers. Within these institutions, there is close collaboration between government bodies, other research institutions, and local farms and businesses. Before 2020, however, there already existed several businesses and social enterprises that were focused on building a culture of urban farming in Singapore, such as ComCrop and Edible Garden City, both of which focused on utilizing spaces such as rooftops for farming. The Kranji Countryside has also long been home to Singapore's farms, such as the Hay Dairies Goat Farm and Jurong Frog Farm. However, with land increasingly being slated for development or being returned to the military, many existing farms are struggling to find new land to continue their operations. Table 9.2 highlights examples of activisms in Singapore for food security.

Table 9.2 Singapore's sustainability scene—food and agriculture

No.	*Name of organization*	*Type*	*Objectives and impacts*
1.	Singapore Food Agency	Government	Working to ensure that 30% of Singapore's nutritional needs are met through local produce
2.	Food Bank Singapore	NGO/NPO	Collects surplus food from supermarkets, F&B outlets, and wholesalers and redistributes them to over 170 charities
3.	Edible Garden City	Social Enterprise	Designed, built, and maintained over 200 urban edible gardens; Works with more than twenty schools to develop a farming curriculum
4.	Comcrop	Social Enterprise	Created the first urban rooftop in Singapore; Hosts tours and sells produce in some locations
5.	SG Food Rescue	Community Group	Conducts food rescues at various locations (Little India, Pasir Panjang Wholesale Centre) once a week to rescue food that would otherwise be thrown away
6.	Food From The Heart	NGO/NPO	Runs six core programs: Bread Run Programme, Community Food Pack Programme, School Goodie Bag Programme, Toys from the Heart, Birthdays from the Heart, and Market Place; Supports 40,300 beneficiaries yearly
7.	Kranji Countryside Association	NGO/NPO	Represents farmers in the Kranji countryside and helps them with issues such as renewing leases; Organizes the Kranji Farmer's Market to sell local produce and to encourage Singaporeans to take part in workshops and activities related to farming

(continued)

Table 9.2 (continued)

No.	*Name of organization*	*Type*	*Objectives and impacts*
8.	Foodscape Collective	Community Group	Facebook group sharing tips on urban gardening and circular food systems; Hosts workshops and talks
9.	Singapore Young Farmers	Community Group	Encourage more Singaporeans to be proud of local produce and to consider joining the farming profession
10.	Inscetta	Green Business	Urban farm that breeds black soldier flies

Credit Belicia Teo [no copyright issue]

Reflecting on Policies and Justice

National and international policies are influenced by these strands of environmental stances which are likewise moderated by the opinion of civil movements. Debates from scholars, policymakers, and activists are long drawn and revolves around two main dimensions: (1) the role of states in food sovereignty and (2) the role of markets. Both dimensions echo the mismatch and tensions of the food regime–food movements. Food justice and food sovereignty requires intricate networks of production, distribution, and consumptions that are linked to many aspects of the global economy. The discourse of each specific strand tends to be focused too narrowly. A narrow focus lacking the ability to incorporate itself into other aspects of societal pillars and break out of a vicious cycle which is unsustainable. Struggles that are championed should not be viewed narrowly but as an intricate web of market and societal relations (Edelman et al. 2014).

The cross-sections of environmental and food-related tensions are manifold and have captured the attention of farmers, consumers, citizens, activists, and academics. Food security is one of the avenues for contestations against neoliberal projects of privatization, deregulation, and corporatization of global economies. Food challenges compounded by pressures from climate changes presents itself as an urgent undertaking for structural changes in the capitalist global economy—serving as a point of reflection on the trajectory of human development and its sustainability for future generations.

References

Alonso-Fradejas, Alberto, Saturnino M. Borras, Todd Holmes, Eric Holt-Giménez, and Martha Jane Robbins. 2015. Food Sovereignty: Convergence and Contradictions, Conditions and Challenges. *Third World Quarterly* 36 (3): 431–448.

ANGOC (Asian NGO Coalition for Agrarian Reform and Rural Development). 1995. Asian NGO Initiatives in Addressing Hunger and Poverty: Strategies for Empowering Local Communities through People-Centered Development. Regional Paper prepared for IFAD Conference on Hunger and Poverty. Brussels.

Asia Society. 2010. *Never an Empty Bowl: Sustaining Food Security in Asia.* International Rice Research Institute Task Force Report.

Balsinger, J. 1998. Asia-Pacific Forestry Sector Outlook Study: Perspectives of Environmental Civil Society Organizations on Forestry in the Asia-Pacific Region: Outlook to the Year 2010." FAO Working Paper No. APFSOS/WP/37. Retrieved 15 Oct 2018 http://www.fao.org/docrep/w7746e/w7746e04.htm.

Cadieux, Kirsten, and Slocum, Rachel. 2015. What Does it Mean to do Food Justice? *Journal of Political Ecology* 22 (1–26). http://doi.org/10.2458/v22i1.21076.

Chavez, M. 2017. It's not Just About Us: Food as a Mechanism for Environmental and Social Justice in Mato Grosso, Brazil. In *Food Justice in US and Global Contexts: Bringing Theory and Practice Together*, ed. I. Werkheiser, and Z. Piso, 51–66. New York, NY: Springer.

Clapp, Jennifer. 2014. Food Security and Food Sovereignty: Time to Get Past the Binary. *Dialogues in Human Geography* 4 (2): 206–211.

Clendenning, J., W.H. Dressler, and C. Richards. 2016. Food Justice or Food Sovereignty? Understanding the Rise of Urban Food Movements in the USA. *Agriculture and Human Values* 33: 165–177. https://doi.org/10.1007/s10460-015-9625-8.

Donkers, Harry. 2014. Sustainable Food Security, A Paradigm for Local and Regional Food Systems. *International Journal of Humanities and Social Science* 4(12).

Edelman, Marc, Tony Weis, Amita Baviskar, Saturnino M. Borras, Eric Holt-Giménez, Deniz Kandiyoti, and Wendy Wolford. 2014. Introduction: Critical Perspectives on Food Sovereignty. *The Journal of Peasant Studies* 41 (6): 911–931.

Gadgil, M., and R. Guha. 1994. Ecological Conflicts and the Environmental Movement in India. *Development and Change* 25: 101–136.

Garner, R. 2011. *Environmental Policies: The Age of Climate Change*, 3rd ed. New York, NY: Palgrave Macmillan.

Gottlieb, R., and A. Joshi. 2010. *Food Justice*. Cambridge: MIT Press.

Gottlieb, Robert, and Andrew Fisher. 1996. Community Food Security and Environmental Justice: Searching For A Common Discourse. *Agriculture and Human Values* 13: 23–32. https://doi.org/10.1007/BF01538224.

Holliman, Jonathan. 1990. Environmentalism with a Global Scope. *Japan Quarterly* 37 (3): 284–290.

Holt-Giménez, E., and Shattuck, A. 2011. Food Crises, Food Regimes and Food Movements: Rumblings of Reform or Tides of Transformation? *The Journal of Peasant Studies* 38 (1): 109–144.

Jarosz, Lucy. 2014. Comparing Food Security and Food Sovereignty Discourses. *Dialogues in Human Geography* 4: 168–181. https://doi.org/10.1177/2043820614537161.

La Via Campesina. 2009. *La Via Campesina Policy Documents*. Ecuador: La Via Campesina.

Murphy, Sophia. 2014. Expanding the Possibilities for a Future Free of Hunger. *Dialogues in Human Geography* 4 (2): 225–228.

Naylor, Rosamond L. 2016. Oil Crops, Aquaculture, and the Rising Role of Demand: A Fresh Perspective on Food Security. *Global Food Security* 11 (2016): 17–25. https://doi.org/10.1016/j.gfs.2016.05.001.

Pimbert, Michel P. 2019. Food Sovereignty. *Encyclopedia of Food Security and Sustainability* 3 (2019): 181–189. https://doi.org/10.1016/B978-0-08-100596-5.22235-X.

Romer, N., and Farthing, L. 2016. Food Justice + Food Sovereignty Can the U.S. Food Justice Movement Join the Global Movement? New Politics 16 (1): 83–90.

Schanbacher, W.D. 2017. Introduction to Food Justice in a Global Context. In *Food Justice in US and Global Contexts: Bringing Theory and Practice Together*, ed. I. Werkheiser, and Z. Piso, 7–12. New York, NY: Springer.

Serrano, I.R. 1994. *Civil Society in the Asia-Pacific Region*. Washington, DC: Civicus.

Teng, Paul P.S., and Jurise Oliveros. 2015. Challenges and Responses to Asian Food Security. *Cosmos: Journal of the Singapore National Academy of Science* 11: 1–18. https://doi.org/10.1142/s0219607715500019.

UN Environment Programme. 2018. *List of Accredited Organizations*. Retrieved 15 Oct 2018. https://www.unenvironment.org/civil-society-engagement/accreditation/list-accredited-organizations.

CHAPTER 10

Toward a Sustainable Food System in Asia-Pacific Amid Climate Crises

Both climate change and food security are among the most critical issues of our time. They are multi-faceted transcending national boundaries. Among various ways to address these issues, regional initiatives can play a pivotal role while actively engaging global partners to slow down or reverse current trajectories. Using various research tools such as a robust content analysis and institutional ethnography, this book offers a critical analysis across three regional organizations—the Association of Southeast Asian Nations (ASEAN), the Pacific Islands Forum (PIF), and the South Asian Association for Regional Cooperation (SAARC). We also focused on two major countries in the region—China and India by exploring their unique challenges and reprecussions of utilizing foreign land and water grabs as solutions. Lastly, the book examined the notion of food security within urbanized Asian cities as well as bottom-up food movements that will drive the future of environmental and food politics. This closing chapter concludes the book by summarizing the findings, showing patterns and pitfalls across the regions, and pathways for a sustainable food system in the Asia-Pacific region.

M. S. Islam and E. Kieu, *Climate Change and Food Security in Asia Pacific*, International Political Economy Series, https://doi.org/10.1007/978-3-030-70753-8_10

Patterns and Pitfalls

Critical Dilemma

Food is deeply related to not only health and pleasure, but also history, culture, geopolitics, and global economy. Today, the world is facing a critical dilemma: there is an ever-increasing demand for food driven largely by the rapid growth in world population, global income, and meat consumption in the last decades (Capone et al. 2014), while climate change and other environmental problems have significantly affected the productivity and distribution of food. It is predicted that up to 25% of world food production may be lost during the twenty-first century due to climate change, water scarcity, invasive pests, and land degradation (Nellemann et al. 2009). The current levels of consumptions, on the other hand, are unsustainable, inequitable, and inaccessible to majority of humans (McMichael 2012). Despite the availability of food, the number of hungry people across the world remains unacceptably high. The Action Against Hunger (2020) reveals bizarre facts about hunger and malnutrition:

- There is more than enough food produced in the world to feed everyone on the planet.
- About 690 million people worldwide go to bed hungry each night.
- Small farmers, herders, and fishermen produce about 70% of the global food supply, yet they are especially vulnerable to food insecurity—poverty and hunger are most acute among rural populations.
- Conflict is a major driver of hunger: The UN estimates that 122 million of 144 million stunted children live in countries affected by conflict.
- An estimated 14 million children under the age of five worldwide suffer from severe acute malnutrition, also known as severe wasting, yet only 25% of severely malnourished children have access to lifesaving treatment.

Due to massive urbanization and growing rural–urban population resulting in feeding more people from less land, Asia-Pacific region is grappling with both food security and long-term environmental sustainability. Asian countries, India and China in particular, have the highest population density and growth in the world. It is expected that the Asia-Pacific region will witness the urban populations increase by more than

580 million by 2020 as compared with levels in 2000, and the total size of the urban population in the region will overtake the total rural population for the first time in history. China's urban population is expected to increase by a further 308 million by 2020 in its two hundred plus cities. Similar rapid increase will be happening in Indonesia, the Philippines, Vietnam, Bangladesh and a number of other countries. Rural populations, at the same time, will significantly decline in most of the region (Wahlqvist et al. 2012).

Along with a larger population, higher per capita consumption among communities with growing incomes is the main reason behind the increasing demand for food in Asia-Pacific (Vermeulen et al. 2012). Cereals production, for example, would need to increase by 940 million tonnes to reach 3 billion tonnes projected for 2050; meat by 196 million tonnes to reach 455 million tonnes by 2050; and oil crops by 133 million tonnes to reach 282 million tonnes (oil equivalent) by 2050 (Alexandratos and Bruinsma 2012). To match the 1.1% growth in consumption, global production in 2050 would need to be approximately 60% higher than that of 2005/2007 (McKenzie and Williams 2015). There are various factors and forces that drive consumption patterns and lifestyles such as economic forces, technological progress, historical legacy, political settings, environmental issues, sociological and cultural contexts, and psychological determinants. Social consumption drivers include urbanization, demographic change, and changing patterns of consumer needs, preferences, choices, tastes, habits, and practices. Economic drivers include issues of trade, food markets, and their volatility, supply and distribution, regulation, affordability and accessibility, and globalization (Capone et al. 2014).

Over the years, there will be mounting pressures over the global food system. On the demand side, global population size will increase along with growing affluence that will generate greater demand for a more varied, high-quality diet requiring additional resources to produce. On the production side, accumulation, resource grab, competition for land, water, and energy use will intensify, while the effects of climate change will become increasingly apparent and debilitating. Reducing GHG emissions and adapting to a changing climate through adaptation, mitigation, and resilience will become necessary. Globalization will continue and neoliberal forces restricting aspects of global trade will intensify, exposing the food system to novel economic and political pressures. Today, the main challenge for the food and agricultural sector is to supply culturally acceptable food both in quality and quantity, in order to meet the nutritional needs and demands of a growing population in a sustainable way—environmentally, socially, economically (Capone et al. 2014).

The population size and food supplies in the Asia have been increasing in tandum since the 1980s. Yet, Asia has a high number of undernourished, and a rising urbanized population that will increase food demands. The quality of natural resources is also deteriorating due to human activities resulting in lower output and quality of food. Many Asian countries also have inadequate investment in agriculture, research, development, extension, and education (ADB 2017). With worsening climate change, the failure of current regional food initiatives to consider marginalized communities and the emphasis on development will only expand inequality gaps. Currently, there are competing power interest rooted in the notion of development in Asia, which supersedes preventive measures against threats like food insecurity, as evident with ASEAN and SAARC (Islam and Kieu 2020). Challenges to the food policy include willingness to commit political resources, priorities and preferences of policy goals, policy integration with relevant sectors and levels, policy specialization, and the consistency of policy instruments by policymakers and private actors. Many countries also have not actively envisioned an integrated food policy yet (Candel and Pereira 2017).

Although the discourse of climate change is becoming powerful and its effects are becoming clearer, the actions to address this critical problem of our time do not seem to be genuine and remains largely symbolic. As a result, climate change generates a new kind of "resource war" in which the "climate change haves" get more business opportunities with greater access to resources such as green products and services, while the "climate change have-nots" largely languish in the smoke, fumes, toxic chemicals, and illnesses of the old pollution-based economy. Protecting the green image rather than genuinely protecting the environment and addressing the need of the poor seems quite dominant across the world. Regional approaches are optimally positioned to address the critical issues of climate change and food security; however, the trends of resource war, polarizing trajectories, symbolic response to climate change, and other environmental problems largely hinder the success of the various regional initiatives. Economic growth is certainly necessary but not enough to tackle climate change and food insecurity. The growth needs to be accompanied by robust public policies and meaningful participations of the poor.

Climate Change and Food Security: The Tale of Three Regions

Since the 1990s, ASEAN has been very active in shaping institutional development in the Asia-Pacific, making it at the forefront of Asia-Pacific regionalism. Nevertheless, its international credibility has been questioned because of its inability to deal with several important regional events, situations, and challenges such as climate change and food security (Narine 2008; Islam and Kieu 2020). In response, ASEAN underwent a series of institutional reform, focusing on a new ASEAN Charter and building a unified identity of "ASEAN Community," while emphasizing on non-intervention with commitments to human rights and democracy. These efforts, however, are not always in harmony with the political realities of most ASEAN countries. While regional cooperation between ASEAN nations have been predominatly self-interest seeking, ASEAN member states have started to move towards the recognition that nation-building concerns can serve intra-regional mutual interests through cooperative endeavors. However, its diverse membership, its principle of non-intervention, and other local dynamics such as weak institutional and political apparatuses as well as tensions arising from ethnic, religious and politics divide, etc. limit ASEAN's ability to reform (Narine 2008). Hence, there is a vital need to explore social institutional dynamics revolving around power, self-interests, vulnerabilities and, tensions between social entities because these forces have the means to prevent any substantial progress toward building equitable policies to mitigate threats from climate change (Islam and Kieu 2021).

ASEAN's openness to deals and FTAs generated a regional free-trade arms race across the Asia-Pacific and encouraged various forms of regional economic integration such as the Chiang Mai initiative. The South China Sea disputes, however, reveals that the East Asian regional security architecture is weak and underdeveloped due to the structural limitations and weaknesses. Avoiding dominance by regional powers, balancing economic disparities, integrating new members, and strengthening the secretariat to become the center of Asian institutions are among the central challenges of ASEAN today (Kurlantzick 2012; Narine 2008; Islam and Kieu 2020). Yet, the tensions and rivalries between China, Japan and the United States, India, and Russia create a "political space" in which ASEAN may exercise significant regional influence. ASEAN's future therefore depends largely on its role in facilitating the emergence of China as a global power, and as a mediator between great powers of the region (Kurlantzick 2012; Narine 2008).

SAARC, on the other hand, has been progressive in its acknowledgment of climate change impacts on the region. It has attempted to coordinate various efforts over the years; however, they have not been effectively translated into successful programs to address the current and future problems related to food security and climate change. While the region is quite successful in articulating and setting agendas to address the critical problem of climate change and food insecurity, its lack of political will and ongoing conflicts and tension largely hinder translating agendas into active adaptive measures. Avoiding the dominance of India, a dominant powerhouse in the region, and growing tension between India and Pakistan are among the central challenges in the region. Nevertheless, SAARC has been able to pinpoint and highlight its common issues of concern and some critical areas for cooperation among its members, showing a vast potential to becoming a driving force for climate change mitigation and improved food security in the region. Regionally, SAARC has other more pressing issues to deal with, and this is one of the key obstacles to ensuring cooperation among member states and gaining support for non-traditional security and environmental issues.

As we have seen, despite having enormous resources, abilities, and potentialities, PIF lacks robust plans to tackle climate change as well as to manage and supply essential food sources for the entire region. Programs largely concentrate on production systems rather than distributive networks, neglecting the marginalized communities. To date, the six themes of the Framework for Action remain merely a conceptual model, as the implemented programs do not operate in conjunction with the themes. Lack of inclusivity is an issue in the region as programs target only clusters of member states failing to encompass the entire region. Engaging various stakeholders, including international organizations and the private sector, PIF as a regional forum plays only a "facilitative role" in drafting agendas for the region. Priority for the environmental sustainability and food security remains secondary to economic growth. Bolstering economic growth through more productive and economically efficient activities especially by the private sector, emphasizing on strengthening capacities, increasing food production, and developing appropriate policies remain the key focus of the region. Since a "top-down" management to resolve overfishing in the region is not working well, there is a need to empower coastal communities to sustainably manage and use their fisheries resources (Islam and Kieu 2020). Communities with the support of governments and relief organizations have been able to avert food crises relating to natural disasters in Fiji (2009), Samoa (2009), and the Solomon Islands (2007). It was found that social capital particularly contributed to this community resilience, with systems of reciprocity and cohesion. Pacific Islands land tenure systems allow many to have entitlements to land and fishing grounds to carry out subsistence production too.

Taken ASEAN, SAARC, and PIF together, the Asia-Pacific region exhibits a huge potential in addressing critical issues such as climate change and food security, although some local dynamics and ideological differences often hinder the implementation of various policies taken. To put it aptly,

> It may seem unjustified to claim that ASEAN, PIF, and SAARC have been politically passive in terms of addressing climate change and food security, given the various policies and frameworks that exist. Declarations stating the seriousness of climate change were eagerly adopted across ASEAN, PIF, and SAARC. However, these declarations and the assortment of agendas such as AIFS, SPA-FS, the PIF SPREP programs, the PIF Framework for Action and even SAARC's Thimbu agenda have failed to address the crux of the issue. By and large, regional organizations have failed to capitalize on the opportunity that their larger political voice provides to actively address global actors in efforts to slow down or reverse the impacts of climate change in their regions. (Islam and Kieu 2020: 16)

The regional responses to climate change and food security vary. In terms of their planning, implementation, cooperation, legal obligation, and international contribution, we can discern the following responses from ASEAN, PIF, and SAARC (Table 10.1):

Table 10.1 Regional response to climate change and food security

Mode of Analysis	*ASEAN*	*PIF*	*SAARC*
Planning	Extensive	Inclusive	Encompassing
Implementation	Potential	Nascent	Inactive
Cooperation	Performative	Engaging	Lacking
Legal obligation	None	Uncertain	Little to none
International contribution	Minimal	Minimal	Nominal

Source Islam and Kieu (2020: 16)

Chindia Dilemma and Landgrabs

As we have seen, within the Asia-Pacific region, China and India (Chindia) emerged as the two largest emitters of CO_2 due to their massive economic development. Because of agricultural shifts from the impacts of climate change, both countries face similar threats from ecological degradation, food, and water scarcity. However, as emerging players in both regional and global economy, China and India face other developmental challenges such as socioeconomic development and poverty. The critical challenge for Chindia is to balance climate change, environmental degradation, and food security with developmental goals.

The 2007–2008 global financial crisis is considered as the worst global economic crisis since the Great Depression. As countries all around the world were hit hard by the recession, many nations scrambled to acquire water and land in order to secure food and financial security for themselves. We have seen in Chapter 8 why, where, and how both these heavyweight countries have acquired land, the extent of their global land and water grabs, and some far-reaching impacts of this practice in the affected countries. India and China were two such countries that were heavily involved in land and water grabs, with both countries accounting for approximately 10% of the total land grabbed across the entire globe combined. It is both politically sensitive and reputation-damaging activity. Despite some limitations, we suggest that contract farming is a better alternative that involves the agreement between buyer and farmer for agricultural production, and therefore can be beneficial for both farmers and businesses.

Toward a Sustainable Food System

Key factors that lead to higher levels of food security include: economic growth and higher consumer income; higher levels of democracy; lower levels of corruption; eradicating inequality and poverty; investment in agriculture; ways by which food production is organized (cooperatives vs family farming); handling food emergencies & food crisis prevention; diversifying food import sources; regional cooperation; and reducing food waste (ADB 2017). To mitigate the impacts of climate change, prolonged short growth seasons collectively with higher growth temperatures can provide new opportunities for agriculture and should be adapted to each country to suit other environmental factors like soil properties (Uleberg et al. 2014). Agricultural, aquaculture, and marine production in the Asia-Pacific must be raised to attain food security despite the challenges, such as impacts of climate change. Regional corporations for tackling food security should supersede developmental interests. Strategies to overcome food insecurity should also be a global effort, and include protective and regulator policies to ensure sustainable food production, to reduce global inequalities in food security vulnerability (Islam and Kieu 2020). Overall, Asia-Pacific needs to assess their national situations, formulate the most appropriate policies, and make the necessary investments in food systems, improve trade policies and regional frameworks on food, as well as research and innovation in regional food systems (Bevan-Jones 2017). Across all the domains of potential intervention, the most critical elements relate to governance and are often problematic (ADB 2017; Birner 2009a, b; Tripathi et al. 2016).

Global food systems overlap with agricultural systems in the area of food production, but also include the diverse set of global and local institutions, productive and other technologies and practices that govern the way food is harvested, marketed, processed, transported, accessed, and consumed. Food systems influence not only the consumption pattern, production systems, and distributive mechanism, but also the access to and the nutritional value of foods (Capone et al. 2014). A sustainable food and agricultural system will alleviate many antecedents and outcomes brought about by climate change. Some of these include but are not limited to: (1) improve climate change adaptation and mitigation from increased production and income, (2) reduction of GHG emissions to curtail the threat of climate change, (3) balance crop, livestock, fisheries, and agroforestry systems, (4) increase resource use efficiency such as land and water usage, and (5) provide protection of the environment and maintain ecosystem services. The goal is to maximize productivity of both land and seascapes in a sustainable way within humanity's "safe operating space" for the planet (Beddington et al. 2012). This requires changes in both food production and consumption by systemically addressing both demands and supply elements. Fostering smarter, efficient, and appropriate food production and consumption patterns within the bounds of the earth's finite natural resources is therefore necessary. Making food and agricultural systems more sustainable largely depends on the increase in crop and animal productivity, reduction in food losses and waste, changes in consumptions and diets, and maintaining a harmonious relationship with nature. Ambitions of maximum consumption should therefore be replaced by patterns of optimized consumption through, for example, moving toward more sustainable food consumption patterns and diets (Capone et al. 2014).

The entire food chain from the production to the consumption needs to be overhauled through the principles of ecology and sustainability. Reconsidering social and ecological values, developing quality products, providing better rewards for farmers, and aiming for food sovereignty and food safety are among the hallmarks of a sustainable food system. The best way to achieve this is by means of the local and regional food systems that we see re-emerging globally. A region benefits when food products are produced, processed, and consumed within it. The region benefits more when this food system is an integral part of a multi-functional environment in which value is attached to other aspects of life such as agricultural tourism, and care for nature, the landscape, and ecosystems that are not directly related to the production of food (Donkers 2014).

Sustainable food and agriculture lie at the heart of reducing poverty and enhancing nutrition while maintaining environmental sustainability. The Asia-Pacific region, therefore, needs a series of improvements to the production system allowing more productive and resilient livelihoods that maintain the ecosystems. The system should contribute to a more secure, sustainable, and safe food to all providing access to adequate food and nutrition. It should allow poor rural people to escape from and remain out of poverty (Beddington et al. 2012). To achieve these milestones, affordable, safe renewable, and sustainable energy supplies must be among the highest priorities (Wahlqvist et al. 2012). Drawing on Beddington et al. (2012), we can adumbrate the following recommendations for the Asia-Pacific region:

- Integrate food security and sustainable agriculture into policies
- Raise global investment in sustainable agriculture and food systems
- Sustainably intensify agricultural production while reducing greenhouse gas emissions and other negative environmental impacts of agriculture
- Develop specific programs and policies to assist populations and sectors that are most vulnerable to climate changes and food insecurity
- Reshape food access and consumption patterns to ensure basic nutritional needs are met and to foster healthy and sustainable eating patterns worldwide

- Reduce loss and waste in food systems, targeting infrastructure, farming practices, processing, distribution, and household habits
- Create comprehensive, shared, integrated information systems that encompass human and ecological dimensions.

References

ADB (Asian Development Bank Institute). 2017. *Food Insecurity in Asia: Why Institutions Matter*. Tokyo: Asian Development Bank Institute.

Alexandratos, N., and J. Bruinsma. 2012. World Agriculture Towards 2030/2050: The 2012 Revision. ESA Working Paper No. 12–03. Rome, FAO.

Beddington, John R., Mohammed Asaduzzaman, Fernandez A. Bremauntz, Megan E. Clark, Marion Guillou, Molly M. Jahn, Lin Erda, Tekalign Mamo, Nguyen van Bo, and Carlos A. Nobre. 2012. *Achieving Food Security in the Face of Climate Change: Final Report from the Commission on Sustainable Agriculture and Climate Change*. The CGIAR Research Program on Climate Change, Agriculture and Food Security (CCAFS).

Bevan-Jones, Catherine. 2017. Food Security, Trade and Partnerships: Towards Resilient Regional Food Systems in Asia. https://doi.org/10.13140/rg.2.2.35609.11362.

Birner, R. 2009a. Choosing Policy Instruments to Reduce Hunger and Poverty: Is It Possible to Overcome the Feasibility Dilemma? In *The Poorest and Hungry: Assessments, Analyses, and Actions: An IFPRI 2020 Book*, ed. J. von Braun, R. Vargas Hill, and R. Pandya-Lorch, 501–509. Washington, DC: International Food Policy Research Institute.

Birner, R. 2009b. Improving Governance to Eradicate Poverty and Hunger. In *The Poorest and Hungry: Assessments, Analyses, and Actions: An IFPRI 2020 Book*, ed. J. von Braun, R. Vargas Hill, and R. Pandya-Lorch, 529–539. Washington, DC: International Food Policy Research Institute.

Candel, Jeroen J.L., and Laura Pereira. 2017. Towards Integrated Food Policy: Main Challenges and Steps Ahead. *Environmental Science & Policy* 73 (2017): 89–92.

Capone, Roberto, Hamid El Bilali, Philipp Debs, Gianluigi Cardone, and Noureddin Driouech. 2014. Food System Sustainability and Food Security: Connecting the Dots. *Journal of Food Security* 2 (1): 13–22.

Donkers, Harry. 2014. Sustainable Food Security, A Paradigm for Local and Regional Food Systems. *International Journal of Humanities and Social Science* 4 (12).

Islam, M.S., and Edson Kieu. 2020. Tackling Regional Climate Change Impacts and Food Security Issues: A Critical Analysis Across ASEAN, PIF, and SAARC. *Sustainability* 12 (3): 883. https://doi.org/10.3390/su12030883.

Islam, M.S., and Edson Kieu. 2021. Sociological Perspectives on Climate Change and Society: A Review. *Climate* 9 (1): 7.

Kurlantzick, Joshua. 2012. ASEAN's Future and Asian Integration. Working Paper, November 2012, International Institutions and Global Governance Program. https://www.cfr.org/sites/default/files/pdf/2012/10/IIGG_WorkingPaper10_Kurlantzick.pdf.

McKenzie, Fiona C., and John Williams. 2015. Sustainable Food Production: Constraints, Challenges and Choices by 2050. *Food Security* 7 (2): 221–233.

McMichael, Philip. 2012. *Development and Social change: A Global Perspective*. Los Angeles, London, New Delhi, Singapore: Washington, DC: Sage.

Narine, S. 2008. Forty Years of ASEAN: A Historical Review. *The Pacific Review* 21 (4), 411–429. https://doi.org/10.1080/09512740802294689.

Nellemann, C., M. MacDevette, T. Manders, B. Eickhout, B. Svihus, A.G. Prins, and B.P. Kaltenborn, eds. 2009, February. The Environmental Food Crisis—The Environment's Role in Averting Future Food Crises. A UNEP Rapid Response Assessment. United Nations Environment Programme, GRID-Arendal. www.grida.no.

The Action Against Hunger. 2020. The World Hunger: Key Facts and Statistics 2020. Accessed 16 December 2020. https://www.actionagainsthunger.org/world-hunger-facts-statistics.

Tripathi, Ashutosh, Durgesh Kumar Tripathi, D.K. Chauhan, Niraj Kumar, and G.S. Singh. 2016. Paradigms of Climate Change Impacts on Some Major Food Sources of the World: A Review on Current Knowledge and Future Prospects. *Agriculture, Ecosystems & Environment* 216 (2016): 356–373.

Uleberg, E., I. Hanssen-Bauer, B. van Oort, and S. Dalmannsdottir. 2014. Impact of Climate Change on Agriculture in Northern Norway and Potential Strategies for Adaptation. *Climate Change* 122: 27–39.

Vermeulen, S.J., P.K. Aggarwal, A. Ainslie, C. Angelone, B.M. Campbell, A.J. Challinor, J.W. Hansen, J.S.I. Ingram, A. Jarvis, P. Kristjanson, C. Lau, G.C. Nelson, P.K. Thornton, and E. Wollenberg. 2012. Options for Support to Agriculture and Food Security Under Climate Change. *Environmental Science & Policy* 15 (1): 136–144.

Wahlqvist, Mark L., John McKay, Ya-Chen Chang, and Ya-Wen Chiu. 2012. Rethinking the Food Security Debate in Asia: Some Missing Ecological and Health Dimensions and Solutions. *Food Security* 4 (4): 657–670.

Index

M. S. Islam and E. Kieu, *Climate Change and Food Security in Asia Pacific*, International Political Economy Series,
https://doi.org/10.1007/978-3-030-70753-8

The manufacturer's authorised representative in the EU is Springer
Nature Customer Service Centre GmbH, Europaplatz 3, 69115 Heidelberg,
Germany. If you have any concerns regarding our products, please
contact ProductSafety@springernature.com

Printed and bound by CPI Group (UK) Ltd, Croydon, CR0 4YY
30/09/2026
02225321-0007